Understanding
Catholic Christianity

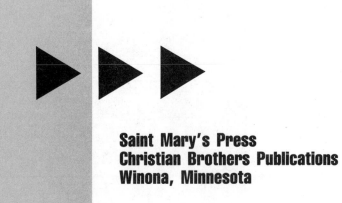

Saint Mary's Press
Christian Brothers Publications
Winona, Minnesota

Understanding Catholic Christianity

by Thomas Zanzig

Nihil Obstat: Rev. Msgr. Roy E. Literski
               Censor Deputatus
               25 August 1987
Imprimatur: †Most Rev. John G. Vlazny
               Bishop of Winona
               25 August 1987

The publishing team included Stephan Nagel, development editor; Carl Koch, FSC, and Rev. Robert Stamschror,
consulting editors; Anna Dolores Ready, manuscript
editor; Lynn Dahdal, production editor; Mary Kraemer,
indexer; and Carolyn St. George, designer and illustrator.

The acknowledgments continue on page 302.

Printed in the United States of America

Printing: 6 5 4 3 2 1
Year: 1994 93 92 91 90 89 88

ISBN 0-88489-182-8

C O N T E N T S

Foreword:
Better Than
One in a Million

Unique in All the World

Fifteen years ago about four billion people lived on this global village that we call Earth. Men, women, boys, girls—four billion human beings with dreams, fears, loves, hates, hang-ups, and hopes. Furthermore, those billions of people represented only a small fraction of the estimated over one hundred billion people who have existed since the beginning of human history.

About fifteen years ago, two of those billions of people were drawn together in love. A man and a woman went through an almost unimaginable series of events—beginning with the awesome event of being born at a particular point in time and leading to the intriguing coincidence of two people crossing paths on a particular day at a particular place. That man and that woman, having fallen in love, then celebrated their union of spirits by becoming one in body as well.

When that man and woman joined in sexual intercourse, literally millions of possibilities were present. In one act of sexual intercourse, the man shared millions of sperm cells with the woman—any one of which might have united with one of her hundreds of eggs or all of which might have died after a short time. Yet one of those sperm cells survived—one unique from all the others in its potential and in its characteristics. That one sperm cell out of millions united with one of the woman's equally unique eggs, and the miracle of human creation began.

Nine remarkable months of human growth followed that union of sperm and egg. The fertilized egg cell split and became two cells, then four, then eight, and then multiplied rapidly into a cluster of thousands of cells called an **embryo.** The embryo settled into the lining of the woman's uterus where, enclosed in a warm sac of liquid and fed through the umbilical cord, it grew.

In only its second month the embryo began to look like a little baby, developing tiny arms, legs, eyes, and ears. In its third month the embryo began to move, nails were forming on fingers and toes, and it was called by a new name, a **fetus**. The fetus grew quickly. At the end of four months it weighed eight ounces and was eight inches long. Teeth began forming inside its gums and hair began growing on its head. Another month passed and the fetus's bones grew harder, and its heartbeat could be detected with a stethoscope.

At six months and then about twelve inches long and two pounds in weight, the easily recognizable human baby kicked against the woman's body. Often creating an exhilarating feeling for the woman, this kicking was the first sign from the baby that it wanted to get out, that it needed to be on its own, that it was an individual apart from its mother. At the end of the seventh month the baby weighed about three pounds and was already sucking its thumb. Its eyes opened and closed.

Finally, by the end of the ninth month the baby had outgrown its first home. It needed more room, more freedom. In response, the muscles of the woman's uterus began to contract. Slowly the woman's muscles squeezed harder and harder around the baby, pushing it out of the uterus, through the vagina, and into the world.

About fourteen years ago, a new human being entered the world—distinct, different, unique.

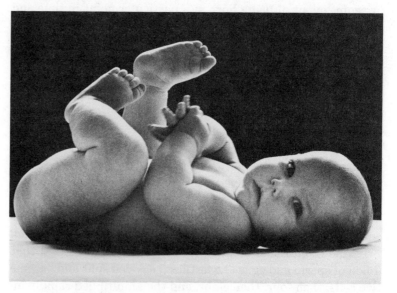

At that moment some fourteen years ago, a new human being entered the world—a new human being sharing many of the characteristics of the one hundred billion who came before. Yet this person was distinct, different, unique. Never before had the world seen anyone exactly like this new being. Never before had this special combination of genes and chromosomes, this combination of blood and bone, this wonderful potential of talent and gift, been born. Never again in the future of the world would that miracle be precisely repeated.

That indescribable mystery of some fourteen years ago, that nearly unimaginable wonder, that never-to-be-repeated moment, was the birth of someone very special—you.

Life Is a Process

Very possibly you have never thought of your own birth with a sense of drama or with a sense of wonder and awe. Perhaps you have never seriously reflected on the fact that the miracle of birth was only the beginning of an ongoing and equally dramatic story—the story of your own life. Since the moment when you burst into the world, you have continued the process of growth. And it has been a total process during which not only your body has been changing but also your mind, your emotions, your attitudes, your values, and your relationships with others. You have continued, for example, the often difficult process of defining that relationship with your parents begun in your mother's womb. Included in this relationship is the conflict between wanting and needing protection and affection, while kicking to be free of its restrictions.

Outside the family you have also been confronted through the years with new experiences, new challenges, new feelings. Many ideas that you accepted unquestioningly before you may now either reject or seriously challenge. Perhaps life has not been an easy time for you, and as you enter adulthood, life will not soon get easier. Yet becoming a loving and lovable adult is a goal that you can achieve, and this course will show you how faith, prayer, and religion can help.

Becoming a loving and lovable adult is a goal that you can achieve.

This Course and You

In many ways this course is about you—about who you are and what you can become; about your relationships with the people whom you have met and will meet in life; and about your response to a lot of the big questions about life and death, about love and hate, about God, and about religion. Perhaps this course might seem no more to you than "just another religion course." In fact, it may be both an opportunity to look in a whole new way at the marvelous journey that is your life and a chance to take charge of the direction that journey takes.

To make this course special, you must demand a few things of yourself.

First, strive to be open and honest with yourself, willing to reflect on both the good and the bad in your life, the strengths and the weaknesses. You need to grapple with the important questions that your life presents you. You must avoid running away from them. Being open and honest with yourself in this course will almost certainly require some time alone, some quiet time for putting things together for yourself and for sorting out ideas and making some decisions.

Second, strive to be open and honest with your teacher and with the other students in the class. This will never mean revealing things about yourself that you do not want people to know. You will never be put in a position in which you will feel that kind of pressure. But being open and honest with others will mean listening carefully to what others have to say. Give them the benefit of the doubt. Allow them to express their ideas, beliefs, and feelings without facing your ridicule or rejection.

Third, if you hope to have this course be all that it can be, you must make a commitment to a sincere search for the truth. During your work with this course you may experience moments of real doubt and serious questioning, times when you simply cannot agree with what is being discussed or presented. You have not only the right but also the responsibility to seek truth—wherever that search leads you. Those of us who freely choose to accept Catholic Christianity have enough confidence in our faith to trust that it will survive and even flourish under the most intense scrutiny and questioning. So we ask that you come to this course with a sincere desire to investigate Catholic Christianity with intellectual and spiritual honesty.

Obviously these few comments suggest that this may well be a different kind of religion course than you have experienced before. It is. Primarily this course is different because you are different at this point in your life. As you begin this course you are a ninth grader, probably entering a new school, and this course is being offered to you as a basic introductory course on Catholic Christianity. (Incidentally, if this description does not fit you, you will have to make a few mental adjustments as you read some sections of this text.) As a ninth grader, you

You have the right and the responsibility to seek truth—wherever that search leads you.

This religion course is different—
primarily because you are different at
this point in your life.

are clearly no longer a child, and you can no longer be treated like one.

This course is an attempt to respond to that fact. It is new in content. Although you have probably heard many of the things presented here before, you have probably never heard them presented in this way. This course may also be different in style from other religion courses you have experienced before high school. As indicated already, the course will be more personally involving than other courses have been, centered as it is on you as a ninth grader and on what you are now experiencing in life. You will have more opportunity than usual to express your own ideas and convictions, as well as your own doubts.

In class you will have the opportunity to discuss the material in greater depth and to personalize what you have read. Your classes will involve many different exercises and activities that can be opportunities for sharing and reflection. You will have some fun times—times for laughing, for simply enjoying the fact that you are getting to know yourself and others in the class. You will have some times for prayer as well, for getting in touch with the Mystery whom Christians call God. Enter into all these facets of the course with that same openness, honesty, and commitment to truth requested above.

Religion only makes sense if it relates to our lives as we experience them. The same holds true for religion courses. You are beginning a whole new stage in your life. The hope for this course is that it will be a time of continued growth for you and of an increased awareness of the unique person you were called to be by God at that moment of conception so long ago.

In this course, you will have time to get in touch with the Mystery whom Christians call God.

A Special Note on Study Aids

You should be aware of some special study aids included in this textbook.

1. One of the goals of *Understanding Catholic Christianity* is to provide students with a basic vocabulary of terms that will help them in religion courses throughout their experience of religious education. Here is how these terms will be handled:

- All special terms and phrases are printed in **boldfaced type.** Anytime you see these terms, make a special attempt to understand and memorize them.

- Every boldfaced word or phrase is defined in the Glossary at the end of this textbook, on pages 283–291.
- Whenever helpful, the pronunciation for these terms will be provided in the Glossary.
- Finally, at the end of each chapter, you will find a list of key terms to identify and remember. These words or phrases are of special importance and will likely appear in quizzes and tests. For obvious reasons, you will want to pay particular attention to these.

2. In the margins throughout this textbook, you will find personal reflection activities. These activities are short exercises or questions directly related to the ideas under discussion in the paragraphs next to or near the activity. At times, your teacher may use these activities to start classroom discussion. Or these activities may be used as homework assignments. Even when they are not used by your teacher, however, you will find that doing the activities on your own will increase your understanding of the material in the course.

1

Identity and Development:
Exploring
the World of Adolescents

Change Can Be Rough

Mobility is one of the most significant characteristics of modern North American society. Not only are we North Americans capable of getting around because of the availability of cars, air travel, and so on, but we also tend to move from one house to another and from one region to another far more often than in the past. In fact, the odds are high that you personally have experienced that kind of move in the last several years. If you have, try to recall the feelings that accompanied that move. If you have not experienced a move yourself, you may certainly have friends who did, friends who shared their feelings with you. What was moving like for them?

The Past Can Be Comfortable

We tend to become very comfortable with our homes, often for reasons we are not even aware of until we leave them behind. Every home has a certain feel to it, an atmosphere, a tone. Each of us can identify certain sounds and aromas as part of our home—for example, the noisy but somehow friendly sound of the kitchen clock or the smell of clean laundry or of our favorite cookies baking. You may even have a set pattern for what you do when you enter your house. Perhaps you always use the same greetings or you throw your jacket on the same chair or you go directly to one particular room.

If you are lucky, you have your own bedroom, or at least one in which you have your own corner. Your bedroom may be a place of refuge for you, a place to be alone with your own thoughts, a place to listen to some music on the radio and to let your mind wander. On the walls hang some of your prized possessions—pictures of best friends; symbols of happy memories; letters from people you care for; posters of your favorite stars, many of whom your parents have a hard time tolerating, much less liking! Your bedroom is your space in your home, and

As you read this material, reflect on either a personal experience of having moved from one home to another or on an experience of having a close friend or family member move away. In the margin next to each paragraph, put a light pencil mark that can be easily erased. Use a plus sign (+) if you agree with the characteristic of moving as described. Use a negative sign (−) if you disagree with what is being described about the experience of moving.

Our feelings about moving may include anger, loneliness, fear, and excitement—all mixed together.

it is a special place. Even in homes where there are hassles, tensions, and arguments, we attach especially pleasant feelings to this private space.

The Future Can Be Scary

Suddenly the time comes to move. Perhaps a parent has a career change that makes the move necessary. The reason for moving does not seem to make much difference—moving is painful anyway. Your feelings may include anger, loneliness, fear, and excitement—all mixed together in confusion. For example: you are going to leave your best friend behind, and although you promise to write and keep in touch, you know deep down the relationship will never be the same. You also have to leave the school where you have had many happy times. Your home—with its sounds and aromas and its special rooms and its many memories—must be left behind too.

What waits at the other end of the move? Entering an unknown future can be even more frightening than leaving a comfortable past. Will you find a home you like in a friendly neighborhood? What will your school be like? Will the kids there accept you or reject you? What is the city going to be like? You feel terrible about what will be left behind and scared about what lies ahead.

Not So Bad After All

When you make the move, however, a rather wonderful thing happens. You find that the house into which your family moves is nicer in some ways than the one you left behind, maybe with a bedroom just for you. During the first day of school you meet two friendly kids who make you feel a lot more relaxed. You slowly begin to participate in various school activities (going to sporting events, maybe even your first dance), and you start to feel part of the school community. Very gradually, the pain of leaving the past begins to go away. Then you find that when you mention "home" you are talking about your new home, not the old one. You also discover that "being home" means a lot more than being in a certain building on a certain block in a certain city. You realize that home is a combination of all kinds of feelings, memories, and dreams.

This description of the process of moving suggests a very positive and happy outcome—the developing feeling of being at home in new surroundings. For some young people, however, this will not be the case. They will face continuing loneliness and pain. List five ways that people can avoid the difficult consequences of moving. Or write down five ways that people might more easily and happily become comfortable with their new surroundings after a move.

Adolescence: A Special Kind of Change

The feelings associated with moving from one home to another can also be very much a part of a different kind of move you are making: the move from childhood to adulthood. You are moving away from the comfort and security of one stage of human life into the unknown of another stage. This change can be frightening, confusing, lonely, yet also exciting and hope-filled.

Childhood is an easy stage of life. Little kids get hurt physically but heal fast, and the bumps and bruises at the end of the day become badges of honor. Children who are friends hurt one another's feelings and swear they are never going to talk to one another again, but five minutes later they are back playing together. About the hardest decision a little kid has to make is what game to play next—not a bad way to live.

Recall your own experiences with younger brothers or sisters or in baby-sitting other children and write a paragraph about the capacity of young children to quickly get over hurt feelings. Can you imagine an adolescent or adult reacting in the same way? Why or why not?

Moving from Childhood to Adulthood

You are moving out of that comfortable "home" of childhood. Just as the move from one home to another can be nerve-racking, so the move from childhood to adulthood that we call *adolescence* can be terribly difficult. Along with most ninth graders, you are facing a great surge of growth and change. At few other times in your future will things happen so quickly, yet so deeply. Rarely in life will you need to adjust to so many changes in so short a time. This is one of the reasons that most people look back to their high school years as among the most memorable in their lives—even though the memories are not always pleasant.

The Whole Is Greater Than the Sum of Its Parts

Most ninth graders are changing dramatically on all levels of life—physically, emotionally, intellectually, socially, and spiritually. We are going to take a look at some of those changes in this and later chapters. Although we can discuss each level of life separately, however, we do not experience them separately.

Ninth graders are changing dramatically on all levels of life but most clearly in terms of their bodies.

Jot down high school events and situations that could generate each of the following emotions:
- pride
- anger
- loneliness
- fear
- satisfaction
- anxiety
- anticipation
- frustration
- joy
- peace
- confusion

For example, many of the emotional changes that you may be encountering are directly related to physical changes that you are undergoing. Likewise, your attitudes toward faith and religion may be changing as a result of your increasing ability to think about difficult concepts and philosophical issues. You are a whole person, not a bunch of separate pieces glued together. So we will look at each part of life separately for the sake of clarity. Yet in reality all the changes we will discuss relate to each other, affect each other, and together make up who you are—a total person.

Please Don't Take This Too Personally

Remember that we are talking in generalities here about *most* ninth graders rather than about *an individual* ninth grader. In reality, picking out any one year in life and describing it in terms of normal adolescent development is not valid. The characteristics we are discussing here actually develop over a period of several years, from about seventh grade through tenth grade. So, if you do not fit the descriptions given, do not worry. The intent is not to wrap you up in a neat little box of some kind, but rather to assure you that many of the things you are experiencing are shared by others.

Given these cautions, let's take a quick look at life through the eyes of an imaginary ninth-grade boy and girl. Later we will take a closer look at the characteristics for each.

The Ninth-Grade Boy

Our ninth-grade boy spends a fair amount of time in front of a mirror—privately, of course—checking out his body and keeping an eye on how everything is developing. Mostly he is concerned about the size of his body. That can be a depressing sight if he happens to be one of the guys who hasn't hit his peak growing time yet. He might still be under five feet, 120 pounds, and embarrassed to death by these facts. Why? Because maybe his best friend, who two years ago was his size, is now six feet, 170 pounds, and has the basketball coach dreaming of a trophy. (Our ninth grader probably doesn't know that his best friend is self-conscious too—in his case because he is often clumsy and hasn't learned to coordinate his rapidly growing body.) All our friend knows is that he doesn't care for what he sees in the mirror. He flexes his muscles and makes up his mind—again—that he is going to send for some bodybuilding equipment right away. When he finally develops the perfect body, in a month or so, then Linda will find him irresistible.

The truth is that our ninth grader has been thinking a lot about Linda lately. That's strange, because he has known her all his life, but things are changing. For the last few years he and his buddies have made all kinds of jokes about sex, and they've all played the game of pretending they know everything about it. In fact, our imaginary ninth-grade boy still talks a great game when the guys are around. The problem is that when he met Linda alone the other day he was scared stiff and embarrassed, blushed like mad, and generally made an idiot of himself. He doesn't even know why. Is he weird or something? He just doesn't know.

Our ninth-grade boy remembers that as a kid he looked through the Sears catalog at the bra-and-panty section. More

Ninth-grade boys spend a fair amount of time in front of the mirror—often deciding that they need bodybuilding equipment.

recently, he sneaked a look at an "adult" magazine. So for quite a while now he has had a pretty good idea of what sex is all about. Except nobody told him what sex is like when it's for real, when there's a real girl involved and you really like her and you want her to like you, but you have the terrible feeling that she doesn't. He would like to talk to someone about sex, maybe Mom or Dad, but that's a whole problem in itself.

He can remember when his family was pretty close. They did a lot of things together, laughed a lot, talked to each other with no problems. Now things are different. He has this feeling that so much is happening in his life, so many questions are hitting him over the head, and his parents just don't understand. Oh sure, they'd like to help all right, but somehow he gets the feeling that his parents were never his age. They must have skipped a grade in there somewhere. That must be the reason that he has so many hassles with them now—about the way he dresses, the hours he keeps, the whole bit.

So rather than trying to talk through his feelings, he decides to keep the peace, to not say too much, and to keep to himself when things get tense. Of course, then his folks think he is hiding something and keep bugging him about it! He can remember kissing his dad good night, but he can't remember when or why he stopped. That nightly ritual just didn't seem right for some reason. And why do his folks have such a hang-up about his friends anyway? If they make one more comment about his buddies . . .

Our imaginary ninth grader just wishes everybody would get off his back and let him get his head straight. School is a drag. How does he know if he can believe half the stuff the teachers say, anyway? The more questions he has, the fewer answers he can find. When he used to feel this way—lonely, confused, and uncertain, he'd talk to God about his problems like his parents taught him, and talking to God seemed to help somehow. Now praying sometimes doesn't work. He finds himself struggling with difficult questions about religion that he never even considered before. For instance, why believe in God at all? Some friends say this God stuff is like the old Santa Claus bit. He wonders. He always believed God existed, and he'd still like to. But why does the world have so many problems? Why are there so many different kinds of religion if there's only one God? How can he believe someone walked on water and cured people? He wonders. Life just isn't as much fun as it used to be.

Parents may wish to help the ninth grader—but were they ever that age?

If you are a boy, evaluate this description of a ninth-grade boy in this way: Lightly pencil your reactions in the margin next to each paragraph using the following codes:
SA = strongly agree that this point is true
GA = generally agree with the point
SD = strongly disagree with what is being stated

The Ninth-Grade Girl

Our ninth-grade girl is pretty familiar with all the things the ninth-grade boy is going through because she went through most of the same things herself when she was a little younger—about a year or two ago. In fact, ninth-grade boys seem very immature to her right now. They're always goofing off, acting tough, trying to be cool. When she thinks about the other sex, she is more inclined to think of more mature boys—like eleventh graders. Of course, this drives the boys right up the wall, but our ninth-grade girl really is more attracted to the older guys. The question is, Do the older guys like her? She figures they will if she looks good to them, so she also goes to the mirror to check things out. And there's a good chance she says "yuk!" when she sees herself. How's a girl supposed to avoid feeling that way, anyway? All day long she sees models in commercials, magazines, and TV shows. Those girls are always beautiful; they have the right figures; their clothes are fantastic—and then there she is! Maybe she still has a figure like her ten-year-old sister—nothing but straight lines. Maybe she's overweight and can't seem to help it. And, oh ick, is that another pimple? Or maybe she is attractive physically, and lots of older guys are calling her. But what are they looking for? And if she goes out with those guys, what happens to her girlfriends who aren't so popular? Will they still like her? You can't win with this body game.

Yet more than just a concern about her physical attractiveness bothers our ninth-grade girl. She admires so many of her friends, and she is glad that they seem to like her, but she has to admit that she gets pretty envious of them at times. Her friend Jeannie seems so sure of herself, so confident around other people. How can she be that way? Her best friend Barb has a sense of humor that always makes her the life of the party. Our ninth grader is sure that at least half the class has to be smarter than she is. She doesn't like feeling envious of people she cares for, but she can't seem to help it. At times, life is a lot harder than it used to be. She feels sad more often. She feels so much closer to her real friends than she ever did before, as if she could talk to them for days on end about life and love and music and school. Yet she feels so lonely at times. One minute she can be laughing like crazy and having a good time, and the next minute she's close to tears and wondering what happened.

If you are a girl, evaluate this description of a ninth-grade girl in this way: Write your reactions in light pencil in the margin next to each paragraph using the following codes:
SA = strongly agree that this point is true
GA = generally agree with this point
SD = strongly disagree with what is being stated

When a ninth-grade girl looks in the mirror to check things out, there is a good chance she says "yuk!"

Although she finds life pretty great, she gets angry about how people have messed up the world or how bored her parents seem sometimes. Her feelings about life just seem to go back and forth. She knows life can be beautiful and love is real and good and the world is full of wonder, and yet everybody keeps messing things up. Why can't people just love each other? Why can't we stop war and prejudice and hunger? Why does her best friend's father drink so much? Why do so many young people die before they've ever had a chance to live? The questions don't seem to end, and whatever answers she used to have for them—answers like "Life is a mystery" or "Just take things that you do not understand on faith"—don't seem to satisfy her anymore.

Occasionally, when she gets to feeling this way, our ninth-grade girl starts to talk to God about her questions and doubts. This God business is kind of weird. Lately Mass is boring her out of her mind. She asks how people who call themselves Christian can act so un-Christlike, why we need priests to forgive us, and a hundred other questions about religion. Yet she feels closer to God in some ways than she ever did when she was a kid. God seems nearer somehow, more like a friend. At least most of the time, that is. She, too, has times when she's not too sure. She wonders: Does God exist or not? Does God really care about me? And, if God is always with me, why do I feel so lonely at times, so afraid?

What's Going On Here?

Remember now, the above portraits are generalizations, and the characteristics described in these sketches may not fit you exactly. However, you may identify with many of the thoughts, feelings, questions, and attitudes expressed by our fictitious ninth-grade boy and girl. Some might find this a bit discouraging or even aggravating. Most of us would like to think that we are so unique that no one else can understand us. At the same time, discovering that the painful feelings we experience are shared by others, that we are not so different as to seem weird, and that many other people can understand our problems can be very refreshing and encouraging. Knowing that others share our pain does not necessarily lessen or take it away. But sharing sure makes it easier to bear the pain and to hope for better things to come.

Discovering that the painful feelings we experience are shared by others can be refreshing and encouraging.

The primary questions that we will address are these: What is causing all these changes in "typical" ninth graders? How long will the process of change continue? Where is all this change leading? How can we best cope with these changes?

The stage called **adolescence** is the transition stage between childhood and adulthood. Adolescence begins with the physical event called **puberty**, which results in our being capable of reproducing sexually. Adolescence ends with our gaining social status as adults at about the age of twenty.

Adolescence is the transition stage between childhood and adulthood.

Puberty itself begins with a period of rapid physical growth and ends in sexual maturity—that is, the capability to beget or bear offspring. Traditionally, puberty is considered to begin about age twelve for girls and age fourteen for boys. Actually it starts as early as ages nine or ten for some people and as late as fifteen or sixteen for others.

Puberty is marked by changes in certain glands that produce chemical substances called *hormones*. We have lots of hormones in our bodies for the purpose of carrying messages to organs about how to function or develop. In this case, a gland in our brains called the *pituitary gland* sends out certain hormones to signal the sex organs—the **ovaries** in girls and the **testicles** in boys—to start working. The ovaries and testicles, in their turn, begin sending hormonal messages to other parts

Find four photographs of yourself taken when you were the following ages:
- two years old or less
- five years old
- ten years old
- a ninth grader

Tape these to the wall or on your desk where you do your homework. As you read and reflect on the remaining material in this chapter, reflect on how you have experienced each facet of human development described during each of the ages represented by the photos. That is, while you read, reflect on how you have experienced at each age the physical, emotional, intellectual, social, and religious changes discussed in this chapter.

Girls begin the rapid maturing process about two years before boys do.

of our bodies, telling them to grow and develop. This results in changes in the secondary sex traits that relate to height, weight, body hair, shape, and voice.

No one's puberty is typical. For example, girls begin the rapid maturing process about two years before boys do, which is a major factor in their frequent interest in older boys. Generally speaking, boys' physical development moves more slowly but then continues for a longer period than does girls'. The greater physical size of boys does not develop until after puberty. Boys at age thirteen are often smaller than girls the same age, a fact that often can be embarrassing for both. Most girls reach close to their full height by age sixteen, while boys often continue to grow in height until age eighteen or later.

Puberty is also a period of *sexual awakening,* and the increased awareness of sexuality creates mixed reactions in both boys and girls. A flood of emotions begins, and attitudes and interests change. The greater your understanding of these changes, the better you will be able to cope with them in your own life. So let's take a closer look at sexual development during adolescence.

Sexual Development in Girls

The first evidence of puberty in the young girl is a change in the breasts, which grow in size and change in shape. A girl can become very conscious of her breast development, not only because of the obvious physical changes she is experiencing but also because of the common attitude in our culture about the importance of breast size.

Other cultures hold completely different attitudes about what is attractive. In Asian countries, for example, large breasts are considered very unattractive. Each culture, however, exerts a great deal of pressure to conform to a particular standard of beauty. This cultural pressure can have great impact on a girl's self-image—the way in which she accepts or rejects herself. Sometimes she may be led to think mistakenly that she is a less likable or worthy person because of her figure.

As her development continues, the adolescent girl's hips broaden, and she begins to grow hair on her pubic, or genital, area. Also during puberty her body hair—in her armpits, on her legs and arms, and maybe on her chin and upper lip—gets longer and thicker. Because our cultural standards also lead us to view body hair on women as ugly, however, most girls begin shaving and plucking their body hair as soon as possible.

About two years after her breasts begin developing and about a year after the appearance of pubic hair, the girl's first **menstrual period** occurs. The menstrual period, or *menstruation,* involves a monthly shedding of the lining of the **uterus.** The shed lining flows out through the **vagina** in the form of blood and tissue.

Often a girl's ovaries produce their first mature eggs within a year after her first menstrual period. Once this process called **ovulation** begins, a girl can become pregnant. Sometimes ovulation happens before menstruation, however. So a girl can get pregnant before the first menstrual period.

For health reasons, girls need sound information and advice regarding sexual development.

Ovulation often takes place about age fourteen. Note again, however, that the normal range of ages for this event is wide. A girl might begin menstruation anywhere from ages ten to sixteen and ovulation, then, from ages nine to seventeen.

For health reasons as well as for the self-image of a girl, she must receive sound information and advice regarding her sexual development. Because of cultural and social influences, however, many parents find that discussing these things with their children is difficult. One result of this is that many girls receive no information about menstruation prior to their first experience of it. The unnecessary fear, guilt, and worry that this causes can be tremendous. Parents should be the first and primary source for this kind of information. If they do not provide it, however, a girl should seek out someone she trusts—for example, a friendly teacher—to gain the facts she needs to understand and to deal with the changes she is experiencing.

Frequently our society reverses its opinion of what makes women physically attractive. Fashion models, for example, may sometimes have to be thin and flat chested. At other times, the well-developed look is more popular.
- Based on current magazine and television advertising, decide which of the above looks is currently fashionable for women.
- React in writing to this question: How are most adolescent girls likely to feel about themselves when measured against this standard?

Sexual Development in Boys

In recent history changes in the pattern of physical growth have occurred. These are seen most clearly in the development of boys, who today are considerably more physically developed than in the past. For instance, a nine-year-old boy in the United States is nearly four inches taller and twenty pounds heavier than a boy that age living one hundred years ago.

About age eleven many boys put on weight and go through a "fat phase" immediately before puberty. During this time they temporarily appear somewhat pudgy. Happily this phase does not last long. Also at this time *penile erections*—the stiffening of the penis—occur spontaneously, that is, without apparent cause. About age twelve, a boy's penis and *scrotum*—the pouch under the penis that contains the testicles—begin to increase in size. This is one of the earliest indicators of approaching puberty. Erections occur more frequently but still spontaneously. Generally a boy this age has not experienced **ejaculation,** which is the release through the penis of the fluid and sperm called *semen.*

A boy's pubic hair commonly appears at about ages thirteen or fourteen, followed by a surge of genital growth, that is, rapid growth in the penis and scrotum. Ejaculation is now possible. Growth of underarm and facial hair follows that of pubic hair. *Nocturnal emissions* (commonly called wet dreams) are probable at this time. A wet dream is simply the release of semen during sleep, normally accompanied by sexually stimulating dreams. This is perfectly normal, and a boy does not need to feel guilty when this happens. A change in voice usually occurs in the boy about age fourteen or fifteen, often with some embarrassing squeaks mid-sentence. The voice of a mature man is about an octave lower than that of a mature woman.

Again the need at this age for sound, clear information about sexual development cannot be overemphasized. Seeking out this kind of information can be even more difficult for the boy than for the girl because of cultural attitudes that make the lack of such knowledge embarrassing for a boy. He is often unwilling to let someone know that he does not "know it all." The old saying that "ignorance is bliss" is particularly false, however, in regard to understanding sexuality. The more boys know about their bodies and the changes they are experiencing, the more comfortable they will be with themselves.

For boys, the growth of underarm and facial hair follows that of pubic hair.

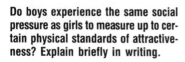

Do boys experience the same social pressure as girls to measure up to certain physical standards of attractiveness? Explain briefly in writing.

More Than Our Bodies Are Changing!

As seen in the brief descriptions earlier of our fictitious ninth graders, the changes brought about by puberty are not all that is happening in the life of the ninth grader. Many other changes—emotional and intellectual, for example—are often directly or indirectly the result of bodily changes. In understanding ourselves, we need to think about this. For instance, consider the impact of these physical changes on our emotional attitudes and reactions to others. Ninth graders are, for obvious reasons, normally very body-conscious, that is, very interested in and concerned about how their bodies are changing and developing. This concern is only heightened by the fact that we live in a very body-conscious society, one in which a person's lovableness and acceptability are too often tied to looks rather than to values and virtues. Think of the unattractive ninth-grade boy or girl, whose body is not developing the way he or she would like, who discovers a new pimple every morning, whose body is not suited to the supposedly important sports. Such persons might easily feel that they are "no good," that no one could possibly care for them.

Now think of the impact of a poor attitude on our relationships with others. If we feel down on ourselves and incapable of accepting who we are, we will likely feel uncomfortable, uneasy, maybe even afraid around others. That kind of discomfort or fear may be demonstrated in many ways. One person might be shy and hide from others, while another person will try to avoid the feelings of inadequacy by coming on strong, acting cocky and in control of the situation. Look at your own attitude. What do you think about your own body, and how does that affect your attitudes and emotional reactions?

Realize, too, that most students who are reading this chapter feel that this is written directly to them. Almost all of them feel that they are the unattractive ones, that they have unlovable bodies, that they are the exceptions, and that no one understands or cares for them. The point is that we all feel that way at times. Very possibly, the girl you think is the most attractive in the class cannot stand the look of her nose, the strongest boy in class is too embarrassed by his lack of coordination to try out for basketball, and the classmate you would give anything to be like wishes he or she could be like you.

Almost all ninth graders think that they are unattractive and that no one understands or cares for them.

We Are More Than Our Bodies

Buckminster Fuller, one of the great creative geniuses of modern times, once reflected on his body and his attitude toward it. He remembered that he had come into the world weighing only 7 pounds, the sum total of all he was. Eventually he grew to be 70 pounds, then 170, then over 200. During that time he ate literally tons of food, some of which became hair that was cut off in regular trips to the barber. Then he dieted and lost 70 pounds. After all that, he asked himself: Just who am I anyway? Who was the 70 pounds lost through dieting? Am I less myself after that? Was I more or less myself before or after the haircut? Fuller realized that his body could weigh 70 pounds less, yet he could feel more fully himself at the lighter weight. Finally, Fuller not only knew but understood in a deep sense a fact we so often miss in our society: we are more than our bodies. Besides bodies we have intelligence—the incredible ability to seek out and grasp truth. We also have emotions—the tremendous gift of our feelings and the ability to identify with the feelings of others. We dream. We reach out to one another in love. We create. And we can do all these things regardless of the shape of our bodies. In fact, those traits that make us truly human—creatures unique from all other forms of life—have nothing to do with our physical appearance.

We must be smart about this. We must judge our own lovableness by more than what we see in the mirror. We must measure our value as human beings by more than the strength or shape of our bodies. For no matter how strong we get, gorillas will always be able to lift more weight. No matter how beautiful we become, we would never win better than second prize if beauty contests included butterflies.

Obviously our bodies are important. We must exercise, keep in shape, and avoid faddish diets and bad habits that can harm us. Our bodies are our primary contact with the rest of the world, the vehicles through which all our values and talents are expressed. So take care of yourself but do not lose sight of what is truly important—the fact that your true beauty will show through your body regardless of its limitations.

Emotional Development

Ninth graders experience some definite changes in their emotional abilities and attitudes too. As mentioned earlier, young children get over hurt feelings very easily. The friend they were

Billboard advertisers say that billboards must use no more than eight words to provide attention-getting information about a product or service. Anything more than this will not be understood by motorists driving by. Try to create your own billboard statement, using no more than eight words, that would advise adolescents on how to accept their physical appearance.

ready to reject one minute will likely be invited to share a favorite toy five minutes later. That is an example of emotional immaturity, however, not a demonstration of the child's ability to forgive. The changing pattern of friendships between childhood and adolescence is a reflection of emotional growth. Young children tend to operate in groups, and they may in all honesty speak of having thirty-five best friends. In adolescence, however, we often begin to develop more exclusive relationships, developing one or two very deep friendships rather than always relating as part of a large group. We will talk more about this in a moment.

Many ninth graders discover another dramatic change with regard to their emotions, a change that again occurs earlier for girls than for boys. They find that they are able to feel more deeply about things than they did before. They may be hurt more easily and be far more sensitive than before. Perhaps you find, for example, that you are more able to relate emotionally to the problems other people have and to feel sincere sadness when you hear of the suffering of others. Or you may find that you are emotionally unpredictable. For no apparent reason, you can be laughing one minute and feeling very down the next. All of these characteristics are signs of maturing emotions. Just as your body is undergoing changes to make your functioning physically and sexually as an adult possible, so your emotions are changing and stretching in order to allow deeper and fuller human relationships. This emotional development can be terribly difficult yet exhilarating for you because it suggests your growing ability to experience mature love with others.

Imagine a teeter-totter that represents your emotional life. The left side represents feeling good or high about life. The right side represents feeling down or bad. Draw a simple sketch to show the position of your teeter-totter today. How often would your teeter-totter go up and down in a day? in a week? in a month?

In adolescence, we often begin to develop deep friendships.

Intellectual Development

Many ninth graders also experience changes in their intellectual attitudes and abilities. Psychologists have found that our ability to think and to reason follows a growth pattern, or series of stages, in the same way that the body gradually develops from childhood to adulthood. Intellectually, young children are unable to grapple with complex, abstract ideas. They live in a world of things, not ideas, and their lives center around trying to gain control of those things through the use of language and through physical development. Gradually, however, we open to the world of ideas and complex thoughts, and a whole new level of living begins. The best demonstration of this is the probability that in your own life you find yourself now seriously questioning things that you once took for granted. You may find yourself wanting or even demanding reasons for what is expected of you.

For example, when you were a child, your parents probably told you which kids in the neighborhood you were allowed to play with. Although you may have occasionally been bothered by this, you likely accepted such parental advice without a lot of argument. As you move through adolescence, however, your parents will continue to try to influence you in your choice of friends, but with far less success! In arguing your point of view with them, you may even be able to make your case using many abstract ideas about the meaning of friendship or your right to freedom in personal relationships. These thoughts would literally have been unthinkable just a few years ago. This same pattern of increasingly independent thinking may also be reflected in arguments with your parents about the hours you must keep or about the question of which school you will attend.

Your developing intellectual capacity is also clearly reflected in your experience of school. For younger children, school is often a matter of accumulating information exactly as the teachers deliver it. Success in school is determined by how well the children can memorize and give back to the teachers the precise information they were given about mathematics, history, religion, or whatever. In high school, however, this changes. Certainly your courses still require a lot of memorization—your algebra teacher will not accept incorrect answers no matter how forcefully you argue for personal freedom of choice! Yet you are beginning to realize that many areas of study have room for, and even the need for, a great deal of disagreement and personal interpretation. The study of history, for example,

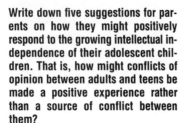

Recall the last time you won an argument with your parent by convincing him or her that your opinion was right. Write a paragraph or two describing and explaining the incident and answering these questions:
- Could you have argued your side of the disagreement as effectively two years ago?
- Why or why not?

Write down five suggestions for parents on how they might positively respond to the growing intellectual independence of their adolescent children. That is, how might conflicts of opinion between adults and teens be made a positive experience rather than a source of conflict between them?

is more than simply accumulating facts about the past; it is a matter of interpreting the events of history and trying to discover their impact on us today. In that effort a great deal of personal opinion exists. You may also find that you now evaluate teachers by the degree to which they allow and even encourage you to think for yourself.

This new attitude of intellectual curiosity and occasional skepticism can be a threat to adults—and to the young person as well. To adults this attitude, which means a loss of the control they once had, is a threat. To the young person this curiosity and skepticism open the possibility of doubt and confusion and the fear that often accompanies these negative feelings. Ninth graders are normally beginning to ask the tough questions about the very meaning of life and how we fit into it. When the answers to those questions are clouded or unavailable, however, the experience can be frightening. Nevertheless, intellectual curiosity is itself another indication of maturing and moving away from the security of childhood to the challenges of adulthood. Like physical and emotional change, intellectual change is both a challenge and an opportunity—the door to a fuller and happier life.

Social Development

Clearly all the adolescent changes that we have been discussing—physical, emotional, and intellectual—have dramatic impact on our relationships with others, on what we might call our social development. We have already noted this by way of example when discussing some of the other areas of development. For example, our changing bodies affect our relationships with the other sex. Likewise, our increasing ability to think can affect our relationship with parents. This course cannot deal at length with all the areas of social development, but we can speak here of what psychologists term *the developmental tasks of adolescents.* Young people must accomplish these tasks if they are to move effectively from adolescence to mature adulthood. Among these tasks three stand out as most important:

1. **The development of a healthful sexual identity:** A person must develop a strong enough sense of himself or herself to be able to relate sexually with others in ways that are positive, life-affirming, caring, and responsible. As noted, this will involve the acceptance of one's own body as well as respect for the bodies of others. Sexual maturity involves far more than

Gradually we open up to the world of ideas and complex thoughts—and a new level of living begins.

List three characteristics—other than the ones mentioned under "Social Development"—that might be involved in developing a healthful sexual identity.

Imagine that you and your classmates have been asked to prepare and lead a three-hour workshop for parents on the subject of parent-teen relationships.
- What topics would you want to raise in such a workshop?
- What goals might you reasonably expect to accomplish in your workshop?
- Write a brief agenda for the workshop based on your reactions to these questions.

List five qualities of your best friend for which you are most grateful. Compare these to the characteristics of friendship described here. If you feel comfortable doing so, find a way to thank your friend for having those qualities.

our bodies, however. Also involved are communication skills, a capacity for developing trust in one's relationships, the ability to care deeply without trying to possess or control the other, and much more.

2. **The development of a more mature parent-child relationship:** Young children must depend on their parents for virtually everything required for survival—food, clothing, shelter, affection, and so on. As we grow older, this dependent relationship has to change; children must more and more assume personal responsibility for their lives. Unfortunately, parents and their children are often very clumsy in the way they handle this transition. They frequently step on each other's emotional toes as they work toward a new adult relationship. Young people want freedom; parents, who are normally motivated by love, often want to continue to protect their children. Far too often parents and children who truly care for each other break apart painfully and angrily. A little understanding of what is taking place could reduce, if not eliminate, much of the tension involved.

3. **The development of a capacity for friendship:** Related to the above developmental tasks and to many other issues that face young people is the need to develop a capacity for friendship. In all the studies that have been done about the needs and concerns of young people, one of the most consistent and highly rated desires of young people is to learn how to make friends and how to be a good friend. Once again, we will have to limit ourselves to simply identifying some of the characteristics and concerns involved in the art of building friendships. You may want to discuss each of these points and add others.

- *Self-acceptance is the foundation of friendships.* If I like and accept who I am as a person, I will likely have the courage and desire to give myself to others in friendship.
- *A friend is committed to the growth and happiness of the other.* Although we obviously gain personally from all our friendships, our goal is to promote the happiness of others, not to use others for our own fulfillment or satisfaction.
- *Friendship takes work.* Friendship requires a commitment on the part of persons to nurture their relationship through both the happy times and the inevitable tough times.
- *Being a friend requires some basic communication skills.* Friends must learn to share their own feelings and thoughts honestly and openly. They also need to listen with their heads and their hearts to what the other is communicating.

Friendship means staying committed through both the happy times and the inevitable tough times.

- *Friendship can only grow when mutual trust is present.* Building trust takes a lot of time, yet trust can be destroyed in a moment. We learn to trust others gradually, based on our day-by-day experiences with them. Trust is fragile, however, and can be quickly shattered. This fact leads to the next point.

- *Friends know how to ask for and accept forgiveness.* We humans are wonderful but also weak. We all make mistakes, and we all hurt one another, most of the time without wanting or planning to. Perhaps what was intended to be a humorous remark deeply hurts a friend. Maybe we forget an appointment or tell others something that a friend considered personal and private. When we hurt someone, finding the words to express sorrow and regret and asking for forgiveness are difficult to do. When we are hurt, accepting once again the risks that trust involves can be even more difficult. Friends must work to learn the skill of asking for and granting forgiveness.

- *In friendship we experience freedom, not fences.* This point relates very much to trust. When friendship exists, we do not feel trapped by the other person. A sure sign of the absence of friendship is the presence of jealousy. If all contacts with others cause a friend to be suspicious or fearful, then friendship did not exist in the first place. This idea relates to our last point.

- *True friendship yearns to be shared and celebrated with others.* We want to share our friendships with others. Constantly wanting to be alone with him or her is often a sign

Writing lightly in pencil, rank order these characteristics of friendship in terms of which you feel is most important, putting number *1* after the most important characteristic, number *2* for the second most important, and so on.

Imagine that your two best friends have had a serious argument. You meet with each of them to try to convince them that they should forgive each other.
- What would you say to them?
- What advice would you offer on how they might resolve their conflict?
- Write a paragraph or two summarizing your thoughts about being a peacemaker.

Jot down three arguments to support the notion that going steady by ninth graders is positive, healthful, and freeing. Then list three arguments to suggest that going steady creates fences between people. Which set of arguments is more convincing?

Try to write down at least three more characteristics of friendship.

that the relationship is not one of friendship but of dependency. When we learn to be friends with another, that experience gives us the skills and desire to build more friendships.

Most of the major developmental challenges of adolescence are touched on in this discussion of friendship. The traits associated with friendship are very closely related to the two key tasks that were mentioned earlier—that is, sexual identity and relationships with parents.

A healthful sexual identity is based on the insight that mature sexual relationships are, in fact, friendships. Of course, they are also more than friendships, but often we treat them

Who Am I?

Don't be fooled by me.
Don't be fooled by the masks I wear.
For I wear a thousand masks, and none of them is me.
I give the impression that I am secure.
Confidence is my name and coolness my game.
But don't believe me.
Beneath lies the real me—in confusion and fear and
     aloneness.
But I don't tell you this because I'm afraid to.
    I am afraid that you will think less of me,
     that you'll laugh at me.
I'm afraid that deep down I'm nothing and I'm no good.
Yet only you can call me into aliveness.
Each time you're kind and encouraging,
Each time you try to understand because you care.
Who am I, you may wonder. I am someone you know very
    well.
I am every man, woman, and child you meet.

                        (Anonymous)

as much less. As you reflected on the traits of friendship, did you picture friends of the other sex as well as friends of your own gender? If you saw these traits as found only in our same-sex friendships, try rereading the list. Ask yourself if they all make sense to you in terms of a relationship with someone of the other sex.

The parent-child relationship can be understood within the context of the need to evolve from total dependency to a mature relationship between adults—in other words, a friendship. We are dependent on our friends, of course, in the sense of trusting them to be sensitive and yet honest with us. We do not depend on friends to make our decisions for us, however, or to pay for the consequences of our decisions.

Each of us would do well to spend significant time—both in personal reflection and in discussion with others—considering the qualities and skills of friendship and discovering ways to grow in our own capacity to nurture friendships in our lives.

Our Religious Lives Also Change

In discussing the journey from childhood to adulthood, we have talked at some length about some of the dramatic changes that ninth graders may be experiencing on all levels of their lives. In this next section we are going to begin dealing specifically with the area of religion—your past experience of it and the questions that you may now be asking about it. We will try throughout this course to provide some answers that make sense of those questions. Before getting into those issues, however, let's deal first with the basic experience of doubt: Are doubts about faith and religion normal? What are the most common doubts young people have about their faith?

Sometimes More Questions Than Answers

As noted earlier, psychologists have found a pattern to our growing ability to think through difficult notions like love, truth, justice, and God. Generally the ability to comprehend abstract and complex concepts begins at about age twelve or so, gradually becoming more mature and sophisticated from that point on. This ability to think in more mature ways can be wonderfully exciting, as one's curiosity expands and as the ability to reflect on all areas of life deepens. Some students

Consider each of the qualities of friendship stated on pages 32–34 in light of the parent-child relationship.
- Based on this list of characteristics, develop a series of eight "Commandments for Parents" that would help parents and adolescents to get along better with each other.
- Then develop a similar list of eight "Commandments for Teenagers" that would help teenagers to improve their relationship with their parents.

During adolescence, our parent-child relationships begin to evolve into adult friendships.

Develop a list of five government policies or social issues that concern you now but would not bother you if you were ten years old.

Maturing young people often find themselves confronting religious doubts and questions.

discover themselves to be vitally interested in areas that completely bored them only a year or two earlier—for example, current affairs or science. This growth can also produce feelings of anxiety and confusion when, for example, it leads students to question their country's foreign policies or their church's moral teachings.

Not surprisingly, young people are also confronted with religious doubts and questions. Life on all levels is full of mystery and rich with questions that can excite, confuse, and even frighten us. Naturally, questions and doubts also arise at this time in the areas of faith and religion. To pretend in this course that such doubts do not exist or simply to avoid dealing with them would be a great disservice to you.

You also need to know, however, that feeling comfortable with your religion is not a sign of immaturity. Your curiosity about life and your search for deeper understanding may not yet extend to the areas of faith and religion. If your past religious life has been positive and enjoyable, you may be content with your present understanding of religious faith.

Moreover, the religious doubts and questions of adolescents are not always related to intellectual difficulties. Some young people develop difficulties with faith and religion because of negative experiences—usually with some person, such as a parish priest, a religion teacher, or a parent. This is, of course, not only an adolescent trait. Many adults make decisions about their religious lives based more on good or bad relationships than on reason. Although personal relationships are vitally important in the experience of our religion, each of us must strive to evaluate our religious beliefs and practices on the basis of what we believe to be the truth. To reject religion because of a conflict with another person is unreasonable, even unfair. Our religious tradition—in fact, any religious tradition—deserves to be judged on its own merits.

In any case, the approach in dealing with faith in this course is *not* based on an assumption that you are experiencing doubt. Nor is the approach based on an assumption that you are totally accepting of religion as you have experienced it. What we hope to do is approach religion, specifically Catholic Christianity, with a sensitivity to your increasing maturity and intelligence. Those who have experienced religious doubt will find both the beginnings of some answers here and some relief from the fear that often accompanies religious questioning. On the other hand, those whose religious convictions are strong will find that these discussions expand and deepen their convictions.

Religious Experience and Development

Religious faith is developmental. This means that faith grows in stages from childhood through adolescence and into adulthood, as do our emotions and our intellects. Let's take a brief look at that development in the settings where it generally takes place: the family, church, and school.

Since childhood, you may have had a crucifix hanging on the wall of your bedroom.

▼

Take an imaginary tour of your home, going through one room at a time in your mind. List anything you can recall in each room that is related in any way to religion—pictures on the walls, statues, books, whatever. Then in writing answer the following questions:
- Do you think that having or not having such things has influenced your own attitude toward religion?
- Why do you think people feel such an apparent need to display these things in their homes?

The Family

Assume, for the sake of example, that you were born into a typical Catholic family. One or both of your parents is Catholic, you regularly attended Mass as a child, you attended either a Catholic grade school or a parish religious education program, and now you are a student in a Catholic high school. Look back over that journey and recall some of the steps along the way.

As a young child you were probably taught certain prayers and religious practices. For example, you may remember saying prayers before meals, particularly on special occasions like Thanksgiving. Other less obvious religious influences probably were at play in your life at that time also. Maybe, like many Catholic children, you had a crucifix hanging on the wall in your bedroom. Perhaps a painting of Jesus hung on the living room wall or at the top of the stairs, which you climbed many times each day. These were all very simple, maybe unconscious, religious influences in your life, but they may have had a deep impact on your initial images of God and on the way you felt about religion.

You may remember enjoying your first religious experiences.

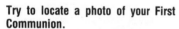

Try to locate a photo of your First Communion.
- In looking at the picture, recall what you felt on that day.
- Write a paragraph or two on this question: How would you compare your attitude toward religion at the time of your First Communion to what you now feel about it?

The Church

Gradually you became more involved in the religious practices of your family. Perhaps you were asked occasionally to lead the family prayers. You were eventually expected to attend Mass each weekend. You may remember enjoying these religious experiences, particularly special occasions like First Communion. They made you feel important, part of something bigger than yourself and your family. This is what could be called the *imitative stage* of religious development. Children do apparently religious things like praying and attending Mass because they want to act like and please their parents. This behavior is not necessarily bad or good. It is simply normal.

Think back also to your early experiences of going to your parish church. Churches come in a lot of different designs. Yours may have been quite old and traditional or very new and modern. The interesting thing is that all churches seem to convey some of the same attitudes, feelings, and sensations. Perhaps you can still remember as a young child the sense of awe created by church music during Mass. Maybe the strange clothing of the priest and others during the religious rites made an impression on you. Something different, something important, was happening. Maybe you remember candles burning, the smell of incense. All of these experiences from your very early life are still part of your religious attitudes today.

The School

You grew older, and as in every other aspect of your life, your religious attitudes were affected by contact and interaction with people outside your family. You went to a Catholic grade school or parish religious education program. You learned more about your faith. In some cases you had great teachers who made you feel important, cared for, and good about yourself. In some cases perhaps your teacher was not so great, and your recollection is of being bored, scared, or maybe even angry.

In understanding your religious attitudes today, you need to realize that all these contacts with religion—whether they were good, bad, enjoyable, or boring—helped shape the person you are today. The decisions many people make about whether or not to believe in God are based on their experiences with teachers and religion classes rather than on whether faith itself makes sense. So you need to get in touch with your past in order to understand why you feel as you do today about religion.

Religious Understanding in Childhood

During your younger school years, you slowly learned more and more about your Catholic faith—where it came from, what Catholics believe about God, and how we express that belief in religious celebrations like the Mass. Remember, though, what we said earlier about the gradual development of the ability to think philosophically or abstractly. The majority of religious concepts are very abstract and very difficult for young children to grasp. For example, how can a young child imagine God? How can a young child understand the meaning of Jesus? How can young children, with no sense of history or even time, be expected to understand a religion that has existed for nearly two thousand years? This is not to say that young children have no understanding of God but only that this understanding of God changes as we grow.

The point here is that you must be open to the possibility that your understanding of religion from your childhood is a mixed bag of some truth, some confused ideas, some genuine understanding, and perhaps some humorous misunderstandings. Little kids often say funny things when they are trying to be serious because they get their concepts and ideas mixed up and their thoughts do not fit together. This strikes older people as funny because they are able to see the lack of logic or common sense in the child's actions or comments. Possibly you are still carrying some confused notions about your religion from your childhood years. That is not bad. What would be wrong is if you judged your religion on the basis of some false notions about it. That is precisely why we have religion courses like this one throughout your growing years, so that gradually

All our contacts with religion—good or bad—help shape our decisions about belief in God.

Recall images of God or religious beliefs held by young children that now seem humorous to you. Draw upon your own childhood as well as that of other children you know. Briefly write about one such humorous incident.

Simple answers to complex questions are all right for little kids, but they will not be accepted by young people.

you can replace childhood knowledge with a more mature understanding.

Adolescent Attitudes About Religion

So where does the growing process bring you today, as a ninth grader? Given all that we discussed earlier about your development, you might be experiencing some confusing religious feelings and questions now. Remember the example used earlier about moving from one home to another and the feelings that accompany that experience? The same holds true for the process of religious growth. Many of your childhood feelings about religion might be good, and you may feel sad—even guilty—about outgrowing them. Maybe as a child your image of God was of a Santa Claus in the sky—a good, jolly old man. Now you are confronted with some frightening and painful problems in the world—war, poverty, and hatred. You may wonder how a good God could allow such things. Maybe as a child you experienced primarily Catholic religious traditions. Now, perhaps, one of your best friends is Jewish or Protestant, and you begin to wonder why your Catholic tradition is any better or more truthful than others. Simple answers to complex questions are all right for little kids, but they will not be accepted by young people. When given only childish answers, some young people end up critical and resentful. They blame adults for what they believe to be the false teachings that they received as children, and they are often unwilling to listen to the new ideas that their teachers now try to present to them.

This negative attitude among some young people is completely understandable given the circumstances just outlined. Throwing off childhood and moving into the unknown can create these kinds of feelings. What is important now is to recognize this tendency and to deal with it creatively. This will require patience because religion is a very difficult and complex subject, which requires a lot more maturity and work than do subjects like math. You might not agree with that example, but at least in mathematics you can be guaranteed that all the pieces somehow fit together. That is not always true when dealing with the mysteries of religion.

The Need for Openness

At this stage in your religious education you will also have to be open to the possibility that you can learn a great deal more about your faith. After eight years or so of religion classes, you might feel tempted to say, "I've heard this all a hundred times before!" You may have heard many of the words before—words such as *Trinity* or *sacraments*—but the realities behind those words are so awesome and so infinite that we can never fully understand them. Always more can be learned, and exciting insights can be gained. Particularly at this time in your life you need to take a fresh look at your faith and see it through the eyes of someone who is leaving childhood behind—a childhood that, in fact, could not provide all the answers that you need and deserve.

Our Uniqueness Brings Pain and Promise

We have covered a lot of ground in a short time in our discussion of the challenging world of the adolescent. We want to conclude this part of the discussion with a comment on one of the most universal and most difficult experiences of young people—loneliness.

This course began with a discussion of the uniqueness of all people. Of all the billions of human beings who have passed through this world, no two have been exactly alike. Perhaps two may have looked alike, but probably they did not think the same way or have the same talents or pursue the same dreams. Never before in history and never again in the future of the world will there ever be another you! This great gift of uniqueness has two major effects: the pain of loneliness and the promise of meaning.

Identify and list five major personal problems often encountered by young people.

The great gift of uniqueness also brings the pain of loneliness.

Loneliness

Because we are unique and because no other person quite like us has ever existed, we are guaranteed occasional and often painful loneliness in our lives. All of us have found ourselves thinking that "no one understands me!" Let's admit that at times this is true. Because we are unique, no one sees life entirely as we do. When someone says, "I know just what you're going through," we often find the comment irritating and even offensive because we know in our hearts that this person does *not* and in fact *cannot* know exactly what we are going through!

The need for people to say consoling things is based on their love and concern, certainly, but also on the false assumption in our society that loneliness is in itself bad and to be avoided at all costs. So we try to escape loneliness anytime that we experience it. We escape loneliness in our homes by turning on the television or stereo. Or we think up any excuse we can to call a friend.

Loneliness is as much a human experience as joy, fear, delight, and anger are.

Yet we often discover that turning to our friends simply does not solve the problem of our loneliness. We find that even with our friends—sometimes mostly with our friends—we feel terrifying loneliness. You may have experienced feeling all alone in a crowded gym during a basketball game or feeling totally isolated while standing at a school dance with hundreds of people around.

Many people try other forms of escape from loneliness: they drink alcohol or they take drugs. In short, they turn to chemical answers for a problem that can never be solved that way. The only way we can endure loneliness is to embrace it as a common human experience, as an experience of our own uniqueness, and as an opportunity to learn more deeply about ourselves.

Loneliness is as much a human experience as joy, fear, delight, and anger are. Some of the greatest lessons in life, in fact, can only be learned in pain, in tears, or in loneliness. We should not try to run away from it, to escape it, or to block it out. The experience of loneliness is a sign of one of our greatest gifts in life, our uniqueness as persons.

Your Life Has Special Meaning

The second effect of our uniqueness is this: the world has never seen or will never in the future see another person just like you. So you have something to contribute to history—some gift to share with humanity—that simply cannot be offered by any other person. The goal of your life is to discover that unique meaning, to embrace it, and to develop it. That search is what the process of maturing is all about. You live in an age in which many pressures are being exerted to make you just like everyone else. You are expected to dress like others, to listen to the same music, to act the same way—in short, to be one of the gang. Some of that pressure to conform is unavoidable and even beneficial—we *need* shared experiences upon which to build deeper relationships with others. Do not get locked into thinking, however, that your worth as a human being is decided by how you fit in with the expectations of others. God has given you both a gift—your uniqueness as an individual—and a **vocation**, or calling, in life to develop your unique self for the benefit and growth of others. We will be discussing in more depth later what that calling means. For now, try to keep in mind the profound meaning of a very simple saying: Your life is God's gift to you. What you do with your life is your gift to God.

Create a small card with the last statement on this page written on it. Tape it to a mirror in your room or anywhere you will likely see it each morning. Try to start each day with a reminder to yourself of the wisdom of this saying.

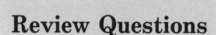

Review Questions

1. Identify three feelings that are common to both moving from one home to another and moving from childhood to adolescence.
2. Why is describing normal adolescent development difficult?
3. What are the ranges of ages for the start of puberty in girls and boys?
4. What is the biological explanation for the fact that junior high school girls are often taller than boys their age?
5. Give an example of how we might experience a change in our emotions that is directly related to our physical development.
6. How are the emotions of adolescents different from those of young children?
7. What is the major difference between the way a young child thinks and the way that an adolescent or an adult thinks?
8. Why is the intellectual change that takes place during adolescence often a threat to both adults and young people alike?
9. What do psychologists identify as three major developmental tasks of adolescents regarding their social development?
10. This chapter lists eight characteristics of friendship. Summarize each characteristic using no more than three words for each.
11. How does the development of the skills of friendship relate to the tasks of developing a sexual identity and growing in a relationship with parents?
12. Why is the experience of religious doubt normal for adolescents?
13. Why do we need to recall and get in touch with the religious experiences of our childhood?

14. Loneliness is commonly viewed as a negative experience. In what way is loneliness also a good thing, a sign of something positive in our lives?

15. This chapter states that the first effect of our uniqueness is occasional loneliness. What is the second effect of our uniqueness?

Key Terms
adolescence
puberty
ovulation
ejaculation

2
Culture and Values:
Becoming Who
We Are Called to Be

Free to Be Me

Your life is God's gift to you. What you do with your life is your gift to God. That motto suggests two meanings, both of which will be discussed in this chapter. The first is that our lives consist of some givens—that is, some things that we have no control over, no say in, and no escape from. Recognizing these givens as gifts from a loving God is not always easy. The second meaning that we will consider is just the opposite of the first or, more accurately, the other side of the same coin. That is, although we cannot control some things in our lives, we do have the freedom to greatly influence who we are and what we will become, to take charge of our lives and to shape our own destinies. As we will see, our ability to accept what we cannot change and to assume responsibility for what we will become is precisely what growing up or achieving maturity is all about.

Gifts or Givens?

Consider for a few moments the many things in your life over which you have had little or no control. For example, although you can now choose whether to remain alive, you did not choose to be born. The initial choice of beginning your life was the decision of your parents, or in an even more profound sense, your life was a gift from God. Other basic features of your life that you did not and, for the most part, cannot control are the following:

- *Your moment in history:* Why were you born in the twentieth century rather than in the Middle Ages? or at the time of Christ? or in prehistoric times?
- *Your country:* In all likelihood you were born and raised in North America, a unique and unusual environment when compared to the rest of the world.

For each item on the list of givens in life, write a two-word or three-word descriptive phrase about yourself—that is, about your own ethnic background, religion, and so on. When you are done, write a brief paragraph using all these phrases to describe yourself in terms of all the givens in your life. Begin the paragraph by completing the statement "I am . . ."

- *Your ethnic background:* You had no control over whether you are black, brown, white, red, or yellow; German, Mexican, Italian, Cuban, or Irish.
- *Your family:* You did not choose your parents. Nor, in the strict sense, did they choose you. They perhaps consciously decided to have a child, but they may not have expected anyone quite like you!
- *Your social and economic background:* Whether you are poor, middle-class, or wealthy and whether you are the child of a prominent or an average family are factors in which you had no say.
- *Your religion:* Although you will have to choose whether to remain a member of the religion into which you were born, you did not have the option of being born into a Catholic, Buddhist, Jewish, or Protestant family or, for that matter, into a family that holds no religious beliefs at all.
- *Your town and your school:* You probably did not choose the school you attended in first grade. Such decisions were made largely by your parents, and even their choices were limited by job opportunities, by the availability of schools, and so on. As you grow older, of course, your influence in such choices increases. You may have great freedom in choosing the college that you want to attend.
- *Your available friends:* You do choose the friends you have, but you choose from among a limited number of people. You can only get to know so many people, and you have no way of predicting who will come your way.
- *Your body:* You have great control over what you do with your body now, but what you started with was not up to you. You never had the opportunity to choose if you would be tall or short, let alone whether you would be a boy or a girl.

Living in a World of *If Onlys*

The above list could be longer, but the point is clear. Much of who we are is beyond our control. For better or worse, that is just the way life is. The sad fact is that most of us—adults and young people alike—spend a great deal of time and effort regretting this reality, denying it to ourselves, and often trying to escape it. We would be much happier if we could accept the givens in our lives.

Here is a simple test about accepting the conditions that we encounter as givens. Try to recall the last time that you started a sentence with the words *if only.* Also, try to remember

Clothes are often seen as a way to improve physical appearance or to gain social acceptance.

when you heard friends, relatives, or others use that expression. A few frequently occurring examples might help to jog your memories.

- If only I could be better looking . . .
- If only I could be richer . . .
- If only he or she would like me . . .
- If only I were taller . . .
- If only I were shorter . . .
- If only I were smarter . . .
- If only I had different parents . . .
- If only I had a nicer home . . .
- If only I had better clothes . . .
- If only I had more understanding teachers . . .

Too often we live our lives in a world of *if onlys*. We look back at our past with regret or anger. Or we look forward to our future with fear or lack of hope. The problem, of course, is that we overlook the possibilities of the present—the here and now. Unfortunately, someday we will recall these moments that we have wasted, these great opportunities for growth that we missed, and will say, "If only I had done that differently . . ."

If you developed the descriptive paragraph about yourself suggested earlier, review that description and circle all those phrases about which you find yourself most often feeling or saying, "If only I weren't that way" or "If only this weren't true about me."

Lemons and Lemonade

For several years now people have talked about the need to "get our heads together." Or we hear people say, "That person's really got her act together" or "He's really a together person." The wording changes but the meaning behind these sayings remains the same—we feel that in some way our minds are divided, separated, disjointed, or confused. Many of us may feel this way. After all, we live in a complex and often confusing world. The people in our family, peer group, schools, society, the media, the Church are telling us what we are supposed to be, criticizing what we are, or warning us about what we should not become. Naturally, we often get confused, frustrated, and bewildered by the often mixed messages that we receive from these sources.

That sometimes trite phrase—*getting it together*—does seem to hold the solution for us. Getting it together means:
1. Discovering what our gifts are and developing them to their fullest potential
2. Accepting the givens of our lives over which we have no control
3. Celebrating our givens by learning to see them as gifts (when we are handed lemons, we can learn to make lemonade)
4. Creating unique lives out of the special set of gifts and givens that shape our lives
5. Leaving behind the world of *if onlys*

Later on in this chapter, we will discuss how education and religion can help us in this process. Right now, let's look at how the values and expectations of others can affect our self-images.

Overcoming the Barriers to Self-Development

In the discussion in chapter 1 of the new world of the ninth grader, we concentrated on what is going on inside the typical ninth grader—those biological, emotional, intellectual, social, and religious changes that he or she is likely experiencing at this time in life. All kinds of events are also happening outside of us that directly affect our lives. Some of these influences are obvious. Others are less apparent but no less significant in their impact on our self-image and on our relationships.

For instance, each of us needs to know that some people care for us, love us, and consider us important. The problem

▼

For each of the five points on "getting it together," write two things that immediately come to your mind regarding yourself. For example, identify two gifts you have that you might develop. Or select two givens in your life that you can choose to view as gifts. Or consider two ways in which you might leave behind the world of *if onlys*.

Getting it together means creating unique lives out of our special gifts and givens.

is that we often feel we must win or earn that acceptance or in some way force people to like us. Too often that means meeting the expectations of others as to who we should be. So we trap ourselves into creating lives based on the demands of others rather than on a clear realization and acceptance of who we are and a commitment to remain true to ourselves.

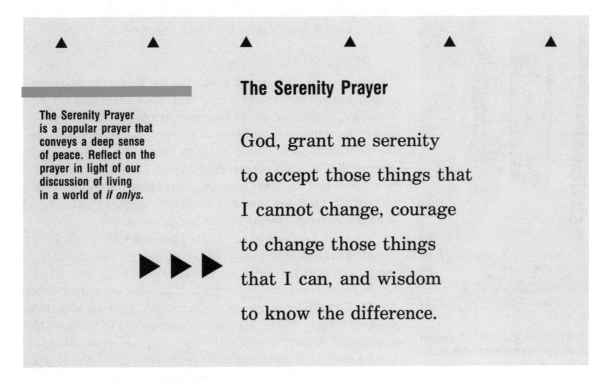

The Serenity Prayer
is a popular prayer that
conveys a deep sense
of peace. Reflect on the
prayer in light of our
discussion of living
in a world of *if onlys.*

The Serenity Prayer

God, grant me serenity

to accept those things that

I cannot change, courage

to change those things

that I can, and wisdom

to know the difference.

Stereotypes as Unfair Expectations

This barrier to self-development is all the more difficult to overcome when others' expectations have hardened into **stereotypes.** A stereotype exists whenever a group unfairly characterizes or judges persons or other groups on the basis of oversimplified and often untrue opinions or information. Clear evidence of stereotyping is the use of the word *all* at the beginning of sentences describing someone or some group. Among the common stereotypical remarks directed at various groups are the following:

Create a list of six stereotypes often associated with young people your age. Begin each statement "All ninth graders . . ."

- All Irish people are alcoholic.
- All men are violent.
- All athletes are dumb.
- All Jews are cunning in business.
- All black Americans are lazy.

- All women are softheaded.
- All Germans are coldhearted.
- All Hispanics are hot-tempered.

As more people accept a particular stereotype as true, it becomes stronger. We may even discover that just as we try to live up to our normal ideals, we can also be led to believe that we must live *down* to certain strong stereotypes. Several examples will help clarify how this can happen.

Physical Stereotypes

In the last chapter we spoke briefly about the body-consciousness of ninth graders and, indeed, of our entire society. Consider the implications of this often exaggerated concern. For example, someone somewhere has determined that white people must have tanned skin in the summer. Why white skin is unappealing has never been determined, but we are thoroughly conditioned to accepting this stereotype. No doubt this stereotype both amuses and confuses blacks, Indians, and others for whom tanned skin is not an issue.

So what happens to all the redheaded white people in the world? Redheaded people do not tan—they fry! Because of this, many of them live with embarrassment, with fear of the laughter of others, and often with a distaste for summer water sports. Consequently we see a wide variety of so-called instant tanning lotions on the market, all guaranteed to increase the appeal and attractiveness of the user. In other words, these lotions promise to make redheads more acceptable and lovable as persons. Consider this: millions of people in this country actually paint their bodies in the belief that cosmetics will make them more lovable. Along with some humor, real sadness exists in this situation because those people are going to learn sooner or later that tanning lotion will not help a bit. In fact, this sort of cover-up can be a step backward from the necessary task of accepting our bodies rather than hiding them.

Far less humorous than the concern about tanning are other examples of the effects of our culture's extreme body-consciousness, especially our obsession with thinness. *Seventeen* magazine reports that 80 percent of college-age teens consider themselves overweight. In recent years a tremendous increase in the incidence of eating disorders, primarily among young people, has occurred. Two such disorders are of particular concern—**anorexia nervosa** and **bulimia**. Anorexia nervosa is an illness in which the person literally starves himself or herself, with 10 to 15 percent of sufferers actually dying of starvation.

Research suggests that 80 percent of college-age teens consider themselves overweight.

On a piece of scratch paper, list ten items popular with adolescents that are advertised and sold with the claim that the items will make young people more physically attractive and acceptable to their peers.

Every new issue of popular magazines announces another fad diet that is guaranteed to make us attractive and fit.

A conservative estimate is that one in two hundred girls from ages fourteen to eighteen suffer from the illness. Roughly one in two thousand boys is anorexic.

The other eating disorder, bulimia, involves what is called *binge eating,* in which persons gorge themselves but then follow that with forced vomiting or with the use of laxatives.

Clearly this is not pleasant information to consider, but it is simply too important to ignore. These two illnesses are extreme symptoms of our cultural obsession with thinness. Every new issue of popular magazines announces another fad diet that is guaranteed to make us attractive and fit. The fact is that we now have available enough medically proven information about nutrition and health to develop reasonable diets, which avoid the silliness and real risks of many of the fad diets. These diets are a particular concern for your age-group, which needs a high intake of nutritious food in order to sustain periods of rapid growth. If you are concerned about your own eating habits or if you know someone else who you fear may be having difficulty in this area, consult a counselor for help.

Emotional Stereotypes

We also discussed earlier the fact that ninth graders are developing emotionally, that they are beginning to experience events more deeply. For a long time in our culture, however, some emotions have been recognized and accepted as being feminine while other emotions have been classified as masculine. What results?

Divide a piece of paper into two columns. At the top of one column, write *boys,* and at the top of the other, *girls.* In each column, list all the emotions that are usually identified with each sex.

- A four-year-old boy falls and hurts himself, begins to cry, and is immediately criticized: "Boys don't cry." So he learns.

Today many of the older attitudes about what boys and girls should study are changing dramatically.

Complete the following sentence by jotting down four endings you believe to be true: "I believe that developing myself intellectually is valuable because . . ."

Eventually he grows to be a man who is no longer capable of expressing joy or sadness.

■ While playing a game with neighborhood kids, a young girl gets involved in an argument regarding rules. Someone tells her that fighting is not "ladylike." She learns, and she grows to be a woman who withholds her opinions or allows others to manipulate her.

Human emotions are universal. That is, some emotions are felt more deeply by one person than by another, but no emotions are restricted to one sex or the other. Some men, in fact, are more emotionally sensitive than some women. More importantly, emotional expression is a characteristic of the mature personality. The emotionally developed man can cry, laugh, and have strong convictions. Likewise the emotionally developed woman can be tender, feel anger, and strive for success in whatever capacity she desires.

Intellectual Stereotypes

We spoke earlier of the intellectual development that many ninth graders are experiencing at this time. In this regard, too, we can often run into conflict because of the expectations of others. Many young people, for instance, are given the impression by their peers that being committed to their studies or seriously pursuing academic excellence is not acceptable. Those who like school are stereotyped as fools. As a result, many high school students get trapped into thinking that to be normal young people they must hurry up and get out of school, close the books for good, and never study or read again. Unfortunately, if they follow that negative dream, if they stop reading and thinking, they will stop growing. By the time they are twenty-five, they will already be old because they will have no great plans, no fresh visions, no exciting hopes for their future.

Another problem that we face at the intellectual level is based again on stereotypes regarding genders. For years we have falsely labeled some areas of study as masculine and others as feminine. So some people feel that boys should not study cooking or fine arts and that girls should not study computer technology or dream of a career in medicine. Today many of these attitudes are changing dramatically, but the effects of a long history of stereotyping are going to take generations to remove completely.

For the sake of our growth as total persons, we must recognize the necessity of developing our intellectual ability by studying regularly and by working hard to learn as much as we can. We do not have to do this only because of commitments to parents or to teachers. In other words, we do not have to develop intellectually to make others proud of us. We can make the decision to do so because of a commitment to ourselves, to become all that we are capable of being.

Religious Stereotypes

We have been discussing how we often judge our own worth and lovableness on the basis of the expectations others have of us. We get trapped when we try to live up to or fit in with the physical, emotional, and intellectual stereotypes of our culture. We also experience similar tensions in the area of our religious identities. Chapter 1 noted that the experience of religious doubt and of boredom with religion is common among young people. This doubt and boredom are rooted, at least in part, in the young person's increasing intellectual ability and in a necessary rejection of earlier, childish religious understandings. However, stereotyping often causes young people to have a negative attitude about religion. How is this attitude expressed and experienced?

- One way to get at this issue is to imagine yourself overhearing a group of your friends and listening as one of them says that you are "the most religious kid in the whole class." How would you feel about that comment? Would you feel complimented or insulted?

Most young people would not feel good about being described as "religious" or "holy." Why?

- Or let's go one step further. Imagine overhearing a group of your teachers and perhaps the school chaplain who are agreeing that you are "the holiest young person in the school." Again, how would you feel? Would you feel proud or humiliated or embarrassed? Would you want to share what you heard with your best friend, or would you prefer to keep it to yourself? Why?

In the section "Religious Stereotypes," you are asked to reflect on a series of questions. On a piece of paper, honestly answer each question.

Quite likely, most young people would not view such descriptions as compliments. Yet, you might argue, most adults would not react too positively in such situations either, and these examples are exaggerated. So let's imagine a more likely situation. If you truly enjoyed attending Mass, would you be comfortable telling your friends that? Would you be inclined to talk to a friend about your experience of personal prayer? How would most of your classmates react if the most popular student in the class announced that she was going to be a nun or that he was considering becoming a priest? If your parish were to begin a youth ministry group, would you want to be part of it?

The purpose of these questions is to illustrate that in our culture being religious or devout is often considered unacceptable. We must be careful not to allow cultural pressures to distract or deter us from growing spiritually any more than we would allow ourselves to be controlled or manipulated by society's images of what we should be like physically, emotionally, intellectually, or socially.

Keeping Up with the Joneses

Examples of stereotypes limiting our choices could go on and on. As mentioned, these stereotypes gain power as they gain acceptance. For instance, consider the following ways we behave when around others our age whose opinions are important to us:

- A group of boys stands in the hallway and makes fun of an unattractive girl who walks by. One boy wants to be accepted by the gang, so he joins in the ridicule even though he knows he will later feel guilty about doing this.
- A group of girls spreads rumors that could destroy someone's reputation. One girl says nothing in protest because she doesn't want the group to lash out at her.
- Everybody who is anybody is going to get together on Friday night to "get high." One girl doesn't really want to get into that, but she doesn't want to be rejected by those who do.
- If a person wants to be popular, the group says, he or she has to be sexually "free"—meaning that he or she must behave in the way that the group demands. Although afraid of the results of sexual experimentation, many ninth graders feel terribly pressured to become sexually active.
- One boy enjoys religion—even likes going to Mass. But someone tells him that religion is boring and that those who like it are still little kids.

None of the above examples is unusual or exaggerated. So we must consider carefully what happens to the persons whose lives are based solely on what others consider important. They are locked into a prison that will suffocate their individuality, their uniqueness. Struggling to live up to what others expect

We must be careful not to allow cultural pressures to deter us from growing spiritually.

For each of the five examples given under "Keeping Up with the Joneses," suggest a positive, realistic, and mature way in which a young person might respond.

of them, they live in constant fear that they will never succeed. They do things that directly contradict their own values. Unhappily, they may set a pattern that will last into adulthood when they will be trapped by the never-ending battle to "keep up with the Joneses."

This is a bleak, depressing picture to paint. Perhaps the situation is slightly exaggerated to make a point but not greatly so. By giving up the freedom to determine our own lifestyles and our own values, attitudes, and behavior patterns, we give up our ability to be ourselves. We will always be struggling to be someone else—some perfect image of a person thought up by someone else. Our uniqueness, the quality that makes us special and different from all others who ever existed, is precious beyond price. We cannot afford to lose it or to give it away. Besides, we can never escape from who we are. The attempt will only cause us to be unhappy, confused, and frustrated.

Cultural Influences on Self-Development

Many of the ideas we have been discussing relate to or are part of our North American culture. In our search for who we are and in our struggle to develop our own potential, we must be conscious of the nature of our culture and its influence upon us.

What is **culture?** In the sense used here, it means the total pattern of thought, speech, behavior, and social values that has been passed down from one generation to another within a given society. In a more restricted sense, *culture* often refers to the means by which those things are passed on from generation to generation—for example, through the arts, music, literature, social customs, and traditions. Culture is, therefore, a difficult concept to catch hold of because it seems to include just about everything around us. In a sense, it does.

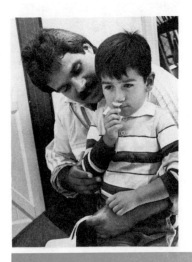

In our search for who we are, we must be conscious of the influence of culture.

Comparing Cultures

Perhaps the best way to understand the nature of culture is to compare the North American way of life to that of a very different society. Consider, for example, the differences between growing up in the United States or Canada and growing up in a remote South American village. Think through your typical day in our society—what you do from when you get up in the morning to when you go to bed. Then try to imagine what you would be doing during the same day if you were part of South American society and culture.

- As a North American, you will likely get out of a warm bed with a thick mattress and blankets, leave your bedroom, and go to the bathroom, where you will wash up and brush your teeth. In a South American village, someone your age might sleep on a hammock in a simple hut, with all the family members gathered in one room and with no indoor plumbing.
- In either country one would likely eat something for breakfast. But your food will likely come out of a brightly designed box while your South American neighbor may well eat something left over from last evening's dinner.

A typical day in a South American society can be very different than one in a North American society.

- Then you will hop on the bus to go to school. The South American in the remote village will certainly not have buses and modern roadways, and he or she would be amazed at the large school systems in North America. Indeed, he or she may not attend school at all.
- After school you might get together with friends to play some games. Your South American neighbor will gather with friends in the same way, but the games they play will be completely different.
- During the day and evening you will be listening to particular kinds of music over radio and television. In the villages of South America the young people will likely be making their own unique music because electricity and all the conveniences that go with it are not available.
- You will read newspapers and books and gain ideas from them that will be very distinct from those learned by your neighbors to the south.

■ You will carry on family traditions, eat with specific routines, act in certain ways, and follow a whole pattern of behavior that would be almost unimaginable for the South American. Likewise his or her way of life would be completely unfamiliar to you. That distinct way of life, that pattern of values and behavior, is what is meant by *culture*.

About fourteen years ago a very unique person with almost unlimited potential—namely, you—was born into the world, but not into the whole world. Rather, you were born into a particular country and into a specific region of the country with its own special cultural patterns. You cannot help but be significantly affected by that culture. This influence is not bad in itself. Every culture has its strengths and weaknesses, its good ideals and bad ones. Nor would life be as rich if all cultures were identical. The variety of human cultures is perhaps one of the most enjoyable and interesting human realities.

Recognizing Cultural Values

We need to learn about and respect other cultures and societies. Equally important for our own development, we must become very conscious of our own culture and its influences upon us as individuals. The television shows that we watch, the music that we listen to, the clothes that we consider fashionable, the dances that we want to learn, and the movies that we go to are all part of a culture that directly influences our values and behavior. So we have to approach these realities with full awareness and with the complete freedom to accept or to reject them.

We know that a key to maturing as an individual is the ability not only to accept those things that are givens and part of our lives but also to assume responsibility for what we are to become as persons. We are North Americans—citizens of free and affluent societies. We should be grateful for the many things that implies: the high standard of living most of us enjoy, the ability to exercise our talents freely, the opportunity to attend good schools, and so on. Yet other values in our culture are not good, and these cultural influences touch us and can harm our attitudes toward ourselves, our hopes, our dreams, and all that we are as persons. Many of the stereotypes that we discussed earlier are obvious examples of negative cultural values.

Without pretending to engage in a thorough analysis of our culture, let's briefly discuss some more subtle, yet powerful,

Cultural influences affect our attitudes toward ourselves, our hopes, and our dreams.

values of our culture—values that might affect us in ways that are not healthful or humane. Of course, what one person describes as not good another might claim as the best thing in the world. This again is why each of us must reflect carefully on who and what we wish to become in life. In that way we will choose those values upon which we wish to stake our lives, rather than have values forced upon us. The following paragraphs examine a few North American cultural values that warrant much reflection and discussion.

Consumerism

Consumerism is a very complex issue but a vitally important one. Much about our economic system is good and valuable, generating the highest standard of living in the world. Yet our economy is driven in large part by the notion that people are primarily consumers, seeking and acquiring new products, many of which are totally unnecessary. So while much of the world goes hungry, we spend billions of dollars each year on junk food. While many in the world do not have enough clothing, we buy and then quickly discard the latest fashions. Young people are a major target of tremendous investments by advertisers who try to pressure them to buy everything from junk food to brand name shoes to the latest in stereo equipment. Each of us must carefully weigh the degree to which we are influenced by this cultural drive to acquire more and more things that bring little real and lasting joy.

Young people are a major target of advertisers, who try to pressure them to buy new and often unnecessary products.

Individualism

Like consumerism, **individualism** can be positive in one sense but negative when taken to an extreme. The commitment to the dignity and rights of the individual is at the center of our way of life and, indeed, central to our religious beliefs as well. A tension arises, however, when individuality is over-stressed so that any sense of responsibility to others and to the community as a whole is lost. Service to others is being replaced by the belief that I must take care of myself first. The notion of sacrificing one's own desires for the sake of "the common good" has become labeled as old-fashioned. The single moral guideline of our society seems to have become Do your own thing. In our cultural quest for individuality, we have forgotten our need to be part of a caring community. Many in our society have apparently achieved success on their own, only to find that they are now dying of loneliness.

For each of the four cultural values listed, state two practical ways in which a young person might resist or positively respond to the value. For example, what are two ways in which someone your age might resist the cultural pressure to acquire unnecessary items? Likewise, give two suggestions for helping young people resist the desire for immediate gratification.

Immediate Gratification

We have become a "feel good" society. Much of our behavior is based on the conviction "If it feels good, do it." We view any experience of suffering as evil, even if the suffering is done out of care and concern for loved ones. As a result, when people experience the inevitable loneliness or pain in life, they immediately want to block it out with alcohol, drugs, or perhaps more consumerism ("I'll feel a lot better if I just buy something new"). The term *immediate gratification* means that we want and expect our needs to be met right now—not tomorrow and certainly not in a few years. Obviously this has tremendous effects on our relationships with others. Many people view as friends only those people who always make them feel good. As soon as relationships become more demanding, they feel as free to discard friendships as they would a pair of jeans that is no longer fashionable.

Sexual Permissiveness

This issue is difficult to discuss without being labeled a prude or worse. Admittedly, some of the past attitudes toward sexuality were unhealthful and even destructive—leading some, for example, to feel ashamed of or guilty about normal sexual feelings and experiences. Our contemporary sexual attitudes and values, however, are equally bad if not worse. To appreciate this, let's look at **sexual permissiveness** in terms of the values already discussed.

- For many people in our society, sexual relationships are just one more consumer item to be tried out and discarded as easily as a pair of shoes.
- Because of our emphasis on individual freedom, many people are terrified of the thought of true commitment to another person, the kind of commitment that is required if sexual expression is to be wholesome and life-giving.
- Finally, because of our desire for immediate gratification, many people are incapable of struggling through the difficulties that will always be part of caring relationships.

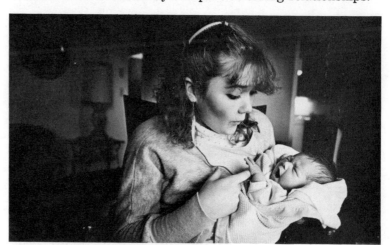

The negative side of our current approach to sexuality is reflected in the nearly epidemic problem of teenage pregnancies.

These negative characteristics of our contemporary approach to sexuality are reflected in the nearly epidemic problem of teenage pregnancies—about one million teenage girls become pregnant each year. Many of these girls and the boys who were involved with them probably engaged in sexual activity thinking that it was the thing to do, that it was so natural that there was nothing wrong with it, or that it was a response to a desire for immediate gratification. Certainly many others thought that they were expressing an honest love and commitment. Yet the sad fact remains that most of these girls discover tragedy and pain rather than joy and that they are often left to suffer the consequences alone.

Our society is so dominated by these negative values that we cannot escape their influence. Yet one could counter each of these with other examples of positive values that our culture also represents, optional ways of life that are life-giving and caring. That is precisely the point: We all do have a choice; in fact, we all *have to choose*, or we risk handing our lives over to the influence of the kinds of values identified above.

Evaluating Our Culture's Media

In our earlier attempt to define culture, we noted that culture is often understood as the means by which a society's heritage and values are passed on. That is, culture is often defined as music, art, literature, and so on. Regarding culture in this sense, we need to become particularly conscious of the values and messages conveyed by several very influential sources of entertainment and information in our culture. These means are commonly known as *the media* and include television, movies, newspapers, radio, and popular music. Let's look briefly at the three most influential media in the lives of young people: television, movies, and music.

Television

Television viewing is the number one recreational pastime in our culture. More to the point, television has been the most influential single cause of the rapid rate of cultural change. At the touch of a button, we are now almost immediately affected by and involved in world events. Also, television has dissolved many of the characteristics that at one time gave each region of the United States and Canada a unique flavor. For example, regional patterns of speech are slowly merging into a kind of national dialect as more and more people sound like the person we hear every day on television.

This apparent power of television to serve as a source of unity and global communication is, according to some people, one of its greatest assets. We have to be clear as well, however, about the potential of television to influence each of us in negative ways. Just listen to some of the statistics that have emerged in recent years about the television viewing habits of people in the United States.

- Children watch an average of four hours of television every day, spending more time in front of the television than doing any other activity except sleeping.
- By the time the average child enters kindergarten, he or she will already have spent more hours learning about the world from television than the total number of hours one would spend in a college classroom earning a bachelor's degree.
- In an average family, the television set is on for about forty-four hours a week.

These figures are in themselves quite staggering, but now reflect on what people are actually exposed to while viewing television.

On a piece of paper, create a log of your own television-viewing habits for a typical week, as follows:
- Down the left side of the paper, list the days of the week beginning with Sunday. Allow some space between each day.
- Across from each day and in the middle of the page, list the television shows that you regularly watch on that day.
- Then, on the right side of the page across from each day of the week, state the total number of hours you normally watch television on that day.
- Finally, in the lower right-hand corner, total the number of hours that you watch television each week.
- Evaluate the results in writing. Is there a pattern to the kinds of shows you watch? Are you surprised by the total number of hours you watch television?

In an average week, television shows portray twenty-two hours of violence.

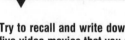

Try to recall and write down the last five video movies that you rented on your own or with friends—that is, not as a family activity.
- Are any themes or values common to all or most of the films?
- What does this suggest about the values of your age-group?

- In one study researchers counted twenty thousand sexual scenes on prime-time network television annually, *not* counting soap operas. Yet the shows mentioned virtually no consequences of such activity, such as pregnancy.
- Speaking of soap operas, consider this: an astounding 94 percent of all sexual encounters portrayed in soap operas are among people *not* married to each other.
- During an average week of television programming, the shows portray twenty-two hours of violent acts.

Often we say that statistics lie, that numbers such as these can be interpreted in many ways. Yet people cannot help but be influenced in their values and attitudes by a medium of such power and constant presence. This is not the place to discuss in detail television viewing and its impact on our lives. Our purpose here is primarily to raise the following questions for your reflection: Assuming that we will continue to be avid viewers, must we not become more critical viewers? Must we not carefully choose what we will watch? Should we not be wary of accepting too easily all the messages that we receive from television advertising and programming? By not reflecting on such questions, we may give television too much power over our lives.

Movies

At one time many people believed that the invention of television would destroy the movie industry, that people would no longer go to theaters to see new films. Today we hear similar warnings about video tape recorders and players and the low cost of renting films for viewing at home. Regardless of whether we watch the films in the theaters or in our family rooms, they continue to be a highly popular and powerful cultural medium. Young people seldom have parties or overnight guests without a video player and a stock of tapes—at times enough for all-night viewing.

As is true in all facets of culture, much that is valuable as well as much that is disturbing can be found in today's films. Contemporary films not only reflect sexuality but help to create a new, permissive attitude toward it. An even more disturbing quality of films today is their treatment of violence. Viewers become almost immune to highly realistic scenes of physical brutality. Moreover, in recent decades, the trend in movies is toward combining sex with violence. In these films, young women are most often portrayed as the victims. What can account for these trends, and what do they say about our culture? Certainly we as individuals do not like being treated brutally. Why then do we seem to enjoy films that show others being abused, raped, beaten, or murdered?

Music

More than any other medium, music is identified as representing what today's young people are and what they believe. As is true in the case of all our cultural expressions, contemporary rock music contains some good news and some bad news for us. Again, what one identifies as bad will vary dramatically from one person to another. For example, some religious denominations use rock music in liturgy or prayer, while other more conservative churches condemn such music as the work of the devil. In any case, so much good rock music has been composed that we cannot make a blanket statement condemning it all.

More than any other medium, music represents the values of today's young people.

This is not to say that *all* rock music is positive or healthful. Many of the songs of today, not surprisingly, promote the negative values that were discussed above—consumerism, individualism at the expense of community, a search for the immediate satisfaction of a desire to feel good, and a treatment of sexuality as a casual matter. We do not propose that you stop listening to music; such a suggestion would be absurd. We do suggest that you *listen consciously and critically* to the music of your generation. Reflect on the lyrics of your songs and the values that they suggest. Ask yourself if you really

The text suggests the need to listen consciously and critically to the music of your generation. Develop a list of five questions a listener might ask himself or herself regarding popular songs, questions that would help one become his or her own best music critic.

want to accept as a guideline or characteristic of your own beliefs and behavior the kinds of values and attitudes supported in each song. In that way you will become your own best music critic.

How Can I Remain True to Myself?

Your own experience may have verified much of what we have discussed in this chapter. That is, you may have found these things to be true in your own life. Quite possibly much of what we have discussed is frightening, if not downright depressing. With all these pressures—from friends, from community, and from culture—how can you hope to remain free and true to yourself? How can you possibly become who and what you want to be in life?

The Value of Education

A partial answer, but a very important one, to the above questions can be found in the very process that you are presumably beginning as you read this book: your high school education.

A Dream of Hope

In a letter to a friend, a college student once shared his dream of the kind of person he wished to become. His thoughts summarize well many of the themes of this chapter.

I hope that I will always be for each person
    what he or she needs me to be.
I hope that my love for those whom I like
    will never lessen my love for those whom I do not.
I hope that everyone will accept me as I am,
    but that I never will.
I hope that I will always ask for forgiveness from others,
    but that I will never need to be asked for my own.
I hope that I will always recognize my limitations,
    but that I will construct none.
I hope that loving will always be my goal,
    but that love will never be my idol.
I hope that everyone will always have hope.
          (Paraphrased from Henri Nouwen, *Intimacy*)

The next few years can be among the most important in shaping your life.

The next few years can be among the most important in shaping your life. This is not simply a statement in support of the school system. It is plainly and purely the truth. The opportunity for education that will be presented to you during the coming years is your surest chance both for getting in touch with who you are and for taking charge of who you will become. Day in and day out, you have the opportunity to learn more and more about yourself, about getting along with others, and about your own culture and that of others. The more you know, the more freedom you will have to chart a true course for the journey that is your life. After all, the most powerful medium on earth is not television, movies, or music, but the human mind. Early in your high school career you must recognize the great value of all the areas of study that are open to you now and in the years ahead. Consider these examples.

- We have talked in this chapter and in chapter 1 about ninth graders as individuals. In the years ahead you will have the opportunity to study biology and psychology, fields of study that can help you tremendously in furthering your self-understanding.

- We have also talked about ninth graders in relationship to others. You are going to have more opportunities to learn about communication and getting along with others—primarily through the social interaction with fellow students and teachers that is such a big part of the high school years.

■ Finally, we have talked in this chapter about culture. In your high school years you will have the opportunity to study the history of the culture that so greatly influences who you are. You will be able as well to learn more about the cultures of others and thus broaden your understanding of the fascinating world beyond your own society. You will be able to study literature and art, the marvelous treasury of ideas, hopes, and dreams handed down by those who went before us. You will also learn about the art now being created for those who will follow us.

All of this lies ahead for you—an invitation to dramatically grow as a person through education. How will you respond to this invitation?

The Role of Religion in Education

Education can be frightening in a couple of ways. First, discovering that the world is much larger and more complex than we used to think makes our place in the universe smaller by comparison. Naturally we do not feel as safe in the world when we realize how little control we have over what goes on in it. Second, looking critically at the faults in our communities and culture can be threatening because a clear view of reality suggests that even the tiny part of the world that we think of as ours is not the safe place that we assumed it was when we were children. Anyone who takes his or her education seriously will often have moments of doubt when ignorance seems to be bliss—especially when compared to truths that are sometimes painful and scary.

If we are to avoid the temptation to run away or hide from the difficulties of life in a very complex world, we must have some source of personal security and some convictions about the deeper meanings of life. This is where faith and religion come in. Religious faith involves a way of looking at reality, a kind of personal vision that can help us make sense of an often confusing world. The next chapter takes up the crucial topics of faith and religion—and how they can fit into our lives.

Education is an invitation to dramatically grow as a person.

Review Questions

1. What is the meaning of the motto Your life is God's gift to you. What you do with your life is your gift to God.
2. What is the major problem with living life in a world of *if onlys?*
3. What tasks are involved in "getting our heads together"? Try to express each one in your own words.
4. When does a stereotype exist?
5. What does the growing incidence of eating disorders reflect about our society and its values?
6. What is meant by the statement that human emotions are universal?
7. Under what conditions might we say that a twenty-five-year-old person is already old?
8. Give three examples supporting the position that, in our culture, being religious or devout is often considered unacceptable.
9. What is the likely result of attempting to live according to the expectations that other people set for us?
10. Name the four cultural values that the text identifies as being unhealthful or inhumane.
11. For an average family, how many hours a week is the television on? During an average week, how many hours of violent acts are portrayed on television?
12. How might one become his or her own best music critic?
13. What role does education play in the struggle to remain true to oneself?

Key Terms
stereotypes
culture
consumerism
individualism
immediate gratification
sexual permissiveness

3 Faith and Religion:
Searching for Answers to the God Question

A Question of Worldviews ▶ ▶ ▶

We begin this chapter with a Jewish folktale.

Two men set out on a journey together. The friends took a donkey to carry their packs, a torch to light their way at night, and a rooster. The rooster sat on the donkey's head during the entire journey.

One of the men was deeply religious; the second was a skeptic, one who doubts all forms of faith. On the journey they frequently spoke about the Lord. "In all things, God is good," said the first companion.

"We will see if your opinion bears out on the trip," said the second.

Shortly before dusk the two men arrived in a small village where they sought a place to sleep. Despite their frequent requests, no one offered them a night's lodging. Reluctantly, they traveled a mile outside of town, where they decided to sleep.

"I thought you claimed that God is good," the skeptic said sarcastically.

"God has decided this is the best place for us to sleep tonight," replied his friend.

They fixed their beds beneath a large tree, just off the main road that led to the village, and tethered their donkey about thirty yards away. Just as they were about to light the torch, they heard a horrible noise. A lion had killed the donkey and carried it off to eat. Quickly the companions climbed the tree to stay away from danger.

"You still say God is good?" the skeptic asked with anger.

"If the lion hadn't eaten the donkey, he would have attacked us. God is good," his companion declared.

The believer in the Jewish folktale could be considered either a person of deep religious insight or a simpleton. Write a paragraph defending each of these two possibilities.

Moments later a cry from the rooster sent them further up the tree. From this new vantage point they saw a wildcat carrying the rooster away in his teeth.

Before the skeptic could say a word, the man of faith declared, "The cry of the rooster has once again saved us. God is good."

A few minutes later a strong wind arose and blew out the torch, the only comfort the men had in the black night. Again the skeptic taunted his companion. "It appears that the goodness of God is working overtime this evening," he said. This time the believer was silent.

The next morning the two men walked back into the village for food. They soon discovered that a band of outlaws had swept into town the previous night and robbed the entire village of all its possessions.

With this news the man of faith turned to his friend. "Finally it has become clear," he cried. "Had we been given a room in the village last night, we would have been robbed along with all the villagers. If the wind had not blown out our torch, the bandits who traveled the road near the place where we slept would have discovered us and taken all our goods. It is clear that in all things, God is good."

As the story above suggests, our **worldviews** shape our experiences in life. That is, our general understandings of what life and reality are all about influence how we see particular events. Some people, for example, experience life as an unending series of difficulties or failures. Others might see the same events as exciting opportunities or challenges.

Our worldviews may be reflections of the personalities or temperaments that we have inherited. Or they may result from our upbringings. For instance, if the people who surround us view the world with fear and gloom, only with great effort will we learn to be optimistic and hopeful. So some people come by positive attitudes quite naturally, while others must work at them. No doubt our relationships with other people have a great deal to do with how we view life. Yet when all is said and done, we as individuals must choose our own worldviews, freely and consciously creating a perspective that will give focus to our life experiences.

This chapter is about our worldviews, which are intimately related to the topics that will be our primary concern in this chapter and for the remainder of this course. These major themes are the roles of faith and religion in our lives, especially as they are reflected in the Catholic Christian tradition.

We will be discussing what may be the most fundamental decision that people ever make. This decision may affect whether we view our lives as meaningful and rich with promise or as essentially absurd and tragic. We may have never thought of faith and religion in these terms, but discussions of faith ultimately revolve around questions about our worldviews.

As we begin this discussion, we must deal with a number of basic issues or questions, the responses to which will serve as a foundation for all that will follow.

- What is the meaning of religious faith?
- What is the purpose of religion, and why do we have so many religions in the world today?
- Why should we believe that God even exists?
- If there is a God, how do people come to know of that God? Is what we believe about God merely a matter of personal opinion?

Discussions of faith and religion ultimately revolve around questions about our worldviews.

- How do we determine which of the many religions is closest to the truth? Which will help us understand what God is really like; which is most able to respond to our needs as persons? These are certainly difficult questions. We must grapple with them, however, if we hope to understand and live our lives fully. In this chapter we will begin to explore these questions by looking at the mystery of God and how we might experience and respond to God. At times, the material may become complex and difficult for you. Try as best you can at those times to grasp the concepts that are presented. Doing so will help you fully understand the rest of this course. As a bonus, grasping these concepts will help you develop a worldview that can give you a deeper sense of meaning and peace in life.

Struggling to Speak of Great Mysteries

An immediate problem that we encounter in a discussion of matters of religion is the limitation of words. Finding words and expressions that capture the realities we are trying to deal with is difficult. What makes the situation even more awkward is that even the words that we *do* have for these realities are often misused or misunderstood. Take, for example, the implications conveyed by the word *religion*. For one person, the term may mean going to Mass on Sunday. For another, it may be associated with a deep love for Jesus. For a third person, *religion* may mean teachings about moral issues. For still another, it may summon up bad memories from childhood.

So what happens in a discussion between these people? For example, the question posed for discussion might be this: what do you think about religion? One person will reply merely that it's all right. Another will respond that it's the greatest experience in his life. A third will say she gets mad every time she thinks about religion. Still another person will say he disagrees with some of the teachings but not all of them. Do you see what happens here? Each of these people assumes that he or she knows what all the others are saying. Actually, because each person has a different idea of what the term *religion* means, very little communication is taking place.

Our becoming conscious of the limitations of words is extremely important. We need to do more than just hear words. We must discover what people mean by the words that they use. One primary goal in this course will be to develop a shared vocabulary—a mutual understanding of basic Christian terms and concepts—so that you can carry on effective discussions about religion with other students and with your teachers.

Working from our example above, the terms *religion* and *faith* are often used interchangeably as if they are synonymous. In fact, they do not mean the same thing, and confusion over these two concepts is a major cause of the difficulties that exist for many people today—old and young alike—regarding religion. If we can clearly distinguish between these two concepts in this chapter, we will achieve better communication.

The Meaning of Faith

To begin our discussion with the meaning of the term *faith*, we need to look at a basic human trait at the heart of faith. To do that, let's reflect on two fictitious but familiar incidents in the lives of people who may be very much like you.

The Watch

Jack and Frank lived in the same neighborhood as kids and attended the same schools. They had been friends since the fifth grade. In high school they still swapped stories of the forts that they used to build every summer in the field near their homes. In those days they would spend hours talking about their dreams for the future—the sports they would play together in high school, their secret hopes about careers. Jack and Frank went through the tough times of early adolescence together, talking about their changing relationships with parents and, of course, about their new feelings toward girls. The two boys shared feelings and thoughts that they could share with no one else. Jack and Frank had in each other the sort of friend whom people seldom find.

Frank always received a pretty good allowance from his folks, and during the summers, he did yard work for several neighbors, so money was never a concern for him. Jack, on the other hand, came from a larger family and his allowance was far smaller than Frank's. And, to be honest, Jack was not ambitious. So Jack always looked to Frank for occasional loans, which Frank knew would not be repaid. But Frank always just accepted that side of Jack. He even joked about it, simply saying, "What are friends for if not to help each other out once in a while?"

Last year, when Jack and Frank were on the football team, a serious problem was destroying the team spirit. Someone was regularly breaking into the players' lockers and stealing wallets, watches, and other valuables. The room was locked to everyone except the team, so one of the players was clearly responsible. Suspicion of one another led to frequent arguments and distrust. Frank and Jack spent a lot of time trying to figure out who the thief was, especially after the thief took Frank's watch.

One day that December Frank was at Jack's house listening to music in his bedroom. When his mother called Jack out of the room, Frank decided to go through Jack's tapes to find some different music to listen to. As he lifted the tapes off the shelf, Frank accidentally dropped one behind Jack's bed. When he bent down to retrieve the tape, he discovered a box under Jack's bed. Frank felt a little uneasy about opening the box, but his curiosity got the better of him. Inside the box Frank found some money and several watches. One of them was his.

When Jack returned to his bedroom, he found Frank staring at the box in disbelief. Neither knew what to say. Almost in tears, Frank picked his watch out of the box and, without looking at Jack or saying anything, stormed out of the room. They haven't spoken to each other since.

Imagine yourself as a friend of both Frank and Jack. You want to help them restore their friendship after this incident. Write a brief description of what you would say to each of them.

Faith Is Trust

The story "The Watch" is about a basic human need—the need for someone to rely upon in our lives. Before Johnny Carson gained fame as the host of "The Tonight Show," he starred in a popular afternoon game show. The title of the show—"Who Do You Trust?"—was meant to be humorous. In real life, however, this question is often a painful cry for some sense of meaning, security, and understanding. To get at the meaning of faith and religion, we must also raise this question because, at its very heart, faith is trust.

We all yearn for people who care for us in such authentic ways that we know we can trust them. We all want people whom we can depend on, friends with whom we can share our deepest feelings and thoughts, and people whose love can give energy and purpose to our lives. When we find a trustworthy friend, we realize that we have been given a special gift.

We all want people whom we can depend on, friends with whom we can share our deepest feelings and thoughts.

We can also grasp the significance of trust in our lives by reflecting on what happens when our faith in another person is destroyed. For example, put yourself in Frank's place in the story of the watch. Play out in your imagination what will happen between Frank and Jack in the future. Then reflect on the impact Jack's thievery may have on Frank's ability to trust others in the future. We hope that Frank will maintain the ability to trust others. We hope he will not prejudge other people because of what Jack did. We might even hope that Frank's love for Jack will be so mature and so deep that he will somehow find in himself the capacity to forgive Jack. Movies are made about that kind of heroic love. In real life, it is a rare gift.

So we see that the capacity of people to face life with an attitude of trust and openness is very much bound up with our relationships with other people. Yet there is another level of trust that is called for in life if we are to understand the deeper meanings of faith and religion. The issue that we are dealing with is not only one of whether or not we can find an occasional friend in our lives whom we can trust fully. A more fundamental and challenging question is whether life itself is trustworthy. That is, is life basically good and can we embrace it with hope? Or must we live with an attitude that trouble is around the corner, that "someone is out to get me"? Life has a way of posing that question more often than we may realize. Listen now to another story about trust.

The Pyramid

Brenda was one of those special persons who comes along so rarely in life that people wonder if the world deserves them. Although naturally bright and a great student, she never bragged about her accomplishments or acted superior. In fact, Brenda often offered to help friends study for exams, and she volunteered to work as a tutor for kids in lower grades. Brenda had a low-key wit and said funny things in such a quiet way that she immediately put people at ease. She was especially popular at parties because people felt comfortable whenever she was around.

Brenda was also a gifted athlete and, as a gymnast, seemed to be totally at home on the parallel bars. Yet what impressed people was not just her routines on the bars. Rather, they were captivated by the joyous look on her face and the sparkle in her eye. She was a young woman in love with life and everything and everyone in it, and her spirit warmed anyone who met her.

When Brenda wasn't involved in a sport herself, she was leading cheers for others. Last year she was a cheerleader for the girl's basketball team. The cheerleaders were known for their popular pyramid cheer. Naturally, Brenda was the one who would balance on top of the pyramid and then leap off to be caught by two other cheerleaders. The risky routine brought all the fans to their feet, so the cheerleaders would save it for that time in a game when the team either needed a great boost in a tough situation or needed to celebrate a game that was going their way.

One night last winter the team was flying high—playing their best game in memory against a school that had won the conference championship the year before. People were as excited as they had ever been, and the crowd started yelling for the pyramid cheer. The cheerleading team responded at the next time-out, and the crowd went wild with enthusiasm. Brenda crowned the top of the pyramid, her incredible smile lighting up the gym, and then soared off in a free-fall through space, to be caught by her friends below. . . .

Brenda died nearly a year ago. People still try to figure out how the accident happened and, even more, to understand *why* it happened. That night, when Brenda's hurtling body hit the arms of her friends, she seemed to land awkwardly, off balance. Her body slipped through the straining hands, and her head and shoulders crashed onto the gym floor. Brenda quickly tried to stand up, then sat back down. Her fellow cheerleaders crowded around. A doctor hurried to her aid. Her parents were there moments later. Brenda was carefully helped off the floor and to the training room near the gym. The doctor said that she had to go to hospital's emergency room for X rays. "Just as a precaution," he said. Brenda said she was okay and wanted to return for the end of the game. Her parents insisted that she listen to the doctor, and Brenda finally agreed.

The next morning the news swept through the school. It was all a mistake or somebody's idea of a sick joke. Then over the school's P.A. came the announcement: Brenda had died during the night due to bleeding in the brain. "There was nothing that could be done."

A year later, the memories of Brenda's funeral and all the tears have not dimmed. Yet her teammates have begun to heal from the shock and unearned guilt. Some of her friends are now able to recall fond memories and even to tell an occasional funny story about Brenda. Others will laugh, for a brief moment forgetting that she is gone. Then the pain comes back, and the agonizing question lingers in the air like a plea: "Why? My God, why?"

Imagine yourself as the student editor of the school newspaper. For your column, you are asked to write a statement in response to the question that ends this story, "The Pyramid": "Why? My God, why?" What would you write?

Few of the details of this real story have been changed in this account. You may know a similar story involving the death of a very special person. Every year high school students all over the country grieve the loss of friends who die in car accidents or drown during picnics. They watch in silent horror as classmates with cancer suffer through their last months of life. The same question haunts many of us: "Why would God let this happen?"

Life's tragedies focus our attention on questions about life's meaning.

This question focuses on the issue of trust in an even more profound way than do our questions about a friendship gone sour. In Brenda's death we are faced with the very basic questions of life that eventually confront each of us: What is the meaning of life? Is life basically good or evil? Is there someone or something that can make sense out of our frequent loneliness? Is life itself trustworthy, in the sense that someone cares for us and, therefore, gives our lives meaning? Can we say with any kind of confidence, as can the religious man in our opening story, that "in all things, God is good"? Now our questions of trust become questions of religious faith.

Recall and briefly write about an incident from your own life that prompted the question: "Why would God let this happen?" Explain how you answered that question.

The Meaning of Religious Faith

Religious faith differs from other human experiences of trust primarily in the object of that trust. That is, in our friendships with one another, we put our trust in another person. In religious faith, we invest our trust in God. In a general sense, then, we can define **religious faith** as the sense of trust that we have in a power beyond ourselves—in a supreme being or creator of the universe. People have given this power a lot of different names throughout history, but in our language and culture we use the name *God.* (We will discuss the unique meaning of *Christian faith* later in this course.)

A final crucial connection between faith and trust deserves explaining here. Although the act of trusting another person may partly result from an intellectual conviction that he or she is trustworthy, the actual act of trusting is more a matter of the heart than of the head. We even find that occasionally our hearts or guts tell us to trust a person even though logic wars against the decision. The opposite may also be true: We may have no rational reason for doubting the trustworthiness of a person, yet a feeling inside us simply will not allow us to do so.

The point here is this: In our discussion of the realities of faith and religion in this chapter and throughout this course, we will be trying to speak to both the head and the heart sides of the topics. Sometimes we will discuss what we *believe* or what we might *understand* about certain issues. At such times we will be in the realm of the head. At other times we will discuss faith and religion in terms of *trust* or *feelings* or *intuition*—at which times we will be emphasizing the heart of the matter. This distinction helps us to realize that we have many ways of dealing with realities as complex as matters of faith and religion.

Develop a list of five "head questions" regarding religious faith—questions about the whats and whys of believing. Then develop a list of five "heart questions" that focus on trusting.

Why Believe and Trust in God?

When discussing faith, a more important question than "Why believe and trust in God?" would be difficult to find. Yet many of us have never seriously asked this question of ourselves. Maybe the answers that you have received in the past have been adequate for you. Maybe a friend asked the question the other day, and you realized that you did not have an answer. Perhaps that scared you. Maybe you never felt comfortable taking the question seriously. Perhaps just asking it made you feel guilty.

We have to deal with this question if any of the other material in this course is going to make sense. Discussing the truth of Christianity or Catholicism, for example, makes no sense without spending some time on the more basic issue of the very existence of God.

Lots of easy answers to what is sometimes referred to as the *God question* are available.

■ That's just the way it is.

- You have to take it on faith.
- I always have believed.

Nothing is wrong with these simple answers if they meet persons' needs. Frequently, however, these answers no longer satisfy young people. More sophisticated answers are expected —and deserved.

Proof Is Impossible; Words Fall Short

Identify the qualities of a caring person by completing this sentence: "I know my friend (or parent or other caring person) truly cares for me because . . ." Based on your reflection, write up four "Commandments for Caring People." Finally, complete this sentence: "I know that God follows these commandments because . . ."

In a moment we will begin looking at the evidence for believing in God. We must acknowledge two limitations of this discussion, however. First, undeniable logical proof for believing in God does not exist. As we shall see in a moment, there are many very sound reasons for choosing to believe in God. By the same token, nonbelievers can pose some challenging arguments against such belief. So belief in God contains a risk.

Yet every decision that we make in life has an element of risk. Whenever we make decisions, we look at the available evidence, including our life experiences, the logic of what others have told us, the history of those who have gone before us, and so on. Then we choose. Yet as humans we know that we can make mistakes, and experience teaches us that our powers of reasoning are limited and can lead us to incorrect conclusions. We know that we cannot always trust our own judgment.

We encounter this same sense of risk when deciding whether or not to believe in God. Even those who have already chosen to believe in God can experience moments of doubt. An airplane crashes and hundreds perish. An infant dies because of the physical abuse of her parents. A close friend betrays us. When such events occur, even the most committed believer may wonder, "Can I be wrong about this God in whom I believe?" Surely this is a major lesson of the story of Brenda the cheerleader. That tragic accident left all who knew her asking the haunting question, "Why? My God, why?" Such doubts are as often directed at ourselves as they are at belief in God.

A second limitation is often encountered in the discussion of belief in God. That is, we must acknowledge and emphasize once again the severe limitation of words. As a reality beyond our human understanding, God must be clouded in mystery. In fact, we might say that God is Mystery with a capital *M*. So any attempts that we make to approach that Mystery will fall short, and any words we use to describe God can only hint at a reality that is beyond words. Trying to define God in words will be like attempting to catch hold of a rushing river with our bare hands. At times we will surely share the feelings of the sorely tested Job of the Bible:

> If I go to the east, he is not there;
>> or to the west, I still cannot see him.
> If I seek him in the north, he is not to be found,
>> invisible as ever, if I turn to the south.
>>> (Job 23:8–9)

Yet we continue our search for Mystery in the spirit of hope and conviction that sustained Job in his struggles:

> And yet he knows every step I take!
>> Let him test me in the crucible: I shall
>>> come out pure gold.
>>>> (Job 23:10)

As a reality beyond our human understanding, God must be hidden in mystery.

The Evidence for Believing and Trusting in God

The Convictions of Persons Who Care for Us

We can believe and trust in God because our parents and others have taught us to do so. Believing in God is not acceptable *only* because others have taught us to. But this can be a very good reason for initially accepting faith.

As an example: Your parents presumably love you more than anyone else does—even though you may not always feel that way. You were born of their flesh. Thus far they have cared for and nurtured you through life. In many ways they have tried to teach you the treasured values of our history and our culture.

One of the treasures that your parents want to share with you is their faith in God. They have struggled to live up to Christian values, trying to demonstrate to you the importance of

Write a brief account of an occasion when the faith of some adult made a strong impression on you.

those values. Because of their faith, for instance, your parents have likely paid far more for your education than was necessary. Why would they do so? Why is religious education so valuable to them? In forty or fifty years of living, why do they still hold on to their faith in God? The conviction of faith discovered in believing parents is a very sound reason for at least taking the God question very seriously.

Yet we cannot rely completely on others for a reason to believe in God. Faith in others can lead us to faith in God, but we must not mistake one for the other. People can let us down. For example, what if those for whom we care choose *not* to believe and trust in God? Does that mean that we follow their lead away from faith? What about those who are tragically abused by the people close to them? Certainly such victims would seem to have more evidence against than for faith in God. So we must look for other sources of evidence upon which to make a sound decision about God.

The Classical Arguments

Naturally, such a significant topic as the existence of God has been the object of much discussion, argument, and theorizing throughout history. In the Christian tradition, discussion of the God question was strongly influenced for many centuries by Saint Thomas Aquinas, the theologian regarded by many as the greatest in the entire history of the Church. By the way, **theology** is the academic field devoted to the investigation of God and of God's relationship with the universe. The term is often used in reference to particular religious traditions—for example, Christian theology or Jewish theology. The scholars who are trained in this discipline are called *theologians.*

Thomas lived in the thirteenth century in Italy. He spent much of his life teaching, thinking, and writing about believing—the "head" dimension of faith. To arrive at what he believed to be proofs of the existence of God, Thomas used a logical way of thinking developed by the ancient Greeks. Thomas felt that, if we look closely enough at the world, we can come logically to the conviction that God exists.

Thomas reasoned, for example, that we can identify a cause for everything in the world. Moreover, if we keep going back in time, trying to find causes for every reality, eventually we will arrive at a *first cause,* or an *uncaused cause.* In Thomas's thinking, this reality is God.

As another example, Thomas argued that the remarkable

sense of order in the universe reflected the existence of an infinitely intelligent being whom we call God. Until very recently these and other similar arguments formed almost the total foundation of the Church's teaching on the existence of God. If your parents are forty years old or older and attended Catholic schools, they probably remember arguments like these.

Although modern theologians do not accept Thomas's arguments as complete proofs of the existence of God, his logical, almost scientific, approach to the question has helped many people. As noted earlier, each person must seek out answers that respond to his or her own needs. Yet the need of many people today is not only to accept God's existence as an intellectual possibility but also to come to a deep sense of trust in God's care and intention for us.

Write a short paragraph in response to this statement: "The proofs of the existence of God developed by Saint Thomas Aquinas do (or do not) convince me because . . ."

Universal Belief in God Throughout History

The vast majority of the world's people claim a belief in sacred Mystery. Perhaps they were all taught this belief and merely accept what they have been told. More likely, many of these people find their religious beliefs confirmed in their own personal life experiences. Something beyond their family background and upbringing convinces them of the reality of a god—or sometimes of multiple gods.

Note also that the belief in God has been a common human characteristic throughout history. Through sophisticated advances in sciences, we are now able to trace the history of human culture back some forty thousand years to the time of the cave dwellers. Throughout history, all cultures have developed religions, with ritual and worship as a part of them. Thus, belief in God—at least as the belief in some power beyond us—is a basic trait of human culture.

Belief in God has been a common characteristic of human culture throughout history.

The glories of nature may give us a very personal sense of Mystery.

The Wonders of Creation

Another argument for the existence of God reflects Saint Thomas's idea that the order of the universe proves the existence of an infinitely intelligent being. Today, however, many people do not respond to the orderliness of the universe so much as to its mysterious qualities. We have witnessed a religious version of the "back to nature" movement in our society. Many young people, for example, claim that they believe in God but that they more fully experience that God while taking a hike in the woods or climbing a mountain than they do in formal worship.

If you have never done so, take the opportunity some time to go outside on a clear, peaceful night and stretch out on the grass. Watch the night sky and simply let it speak to you. Avoid trying to analyze or understand the mystery reflected in the stars. Just relax and observe. These can be profoundly moving moments that can expand our worldviews.

Is the experience of nature a proof for the existence of God? Certainly not. The glories of nature may give us, however, an interior, very personal sense of mystery that is far more convincing than highly reasoned arguments. When we consider creation—from the immensity of the universe down to the infinitely tiny world of the atom—and realize that all of nature holds together somehow, we want to ask how or by whom.

A simple Hindu story reminds us of what truly seeing the power in nature means:

"Excuse me," said an ocean fish.
"You are older than I, so
can you tell me where to find
this thing they call the ocean?"

"The ocean," said the older fish, "is the thing
you are in now."

"Oh, this? But this is water. What I'm seeking
is the ocean," said the disappointed fish
as he swam away to search elsewhere.

If pressed to explain the tale, the wise Hindu storyteller might express the moral this way: The disappointed fish must come to know that he is not to *look for* something. Instead, he must *look at* the reality that is constantly surrounding him. The same might be said of our search for God.

The Moments of Transcendence

Transcendence is a difficult concept with which to deal, but we must try. Although related to the deeply personal experience of viewing the night sky, it is more than that. **Transcendence** refers to the experience that we often have of moving out from or beyond ourselves. For example, the suffering or death of someone whom we know or about whom we read can create feelings of transcendence. In these moments we realize that the world is filled with events that make our personal failures and victories seem trivial by comparison. These compassionate feelings can be powerful enough to lead people to dedicate their lives to easing the suffering of others.

We all experience an ongoing yearning for something more in our lives—as if we were always called to reach beyond who and what and where we are and to strive for something better. As humans most of us cannot conceive of our lives ending with death. Something more than the desire for self-preservation is at work here. We seem to possess the natural conviction that life is more than just our limited experience of it.

Imagine that you have been hired to create a poster that captures the meaning of the statement "Life is more than just our limited experience of it." What photo or design would you choose for your poster? What words would you use to express your message?

The Experience of Love

Moments of transcendence often accompany the experience of love. Love relationships can be profound encounters with the sense of mystery in life. This is true both when we reach out in love to another and when we experience the remarkable gift of another person's love for us. Even the early stage of many love relationships called infatuation seems to provide us with a sense of the deeper richness and meaning of life. Profound experiences of love—such as a seasoned friendship in which we express a total trust in and care for another person—give us a deep sense of value and purpose in life. For some of us these experiences can stand as proof of the existence of a higher and caring power in the universe.

Almost more remarkable than the experience of loving someone is that of being loved by another. Most of us doubt our own value, worth, and goodness. When someone loves us for ourselves, however, the experience can be indescribably freeing. By the same token, we should not be surprised to discover that lonely, hurt, abused people find that believing in God is difficult—at least when God is pictured as loving and caring. The gift of another's affection and concern, however, can fill us with the sense of the basic goodness of life and with the belief

When someone loves us, the experience can be indescribably freeing.

that such goodness can come only from a gracious and loving creator.

The Lack of Meaningful Alternatives

Explaining the world, history, and our own personal lives without some kind of God seems difficult if not impossible. The only alternative is the conclusion that creation was an accident, that the universe is merely an organic machine, and that we are headed nowhere. In other words, believing in God seems to make more sense than assuming that life is meaningless.

Believing in God seems to make more sense than assuming that life is meaningless.

Religious Faith as an Act of Fundamental Trust

Jot down four events in nature or in history that have most challenged your belief in God.

Have we provided proofs of the existence of God? No, we have admitted that such proofs are impossible. Do sound arguments against believing in God exist? Certainly atheists raise difficult questions. (**Atheists** are people who deny the existence of God.) The suffering of innocent people, natural disasters that wipe out the lives of thousands, the ability of people to be so incredibly cruel to one another, the memory of the Nazi death camps, and so on are experiences that haunt believers and challenge religious faith. Faith in God is not always easy. Religious faith has stood the test of time, however, and has been lived out in the lives of too many billions of believers to be easily rejected.

Some theologians today speak of religious faith in terms of an act of fundamental trust in God. Others would speak of faith as a leap into the darkness. We must acknowledge again that religious faith—like all human experiences of faith—involves taking a risk on a Mystery that we might only briefly glimpse. Those who have taken the risk and made the leap of faith suggest that we can experience the reasonableness of such trust only in the actual act of trusting, that we can prove that faith makes sense only by taking the risk it demands and then sharing and celebrating the experience with others.

The idea of sharing faith brings us naturally to the topic of religion and back to the question of how faith and religion differ.

The Meaning and Purpose of Religion

When we feel something deeply, we have to express that feeling. For instance, if we want to encourage somebody during an athletic event, we may applaud and cheer. If we care a lot about some people, we may hug them, kiss them, or give them gifts. If we feel angry, we may scream and pound the wall. All these actions are natural and necessary attempts to express inward feelings in outward ways.

Our wonderfully human need for expression is part of our experience of religious faith too. Throughout history people have struggled to find ways to express outwardly what they have experienced and come to believe about God. This is precisely what religion is all about. **Religion** is the attempt by communities of people throughout history to express their shared faith through outward signs—including symbols, celebrations, statements of belief, and codes of behavior. Precisely *how* this is done in any one community depends both on its particular understanding of God and on the available expressions—symbols, celebrations, statements, and codes of behavior—that are recognized and understood by that community. This is the major reason that we have so many different religions in the world even though, at least according to Christian belief, only one God exists.

Faith and Religion Need Each Other

So *faith* and *religion*, in the sense that the terms are being used here, are not the same. Yet they are closely related and complementary realities. In other words, they need each other. Faith—the personal trust in and relationship with God—

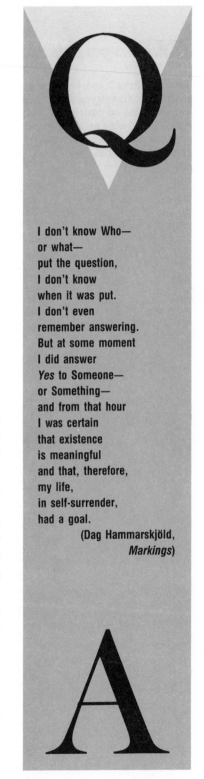

I don't know Who—
or what—
put the question,
I don't know
when it was put.
I don't even
remember answering.
But at some moment
I did answer
Yes to Someone—
or Something—
and from that hour
I was certain
that existence
is meaningful
and that, therefore,
my life,
in self-surrender,
had a goal.

(Dag Hammarskjöld,
Markings)

Recall two times in your life when you thought that the religious expressions of people had no basis in religious faith—that is, when people performed religious acts that seemed meaningless. Briefly describe these events in writing.

requires the means of expression that religion provides. Likewise, religion, to have meaning, must arise out of a strong interior experience of faith. If a personal faith is not present, religious expressions have no basis and will eventually become meaningless, empty, and boring.

A Crisis of Faith or of Religion?

What meaning might the distinction between faith and religion have for you? Some say that young people today suffer a "crisis of faith." The evidence often given to prove this claim is that young people are bored with Mass, that they have negative attitudes toward religion classes.

Recollecting our distinction between faith and religion, we might ask: Is the so-called crisis of faith truly one of faith? Or is it rather a "crisis of religion"? Are young people saying that they do not believe in God? Or are they in fact saying that they simply do not enjoy or understand the religious expressions used by their particular church or religious tradition? Our answers to these extremely important questions can eliminate much confusion and misunderstanding as well as a great deal of guilt.

Recent surveys demonstrate clearly that well over 90 percent of young people believe in a personal God of some kind and that they pray to that God regularly. That statistic alone suggests that no crisis of faith exists. On the other hand, many young people—and their parents as well—are not completely satisfied with the ways in which their religious faith is expressed. This is hardly surprising and need not be the cause of exaggerated concern. Do we ever find that expressing our deepest feelings is easy? When you feel angry, can you tell a friend clearly why you feel that way? When you love someone, can you easily tell the person what you are feeling? Of course not. Clearly expressing outwardly what we feel inside is extremely hard work and often impossible.

What is true for us as individuals is just as true for religion in its attempts to express the faith shared by its members. That is precisely why religion will not always appeal to us, why we cannot expect to feel excited every time we go to Mass, and why the words that we use to describe or pray to God seem to fall short. As individuals, we never stop trying to demonstrate our love. By the same token, we cannot stop trying to refine the religious expressions for our faith.

Let's take this idea a step further. This crisis of religion can lead to a crisis of faith. For instance, people sometimes feel frustrated with their religious upbringings, with the lack of personal meaning in public worship, or with disagreements over specific religious or moral teachings. Because they are questioning their particular religious traditions, they assume that their faith in God is automatically dead.

For example, you have probably known students who say that they do not believe in God. The first time you hear someone say so can be quite a shock. Maybe the option of believing or not believing never occurred to you. Yet ask those students why they do not believe. At times they talk about priests and sisters with whom they had trouble. Or they are angry with their parents, and they use the rejection of faith as a good way to get back at them. The danger here is that they are "throwing the baby out with the bath water." In other words, they are rejecting faith because they are not happy with religion as they have experienced it.

An equally dangerous possibility exists. Each generation passes on its religious symbols, teachings, and traditions to those who follow. The danger is that with such concern about teaching religion—making sure everyone "gets it right"—the personal sense of faith in God can be lost. If faith is lost, religion becomes boring and meaningless. When a shared faith relationship with God is present, however, people hunger for the expression that only the richness of religion can provide.

In the remainder of this chapter we are going to look more closely at the topic of religion. We will be exploring two complex but vitally important questions:

- If we do choose to believe in and trust God, how do we know *what* to believe about that God?
- Do we need organized religions, and if so, how do I decide which, if any, religion to call my own?

In many ways the responses to these difficult questions will serve as the foundation for the rest of this course.

Recent surveys demonstrate clearly that well over 90 percent of young people believe in a personal God.

If God Is, Who Is God?

If we choose to believe that no God exists, our discussion ends at this point. If God does not exist, all discussions about religion in general or Catholicism in particular become meaningless. If no God exists, religion of any kind becomes unnecessary if not foolish.

Imagine that a friend tells you that she no longer believes in God. In light of this chapter, list five questions that you would like to ask her about her reasons for not believing.

Assuming that we do believe in God, what *kind* of God do we believe in?

Yet what if there *is* a God? If we choose to believe that God does exist, then in a very real sense our discussion is only beginning. For if God does exist, we must immediately ask questions such as these:

- What is this God like, and how do I discover that?
- How do I personally respond to God, that is, what does God expect of me if anything, and how do I learn about these expectations?
- Is there a need for religion, and if so, how do I choose which religion to follow?

This questioning may seem quite peculiar to you. We have been discussing, among other things, the tremendous importance of words and the need to arrive at some shared understanding of what the words that we use actually mean. Consider the fact that we routinely use a word like *God,* and we assume that everyone knows what we mean by this word. How can we make that assumption? When you use the word *God,* you may have in mind a reality very different from mine.

- For you, God might mean a heavenly Father who, out of love, has created you and all the world, and who is constantly caring for you.
- Perhaps I have not yet heard of or experienced that kind of God. Perhaps to me God is a divine being full of anger, a judge who is waiting to punish me for all my wrongdoings.

■ Someone else may not think of God in such personal terms
at all. Perhaps she sees God as an impersonal superintelligence
that created the world and holds it in existence. This God has
no personal concern for or contact with us as individuals.

So we see that, in our discussion of God, we are dealing with
more than the basic question of whether or not this power exists. We are also dealing with this profound question: If God
exists, what kind of God is he or she or it? By this time you
may be asking another question: Whoever said religion courses
are easy?

From this point on we are naturally going to presume that
God exists. We need to do that to justify continuing this course!
Given our belief in God, however, we must now confront the
questions about religion that such a belief raises.

The Meaning of Revelation

Assuming we do believe in God, what *kind* of God do we believe
in, and how do we decide that? Where do we get our understandings of God? How do we arrive at certain beliefs about the
qualities possessed by God and about the nature of the relationship between God and people or, more personally, between
God and myself as an individual?

God Explained by God

If God is to be known, we must rely upon God's *self-disclosure*.
That is, we must rely upon God to reveal freely to us all those
complex dimensions of Mystery that we could never discover
on our own. This insight helps us define and understand a basic
concept in our discussion of faith and religion. That concept is
revelation.

What is *revelation?* The word literally means "to reveal"
or "to unveil." A brief but accurate definition is as follows:
revelation is the self-communication or self-disclosure of God,
in which sacred Mystery is made known by God to people. This
definition might answer the question, What is revelation? Yet
other questions immediately come to mind, chief among them:
Why does God wish to reveal or disclose sacred Mystery to us?
Also, how does that revelation take place? We can look to our
own experience as human beings to gain some hints at answers
to these difficult questions.

Faith and Religion

Write a paragraph responding to this statement: "If religious faith is a gift from God, then people who do *not* have faith have apparently not been given that gift. Therefore, God is completely responsible for whether or not people believe."

Revelation implies a God who loves and cares enough for people to become one with us in our history.

Faith as a Gift from God

As humans we share the desire to be known by another, to have someone understand us fully. That understanding can only happen, of course, if we choose to let another person into our life. We must take the risk involved in revealing to another those parts of our lives about which we are perhaps embarrassed or ashamed. Even in our friendships, we hesitate to reveal our history. As our trust for our friend grows, we become freer to reveal our total selves. When two people are able to care for and trust each other enough to freely share all that they are as persons, they experience the tremendous gift of love and true friendship.

The concept of revelation is based on the conviction that God created people in order to enter into a personal relationship in which both parties can fully reveal themselves. God, of course, does not have the fears about being shy or embarrassed that you and I normally have! God's gift of self can be totally free because God *is* God. Clearly God would enter into such a relationship only if God cared deeply for people. So the concept of revelation implies a God who loves and cares enough for people to take the initiative, to become one with us in our history, constantly revealing sacred Mystery to us.

In this context we can understand the perhaps familiar Christian idea that faith is a gift from God. The only way we can ever come to a believing and trusting relationship with God is if God chooses to invite and allow such a relationship. Faith in God can be initiated and sustained only by God.

How Does God's Revelation Take Place?

The revelation of God takes place in many ways. As we have seen, a primary way is the created world itself. The universe reveals important characteristics of God—as the gracious creator, as the source of all that is beautiful, and as the infinite power. God's revelation has also been experienced and understood by people throughout history in four other ways.

Within individual experience: Some believers understand that the revelation of God takes place within the personal life experience of people. In this view, God communicates directly to and with individuals. This results in a deeply personal sense of union with God. The individual then responds with a whole new outlook and attitude toward life. Both the Jewish and

Christian Scriptures include many stories of such deeply personal experiences of God by individuals—for example, the experiences of Moses and Saint Paul. Several Christian churches emphasize the need for this personal religious experience if we hope to gain salvation.

Some believers feel that sacred Mystery is revealed within the life experiences of individuals.

Through the events of history: Other believers feel that sacred Mystery is revealed by God through the events of history. In the tradition of Jews and Christians, this would be understood as what we call *salvation history*. These marvelous events throughout history include the Exodus and, for Christians, the Resurrection of Jesus. Jesus is spoken of by Christians as *the total revelation of God,* a topic to which we will return later in this course.

Within sacred writings or scriptures: Many of the major world religions possess special writings that they feel reveal the wisdom of God in unique and very holy ways. These writings are called **scriptures,** which merely means "writings." The Hindu Scriptures are known as the *Vedas,* and Islam's holy book is called the *Koran.* Of course, Jews and Christians revere the collection of sacred writings that we call the *Bible.* Exactly how

God is revealed in the pages of the Jewish and Christian Scriptures is a subject of much debate and discussion, and we will return to that question later in this course.

Through religious teachings and statements of faith: This narrower understanding of revelation has been central to the Catholic understanding of revelation for a long time. In this view, a particular religion reflects deeply upon the revelation of God—often as it is experienced and expressed through the means noted above—and then attempts to capture or summarize the core meaning of that revelation in clearly stated teachings of faith. We call such teachings doctrines or dogmas.

So we see that the notion of revelation is extremely important in our discussion of faith and religion. The major religions throughout history have developed as the attempts by people to understand, communicate, and celebrate what they believe to be God's revelation. As we noted earlier, these religions express their convictions about God and the meaning of life through symbols, celebrations, statements of belief, and codes of behavior. Each religious tradition emphasizes different aspects of what it believes is God's revelation as well as what it believes is expected of people in response to that revelation. One religious tradition, as we have noted, may emphasize the need for an individual experience of God's revelation, what some would call a *conversion experience* or a *born-again experience.* Another religion may emphasize the need to reflect on God's revelation in history and then ritually celebrate those events. Still others may emphasize the need to understand religious doctrines.

In its teachings, a religion attempts to summarize the meaning of revelation.

The Challenge of Choosing

The challenge that eventually confronts each of us is to make a personal decision regarding all the matters that we have discussed in this chapter.

- The initial decision that we must make is whether or not to believe and trust in God.
- Having made that decision affirmatively, we then confront another choice: How will we live out that relationship with God in our lives? Within which religious tradition—if any at all—do we hope to find a meaningful expression of our faith relationship with God?

Many people—young and old alike—may become very uncomfortable with this discussion. Is the implication here that all religions are the same, that what one believes makes no difference, or that one religion is as good as another? Not at all. Certainly most religions are sincere in their conviction of their own truth, have valuable insights into God and the nature of God's relationship with people, and are worthy of our respect and study. Nevertheless, Christians believe that their beliefs and practices come closer to accurately understanding and responding to God than do those of other religions.

What we are trying to demonstrate in this discussion so far is this rather obvious fact: eventually each of us must search for the truth wherever we can find it. If that search for truth is honest, it must include an open-mindedness, including the study of other religious traditions. The goal is not to window-shop for a religion that appeals to us. Rather, the goal is to discover a truth to which we can commit our lives in maturity and with conviction.

Perhaps this course will be a significant help in your search. This course cannot hope to present all the major religions—among them Hinduism, Buddhism, and Islam—because brief sketches of such religions may more likely lead to misinformation and misunderstanding than to truth. We will discuss one other major religion, however. Because Christianity is grounded and founded on the history of the Jews, we must try to understand Judaism in order to understand Christian faith.

A Framework for Understanding Religions

Out of all that has been talked about to this point, a reasonable framework emerges that will guide us in the study of Judaism and Catholic Christianity. We have already noted many of the characteristics shared by religions in general—namely, a sense of the sacred presence of God and a system of beliefs, symbols, celebrations, and codes of behavior. These many characteristics of religion can be organized in a way that allows us to understand and discuss them in a logical way. For our purposes, we will approach our discussion of Judaism and Christianity in terms of three major components of religion: wisdom, worship, and works.

Wisdom refers to a religion's basic system of beliefs, what it holds to be true about the nature of God and about God's

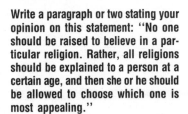

Write a paragraph or two stating your opinion on this statement: "No one should be raised to believe in a particular religion. Rather, all religions should be explained to a person at a certain age, and then she or he should be allowed to choose which one is most appealing."

Most religions have valuable insights into God and the nature of God's relationship with people.

Faith and Religion

relationship with the world. The wisdom of Judaism and Christianity is embodied in their sacred scriptures and in their systems of beliefs or teachings. We will be discussing both of these areas as they are expressed in each religion.

Worship includes all the celebrations and communal prayer forms of a religion. As we shall see, important connections exist between Jewish and Christian forms of worship. Our discussion on Catholic Christian worship will include such areas as the sacraments and its *liturgical calendar*—that is, the way in which the Church organizes its communal worship throughout an annual cycle of seasons and religious themes.

Lighting the eight-branched candelabrum, called the menorah, is a central ritual in the Jewish celebration of Hanukkah. The eight-day festival commemorates the rededication of the Temple in Jerusalem in A.D. 160.

Works refers to the code of behavior that is central to the teachings of a religion. For Christians, as well as for Jews, this code focuses on the Ten Commandments. More broadly, a certain lifestyle or way of life is expected of Christians—one that includes, for instance, a commitment to actions on behalf of justice and peace.

Deciding How to Decide

At some point each of us makes a decision about the role religion will play in our lives. This decision may be to practice actively the religion into which we were born and raised. Or the decision may be to change to another religion or to decide not to practice any religion at all. The unchanging fact is that each of us at some point will make a personal decision about faith and religion. Quite likely you are not yet at that point, but you may be getting close to it. In any case, when the time arrives for you to make that decision, how will you decide? What guidelines will you follow in making your choice?

Let's put the question as directly as possible: Why should you choose to be a Catholic Christian? (Or, if you are not a Catholic but are attending a Catholic high school, how will you make a decision about your religion?) This question may seem odd. After all, you probably already consider yourself Christian. You were presumedly baptized into the faith and raised a Catholic. In such a case, therefore, the question may be better stated this way: Why should one remain a Catholic when given the freedom to choose?

In light of all that we have said about faith, religion, and the religious development of the individual, one reasonable response to this important question might look like this. We would choose to become or remain a Catholic Christian if the following statements are true:

1. The *wisdom* of Catholicism reflects and expresses what we have come to know and believe about God.
2. Catholic *worship* effectively celebrates God's presence in our lives.
3. The *works* of Catholic Christianity suggest a way of life that allows and helps us to become the persons we want to be.

Understanding Catholic Christianity, then, is all about the wisdom, worship, and works of Catholicism. Yet we cannot begin a discussion of Catholicism or Christianity generally without turning first to a discussion of another world religion—Judaism.

Jesus was born into a devout Jewish family. As a child he was educated in the wisdom, worship, and works of the Jews. Jesus became a Jewish teacher and prophet. He proclaimed his profound vision of God and the meaning of life to the Jews. The earliest followers of Jesus were Jews, and they were the founding members of the religious community that today we recognize as the Church. So any accurate discussion of the Church must take into account the fact that the religion of Jesus was Judaism. For that reason the next chapter is devoted to a review of the history, beliefs, and practices of the Jewish people.

Review Questions

1. What point does this chapter make of the story about the believer and the skeptic who went on a journey together?
2. What problem does the use of language present in our discussions of religion?
3. The stories about Frank and Jack and about Brenda illustrate points about the nature of faith. Briefly summarize the point made by each story.
4. How does religious faith differ from other human experiences of trusting relationships?
5. What is meant by the statement that faith and religion are matters of both the head and the heart?
6. What are two limitations that we confront in our attempts to discuss belief in God?
7. Why is it not sufficient to rely completely on the opinions of others as a reason to believe in God?
8. Give two proofs of the existence of God proposed by Saint Thomas Aquinas.
9. What is the lesson about faith in God to be learned from the story of the fish in the ocean?
10. How can the love of another person for us lead us to believe in the existence of God?
11. Explain the statement that religious faith is an act of fundamental trust.
12. In what way can we say that religion is to faith what hugs are to love?
13. What is the major reason that there are so many different religions in the world?
14. Why do faith and religion need each other?
15. Young people suffer more from a crisis of religion than from a crisis of faith. Explain.
16. The experience of religion does not always satisfy us. Why is this not surprising?

17. Why would God want to reveal sacred Mystery to us? How might this be related to the notion of faith as a gift from God?
18. Identify four ways in which God's revelation takes place.
19. Why do we need to study Judaism in this course?
20. Identify three components that are present in every religion.
21. On what grounds should one make a decision about which religion—if any—to follow?

Key Terms
worldviews
religious faith
theology
transcendence
atheists
religion
revelation
scriptures
wisdom
worship
works

4

The Jews of the Bible:
Discovering the Jewish Roots of Christianity

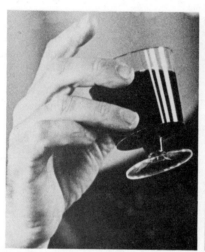

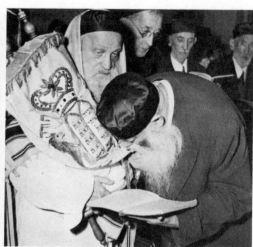

We Need a Sense of History

We have seen the story countless times in television shows: Someone suffers a blow to the head and immediately develops profound amnesia—that is, a complete loss of memory. Suddenly and dramatically, the victim's entire world is thrown into chaos. The faces of loved ones may go unrecognized. All recollection of home and workplace may be lost. Even the victim's name may have to be replaced with John or Jane Doe.

Then begins the slow process of rebuilding the amnesiac's life and, in fact, his or her identity as a person. Small events—a face in a crowd, a song on the radio, an aroma—trigger memories of the past. The person's face lights up with incredible enthusiasm at the slightest recollection. Often the story concludes with one such insight into the victim's past becoming the gateway to a complete recovery of his or her identity.

Without a sense of the past, our present lives, like an amnesiac's, would be filled with confusion and loneliness. The reverse is just as true: our personal histories give meaning and purpose to our present lives. This is true not only for us as individuals but also for the various social groups or communities to which we belong.

- In the United States, for example, citizens remind themselves of their roots as a people through yearly celebrations of national holidays, such as the Fourth of July or Veterans Day.
- In Canada, the various ethnic groups that make up the nation celebrate their unique contributions to Canadian history and culture on Canada Day.
- In your school you likely hear and read about upcoming class reunions—gatherings of graduates, the alumni, who will retell fond stories about events very much like those you are presently experiencing.

Imagine a coming school event of such significance that it could become a story to tell over and over again to your children and grandchildren. Write a brief account of the imaginary event.

Significant events in our pasts, such as a dramatic victory in a sport, helped to build our identities.

Imagine this possibility: Next week you may experience as a class an event so significant—such as a dramatic victory in a sport—that many years from now you will be remembering and telling others about it, perhaps even your own grandchildren!

Treasuring the past as a way to understand and celebrate the present is also very much a part of Catholic Christianity. Annually Christians all over the world recall and celebrate events such as the birth of Jesus and his Resurrection. On a weekly basis, millions of Catholics gather at Mass to listen to the story of Christianity and to break bread in memory of the one who did so with his closest friends on the evening before he died nearly two thousand years ago.

Catholic Christianity has emerged out of a history that stretches back nearly four thousand years! We cannot expect to understand who we are as Catholics without some understanding of that heritage. In this chapter, then, we are going to briefly review the history of the Jewish people and identify some of the most important features of their religion. As noted earlier, we need to begin with Judaism in order to understand Jesus and Christianity. You may experience some difficulty in seeing the significance of this material in your own life or even in this study of Catholic Christianity. Your efforts to learn this material, however, will pay big dividends later when we struggle to more fully understand Jesus and his message. You may even be in for an occasional surprise when you discover how freeing and exhilarating getting in touch with the memories of our religious heritage can be.

A Brief Review of the History of the Jewish People

In such a short space, a detailed summary of the history of the Jewish people and their evolving religion is impossible, so this chapter will simply highlight the major events of early Judaism that most directly come to bear on the life and message of Jesus. You have probably already been introduced to some of this information in your previous religious education.

Throughout this discussion, remember that the entire history of the Jews—and, indeed, of Christianity—can be understood in terms of God's ongoing revelation. The story of the Jews goes beyond *history* in our normal sense of that term for we are dealing with more than a series of historical events involving certain people on clearly defined dates. We are, rather, exploring what is known as **salvation history,** which is the saga of God's loving action throughout the history of the Jews and the Christians. The history of salvation among the Jews centers on their experience of having been chosen by God to play a central role in God's plan of salvation for all humanity. Christians later interpreted Jewish history as a period in which the stage was being set for the ultimate act of salvation in the person of Jesus. More will be said about this view of history as this review of Judaism unfolds.

Judaism's Early History

You may already know more than you think you know about Jewish history from many years of hearing the marvelous stories about this phenomenal religion and its people. For instance, recall if you can the following memorable persons and events.

You may already know more than you think about Jewish history from many years of hearing about this phenomenal religion and its people.

The Patriarchs

Abraham was a wandering shepherd, or *nomad,* who lived in the region of Palestine nearly two thousand years before Jesus. He belonged to a group of people known as **Hebrews.** Perhaps one of the most touching scenes in all of the Scriptures is that of Abraham's decision to sacrifice his beloved son, *Isaac,* in the belief that this sacrifice was the will of his God. God stopped Abraham, however, so Isaac lived to see the birth of his own son *Jacob.* These three men—Abraham, Isaac, and Jacob—are referred to as the **patriarchs,** or fathers, of Judaism.

Jacob, incidentally, was given the name *Israel* by God, and the people who claimed their descent from him became known as **Israelites.** They would only later be known as Jews.

Joseph in Egypt

Remember also that Jacob had twelve sons. Particularly if you have several brothers of your own, you can imagine that having twelve boys in one family was bound to lead to trouble. Yet this family's difficulties seem extreme—even when measured against the soap operas on television. Jacob's favorite son was *Joseph*, and as we might expect, Joseph's brothers were jealous of their father's affection for him. In their hostility, they sold Joseph as a slave to some merchants who were on their way to Egypt. (You think you have trouble in your family!)

Joseph, however, was so talented that he became prime minister of Egypt, a position of great authority. Moreover, Joseph was as virtuous as he was talented. After forgiving his brothers for what they had done to him, Joseph invited them and his father to join him and to live in Egypt.

Jacob eventually died there, more than sixteen hundred years before the time of Jesus. Under a series of kindly pharaohs, the Israelites continued to live prosperously in Egypt. If the story had ended there, we might be able to say that "they lived happily ever after." But the story is only beginning.

Slavery

After about one hundred and fifty years, this time of peace and prosperity ended for the Israelites. They were enslaved by cruel pharaohs who burdened the Israelites with the backbreaking jobs of brickmaking and constructing public buildings. This oppressive slavery devastated the Israelites, and they yearned for freedom. Hundreds of years later the answer to their dreams came in the person of the man most revered to this day by faithful Jews. That man was *Moses*. The story of Moses is at the very heart of Judaism.

Moses and the God Named Yahweh

During personal experiences in which he gained a profound insight into the nature of God, Moses came to a realization of his mission to save his people. Moses' ancestors, beginning as far back as Abraham, had come to a sense of God that was unique. Rather than believing in many different gods in nature, as was typical of the other peoples of their time, the Israelites had gradually evolved the concept of a single God who cared deeply about them as a people. This slowly developing belief in "a God above all other gods" reached a profound new level when the very name of God was revealed to Moses in a scene recorded in the Book of Exodus. God told Moses that he, Moses, was to lead the Israelites from slavery to freedom. Then the scene continues:

> Moses then said to God, "Look, if I go to the Israelites and say to them, 'The God of your ancestors has sent me to you,' and they say to me, 'What is his name?' what am I to tell them?" God said to Moses, "I am he who is." And he said, "This is what you are to say to the Israelites, 'I am has sent me to you.' " God further said to Moses, "You are to tell the Israelites, 'Yahweh, the God of your ancestors, the God of Abraham, the God of Isaac and the God of Jacob, has sent me to you.' This is my name for all time, and thus I am to be [called] for all generations to come." (Exodus 3:13–15)

A statue of Moses, completed by Michelangelo about 1513, in Saint Peter's Basilica

The name *Yahweh* is very difficult to translate into English. The version of the Bible used here translates the name with the phrase "I am he who is." Other biblical scholars have suggested translations such as "I am the One who is present" or "I bring into existence all that is." The name seems to hint at the very nature of God, one who is both present and yet beyond us. The Jews later held the sacred name in such reverence that they refused to pronounce it, even passing over it when reading it in their Scriptures and automatically replacing it with a word meaning "Lord." Later in this chapter we will explore the Jewish understanding of God.

The Ten Plagues

Moses appealed to the pharaoh to "let my people go," but the pharaoh, underestimating the power of a committed person like Moses, refused to listen. However, Moses caught the pharaoh's attention with a series of plagues that Yahweh called down upon the Egyptians. The pharaoh was forced to free the Israelites after the tenth plague in which the firstborn children of all the families in Egypt were killed. The children of the Israelites were spared or "passed over" if their families smeared the blood of slaughtered sheep or goats on their doorposts and then ate the flesh of the animals. Eventually the miraculous liberation of the Israelites from slavery in Egypt would be memorialized and annually celebrated in the Jewish feast of Passover.

The Desert

As the Israelites made their escape through the desert, the bread that they hurriedly prepared before leaving Egypt sustained them. With no time to wait for the bread to rise as it normally would, they had to be satisfied with unleavened bread. This occasion is also remembered in the special Jewish feast of Passover and is even recalled in our own Christian celebration of Eucharist when we, too, eat blessed bread that is unleavened.

Back to the story: Pharaoh changed his mind and sent his armies to pursue the Israelites into the desert. God once again came to the rescue of the Israelites by allowing them to cross through a sea—which then became a watery grave for the armies that pursued them.

This marvelous imagery brings us now to the centerpiece of all Jewish history, to a mountaintop encounter between

The ten plagues, or disasters, experienced by the Egyptians were related to their way of life as a people largely dependent on the land—mosquitoes, gnats, locusts, hail, cattle disease, and so on (see Book of Exodus, chapters 7–12). Imagine that God is to send a series of ten plagues to a modern dictatorship that is enslaving people. What form might the plagues take?

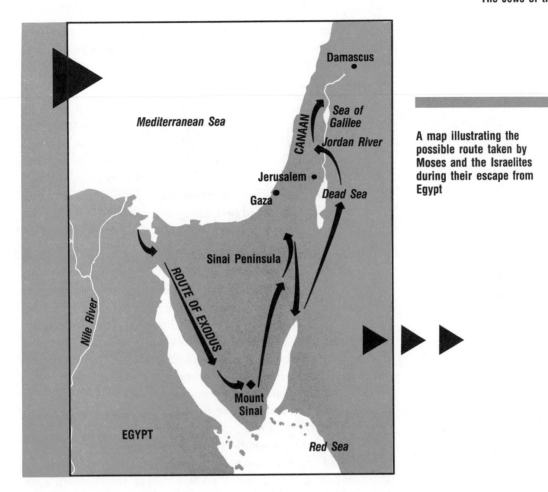

A map illustrating the possible route taken by Moses and the Israelites during their escape from Egypt

Moses and Yahweh that would permanently seal the loving relationship between God and that small community of persecuted yet blessed people.

The Covenant of Sinai

Earlier in this course you read about the wisdom of particular religions, that is, the ways in which religions come to understand and express their beliefs about God. The wisdom of Judaism is, in a sense, summarized in the story of Moses. The understanding of God implied in God's new name is that of a sacred yet saving Mystery. This relationship—between a personal loving God and a Chosen People—was known as a **covenant**, a key concept in Judaism.

The relationship between Yahweh and the Israelites was formalized on Mount Sinai in a dramatic encounter between

Yahweh and Moses. Tradition says that the Israelites had been wandering in the desert for fifty days. When they reached Mount Sinai, Yahweh called Moses to the top of the mountain and told him:

> "Say this to the house of Jacob! Tell the Israelites, 'You have seen for yourselves what I did to the Egyptians and how I carried you away on eagle's wings and brought you to me. So now, if you are really prepared to obey me and keep my covenant, you, out of all peoples, shall be my personal possession, for the whole world is mine. For me you shall be a kingdom of priests, a holy nation.' Those are the words you are to say to the Israelites." (Exodus 19:3–6)

Moses returned to the people and told them what Yahweh had said, and they agreed to do whatever God asked of them. In one of the most powerful scenes in the Scriptures, Yahweh again encountered Moses and presented him with the **Law.** The Law described the Israelites' end of the bargain—in other words, their responsibilities if they wished to enter into a sacred covenant in which Yahweh would be their God and they would be Yahweh's Chosen People. The cornerstone of the Law is what we now call the Ten Commandments.

This event, which we call the Sinai Covenant, is in many ways the birthday of the Jewish people as the people of God. They had begun as a wandering tribe of nomads, then endured hundreds of years as slaves, and finally evolved into a deeply religious community committed to a special relationship with their God. With their acceptance of the Law as a code of both individual and communal behavior, the Israelites forever changed and elevated the human understanding of morality, our sense of what is right and wrong. This new sense of morality will be discussed throughout this course.

Into the Promised Land

After Moses' time, the Israelites entered the fertile land of Canaan, the land that had been promised to them by Yahweh as a country "flowing with milk and honey" (Exodus 3:17). Today this land is variously identified as Palestine, Israel, or the Holy Land.

A savage time followed, filled with virtually constant warfare between the Israelites and other invading tribes, as well as with the city-dwellers of the region. During these struggles,

The Ten Commandments

10

Then God spoke all these words. He said, "I am Yahweh your God who brought you out of Egypt, where you lived as slaves.

"You shall have no other gods to rival me....

"You shall not misuse the name of Yahweh your God, for Yahweh will not leave unpunished anyone who misuses his name.

"Remember the Sabbath day and keep it holy. For six days you shall labour and do all your work, but the seventh day is a Sabbath for Yahweh your God.... For in six days Yahweh made the heavens, earth and sea and all that these contain, but on the seventh day he rested; that is why Yahweh has blessed the Sabbath day and made it sacred.

"Honour your father and your mother so that you may live long in the land that Yahweh your God is giving you.

"You shall not kill.

"You shall not commit adultery.

"You shall not steal.

"You shall not give false evidence against your neighbour.

"You shall not set your heart on your neighbour's house. You shall not set your heart on your neighbour's spouse, or servant, man or woman, or ox, or donkey, or any of your neighbour's possessions."

Seeing the thunder pealing, the lightning flashing, the trumpet blasting and the mountain smoking, the people were all terrified and kept their distance.
(Exodus 20:1–18)

Sometimes we can become so familiar with our religious teachings and traditions that they no longer seem fresh to us. Reflect on this biblical account of the giving of the Law by Yahweh to Moses on Mount Sinai. In this context, the code of morality that we commonly know as the Ten Commandments can take on new meaning for us.

men called **judges** were periodically appointed to lead the people in their fights. (The most familiar judge is Samson, who received perhaps the most famous haircut in all of history!) As the land was gradually conquered, it was divided up among *the twelve tribes of Israel*, each tribe claiming descent from one of the twelve sons of Jacob. Can you think of a much later time when the number twelve would play a significant role in Christian history?

During this time of great struggle, the Israelite tribes spread over the land just east of the Mediterranean Sea. The city of Jerusalem marked the boundary between the region to the south, which was called **Judah**, and that to the north, called **Israel**. Their common worship of Yahweh united the tribes.

The United Kingdom

The Israelites' attempt to establish a homeland reached a high point about one thousand years before the time of Jesus. Israel became a recognized kingdom when *King David* conquered Jerusalem, and his son *King Solomon* built a beautiful temple there. Yahweh remained the acknowledged leader of Israel, the head of both the political and the religious dimensions of the nation.

A brief time of prosperity and peace followed. No doubt the government was tempted to interpret the will of Yahweh to meet its own ends, as had happened in other cultures of the time. In such cases the gods of the nations were simply said to endorse whatever policies the rulers desired.

In Israel, however, great **prophets** constantly questioned the injustices of the kings and tried to call the people back to their covenant with Yahweh. Yet the people continually returned to the worship of other gods. After the time of Solomon, the peaceful period ended, government and religion divided, and only a small number of true worshipers remained.

A New Desert Experience for the Jews

Eventually the greater powers of the region crushed the kingdom, which had split into two after the death of Solomon. About seven hundred years before Jesus, the Assyrians sent the powerful and wealthy citizens of the northern kingdom of Israel into exile. About one hundred and thirty years later, victorious warriors transported the citizens of the southern kingdom of Judah to Babylon, a city devoted to materialism and

▼

Write a brief description of an event in your personal or family life in which a particularly difficult situation turned into a kind of desert experience for you—that is, a time for more deeply discovering and understanding life.

pleasure. This new desert experience reminded the people of their escape from Egypt, but in Babylon they experienced Yahweh in a fresh way. If anything, their faith in Yahweh became stronger than ever. The Israelites realized that Yahweh was not only stronger than other gods; other gods did not exist at all.

The desert is still home to nomadic people in the Middle East.

Separated by Land, United by Faith

About five hundred years before the time of Jesus, the Persians overcame Babylonia. The Israelites who had remained faithful, called the *Remnant*, returned to their homeland. The majority of those who returned were the former inhabitants of Judah. That is why the next five centuries are called the period of **Judaism**, the name from which the title **Jew** is derived. The returning Jews rebuilt the city of Jerusalem, although they did not regain the political power that they had known in the days of the united kingdom.

Having conquered the Persians, the Greeks became the Jews' overlords for nearly three hundred years. Then, just sixty-three years before the time of Jesus, the Jews came under the rule of the Romans. By then the Jewish people were scattered all over the Western world, and Jerusalem had become their religious capital. During this time, many people of deep and simple faith among the Jews recognized that they could not survive on their own. So they put all their hopes in the coming of a savior. Called *the poor of Yahweh,* these Jews believed that from within their group a great leader, or liberator, called the *Messiah* would come.

That briefly outlines the history of the Jewish people to the time of Jesus. During these two thousand years, they progressed from a nomadic way of life to a settled farming life. Then they formed themselves into a nation. Finally, they became a scattered spiritual community united by their faith in God and their dedication to living out the Law. Their story is particularly special and important to our understanding of Christian faith.

The Wisdom of the Jews

The history of the Jews has confused and challenged historians for years. The study of world history suggests that religions evolve through fairly predictable patterns. The Jews fit few of the patterns.

Historically, when a tribe of people turned from a nomadic to an agricultural way of life, their god became just another god worshiped by the people in that locale. This did not happen to the Jews. Through great determination and by fighting against what seemed to have been unbeatable odds, they remained true to Yahweh. Again, after the kingdom was split and the Jews were scattered, a historian might predict that their religion would come to an end. But no, instead the Jews discovered a renewed sense of their faith.

By historical standards the Jews should never have survived. In our own century, the Holocaust destroyed six million Jews—fully one-third of their entire population. Still this remarkable people and their religion survive.

Its extraordinary history alone makes Judaism a religion worthy of admiration. Of even greater significance to us is the nature of the Jewish religion itself. Its religious concepts are

The Holocaust destroyed one-third of the worlds' Jewish population. Still this remarkable people survives.

the ones in which Jesus was raised and from which Christianity emerged. A true knowledge of our Christian heritage requires a basic understanding of key concepts inherited from the Jewish religion. Using the framework that was introduced earlier for our study of religions, we are dealing here with the wisdom of Judaism.

The Jewish Scriptures as Recorded Wisdom

Our primary source of knowledge about the history of the Jewish people and their religion is found in the book Christians normally refer to as the *Old Testament*. The later writings in the Christian Bible, about Jesus and the early Church, are then traditionally called the *New Testament*. A recent trend among Christians seeks to improve these titles. We now prefer to call the sacred writings of the Jews the **Jewish Scriptures**. This change recognizes the fact that, far too often, our sense of the word *old* implies that something is out-of-date or without value. Clearly this is not the case for these scriptures: the Jews hold these writings to be both sacred and alive with meaning; Christians treasure them as part of the Christian Bible.

In a similar way, we now prefer to call the New Testament the **Christian Scriptures**, or even more specifically, the **Christian Testament**. The word *testament* means "covenant," and in references to the Bible, the term refers either to the earlier Sinai Covenant with Yahweh or to the later covenant established with God by Jesus. The term *Christian Testament* acknowledges the fact that the broader term *Christian Scriptures* would include the Jewish Scriptures, which Christians accept as part of their Bible. Because this language is not universally used, you may occasionally be confused when you run across such terms. Try to develop the habit of using these terms, however, out of respect for Jewish people.

The history and stories of Israel grew out of a long *oral tradition,* in which they were passed from generation to generation by word of mouth. About one hundred years before Christ, scribes began to write down these sacred stories. This writing continued throughout the later biblical times. The Jewish Scriptures are really a collection of books, rather than one book written by one author. Some of the individual books took centuries to develop to the point that we now have them. The Book of

---

The Jewish Scriptures

Catholic Christians have adopted the following forty-six books from the Jewish Scriptures:

The Books of the Law
> Genesis
> Exodus
> Leviticus
> Numbers
> Deuteronomy

The Historical Books
> Joshua
> Judges
> Ruth
> 1 Samuel
> 2 Samuel
> 1 Kings
> 2 Kings
> 1 Chronicles
> 2 Chronicles
> Ezra
> Nehemiah
> Tobit
> Judith
> Esther
> 1 Maccabees
> 2 Maccabees

The Wisdom Books
> Job
> Psalms
> Proverbs
> Ecclesiastes
> Song of Songs
> Wisdom
> Ecclesiasticus

The Books of the Prophets
> Isaiah
> Jeremiah
> Lamentations
> Baruch
> Ezekiel
> Daniel
> Hosea
> Joel
> Amos
> Obadiah
> Jonah
> Micah
> Nahum
> Habakkuk
> Zephaniah
> Haggai
> Zechariah
> Malachi

Psalms, for example, was written over a span of some eight hundred years.

Roman Catholics accept forty-six different books in their version of the Jewish Scriptures, while Protestants and Jews officially include just thirty-nine. As a kind of library of books, the Jewish Scriptures naturally contain a variety of different kinds of writing. Some of the books are immediately recognized as histories. Others read more like law books. Still others are clearly poetic in nature, while some have the tone of philosophy, in which the authors ponder the deeper meanings of life.

The Jewish Scriptures also reflect the Jewish people's gradually evolving sense of their God. Just as we grow in our faith as individuals, so too is God only gradually understood by communities of people. This was true of the religious and moral sense of the Jews. Occasionally the cruelty and barbarism of some sections of scripture shocks readers today. Yet, slowly and at times painfully, the Jewish people developed keen beliefs in the nature of God and about justice among people. As the prophet Jeremiah said, Yahweh had declared that "within them I shall plant my Law, writing it on their hearts" (Jeremiah 31:33).

No God But Yahweh

Our earlier discussions of God and religion suggested that some cultures throughout history have evolved a belief in many gods rather than in one God. This belief is called **polytheism** (from the Greek words *poly,* meaning "many," and *theos,* meaning "god"). In polytheism, each force in nature is believed to be controlled by a different god, such as the rain god or the god of fire. Occasionally one god may be recognized as superior to all others, as in the case of the ancient Egyptians' worship of the sun god. The Jewish people arrived at a remarkably different understanding, however. God is one—unique, incomparable, and caring. This belief in one God is called **monotheism** (from *mono,* meaning "one," and *theos*).

Nothing quite like this belief in one God had ever existed before. In fact, a close study of the Bible shows that this belief was only slowly recognized even by the Jewish people themselves, who were often tempted to accept polytheism. In our culture we are so accustomed to think in terms of either monotheism or atheism that we have a difficult time understanding how radical the notion of one God was at the time.

The Jewish belief in the absolute supremacy of Yahweh

caused conflicts for the Jews throughout their history. By proclaiming Yahweh as "the God above all other gods," they automatically denied the power of other gods worshiped by neighboring groups. Also, as in the case of the Romans particularly, other groups often considered their political leaders to be divine. By denying this possibility, the Jews were guaranteed conflicts with their Roman overlords.

The Jewish Scriptures reflect the Jewish people's gradually evolving sense of God as unique, incomparable, and caring.

A Covenantal Relationship with God

The **Sinai Covenant,** as we have seen, is the name given to the special relationship established between Yahweh and the people of Israel. A covenant is much more than a simple agreement; it carries more weight than our concept of a simple legal contract in which persons agree to certain shared responsibilities. The Sinai Covenant involved a solemn oath by God to be in relationship with the Jewish people in a profoundly personal and loving way. Yahweh offered to be their God, that is, to be intimately involved with them throughout their history. God asked the people of Israel to respond to this covenant by living out their end of the bargain, which was summarized in the Ten Commandments given to Moses on Mount Sinai.

We might more easily understand the profound nature of this covenantal relationship if we look at the vows that lovers proclaim in marriage. Marriage is clearly a contract with all kinds of legal implications for rights regarding children, ownership of property, and even paying taxes. Marriage viewed on this level is a mechanical, cold arrangement. However, on a deeper level, marriage is also a sacred bonding of two people in which they pledge their love for each other. Their mutual responsibilities are understood as signs of care and concern for each other, not in terms of rules and regulations. A true marriage is a covenant in the most profound sense.

We cannot lose sight of the powerful insight into the nature of God that is reflected in the Sinai Covenant. Polytheistic cultures, which viewed gods as fearsome forces in nature, surrounded the Israelites. Yet the Jewish people experienced the one God who cared for them in an intimate and tender way. Clearly this was a gradually evolving concept for them. At times in the Bible, Yahweh was also a God who could be extremely angry. Even God's anger, however, was understood by the Jews as that of a caring parent, an expression of "tough love." This belief in a passionately loving and faithful God sustained the Jews throughout a history that should have seen them destroyed many times over. In light of this covenantal relationship, we can begin to understand the Jewish regard for the Law.

The Jewish people experienced the one God in an intimate and tender way—as a caring parent.

Freed by the Law

To get a true sense of the importance of the Law for the Jewish people is difficult for us. Our concept of law is restrictive and negative. That is, we see law as a series of rules and regulations that lock us in and limit our freedom. For Jews, however, the Law promotes freedom in a positive sense. The Law is considered the very word of God, an expression of God's loving intention for the Chosen People. Faithful Jews feel that they directly encounter God by living out the Law. An analogy might explain this: To us, law is like the sign at the bottom of a hill warning skiers not to ski because of the danger of an avalanche. To the Jews, the Law is more like the sign pointing to the ski lift.

Admittedly some Jews were inclined to be more negative in their understanding of the Law, to live by the letter of the Law rather than by its loving spirit. Jesus would condemn those who did so. At the same time Jesus proclaimed that not one word of the Law was to be eliminated. Although for us the Ten Commandments are the most familiar part of the Law, it is far more extensive than that, speaking to almost every part of the lives of the Jews.

We tend to see law in a negative way, as a limit on our freedom.

People with a Destiny

Before the Jews, time was commonly understood as a recurring cycle. Time's cyclic quality seemed apparent in the repeating seasons. In other words, people had no sense of the world or themselves going anywhere and no sense of some long-range purpose for their existence. Because of their covenantal experience, however, the Jews discovered that they were a people with a destiny: they were being called to somewhere by someone. Of course, that *somewhere* was not always clear. At times the Jews imagined themselves as a world military or political power. At other times they saw themselves as a spiritual community in which the kingdom of Yahweh would become visible. About the *someone* who was guiding their history, however, there was no doubt.

God in History

Early in their history the Jewish people recognized that their past as well as their future had significance. This sense of history made Judaism a religion shared best through the telling of great stories about the acts of God in their history. For example, the Jews yearly celebrated the feast of Passover as a memorial of their liberation from slavery in Egypt.

What has been called *salvation history* is grounded on this new understanding of history. That is, both Jews and Christians share the conviction that God's plans for us are being worked out through the events of history.

The Coming of a Messiah

All religions believe that they provide salvation—that is, relief from the pain and evil in the world. Judaism shares this belief, but the Jews' sense of history gives their religion a unique focus. Jews believe that they have a particular destiny in the plan of God, that their future holds something especially marvelous for them. Five hundred years before Jesus' time, that hope or expectation began to take on a very definite form among some Jewish groups. They believed that a leader would emerge from King David's line. That person was the **Messiah,** meaning "the anointed one," the one called by God to rescue the people and to build a new and mighty nation.

This expectation of a coming Messiah grew in later biblical times. Who the Messiah would be was unknown. Some expected a great military leader who would reestablish them as a political power. By the time of the Roman occupation of Palestine, less than a century before Jesus, the dream of a Messiah had reached a peak in the thoughts and hopes of many Jewish people.

The Worship of the Jews

The approach to worship developed by any religion grows quite naturally out of its history and is often based on the attempts by believers to commemorate and celebrate their history and their beliefs through words, symbols, and rituals. Certainly this was the case for the Jewish people of Jesus' time. By that time in Jewish history, individual and communal prayer played a central role in daily life. Greek or Roman neighbors might have been satisfied to offer an occasional sacrifice at a shrine, feeling that such a gesture would protect them from harm and allow them to get on with their lives. For the Jews, however, no aspect of life went untouched by the hand of Yahweh. Their firm faith in Yahweh filled every part of their lives, and their daily, weekly, and annual cycle of worship reflected that fact.

Daily Life Dedicated to Yahweh

Faithful Jews were expected to live lives of deep personal prayer. Every morning and evening Jews recited the famous Shema prayer: "Listen, Israel: Yahweh our God is the one, the only Yahweh. You must love Yahweh your God with all your heart, with all your soul, with all your strength" (Deuteronomy

6:4–5). In addition to this minimal prayer, faithful Jews said prayers of praise and blessing each morning, afternoon, and evening.

The Week Consecrated by the Sabbath

The **Sabbath** was and remains today a weekly day of rest and prayer for the Jews. Beginning at sundown on Friday, this day was meant to remind Jews that the world is the work of the creator, not of humans. Sabbath worship was recognized in Jesus' time as a central and sacred sign of Yahweh's presence with the people. The Sabbath was viewed as so sacred that it was the only day of the week that had a name; all other days were identified as, for example, "the day before Sabbath." Many laws governed the behavior of men and women on the Sabbath, and arguments surrounding the proper way to follow those laws were constant. Jesus became embroiled in debate on this issue during his own ministry. The Christian tradition of Sunday worship finds its roots in the Jewish Sabbath.

The Jewish Year
Consecrated Through Religious Feasts

Religions often develop an annual cycle of religious feasts and observances to celebrate key events in their history. We know this from our own Catholic heritage, and we will discuss Catholic worship and liturgical feasts in a later chapter. What about the Jews of Jesus' day?

The gospel story of Jesus mentions three major religious feasts celebrated each year by the Jews.

1. *Pentecost* (the word literally means "the fiftieth day") celebrates the giving of the Law to Moses after fifty days of wandering in the desert following the escape of the Israelites from bondage in Egypt. Earlier in Jewish history this day was a great springtime holiday, one that served as the time to celebrate the gratitude people felt for the wonderful gifts of Yahweh. The Jews later expanded the holiday's meaning to include the celebration of the gift of the Law as well. This pattern for the development of holy days is common in many religions. Christians, for example, have borrowed for their Christmas and Easter celebrations some symbols and traditions from what were originally pagan holidays.

2. **The Day of Atonement,** also known as *Yom Kippur,* held such solemn significance for Jews that all one had to do was mention "the Day" and everyone knew what feast was referred to. A time for the repenting of sins, the feast included stirring ceremonies, fasting, prayer, and ritual bathings.

3. **Passover,** the holiest and most celebrated of all the major feasts of the Jewish year, memorializes the miraculous liberation from Egypt. This feast, which marked the beginning of the Jewish religious year, lasted a week and included the sacrifice of lambs in the Temple in Jerusalem and the ritual eating of a special meal. This very cheerful feast would play a central role in the events surrounding the final days of Jesus.

Passover, a feast that includes a special meal, is still celebrated by Jews today.

So the daily life of faithful Jews was focused on the covenantal relationship with Yahweh. Religion was not tacked on to life in an artificial way. Naturally some Jews engaged in private and communal worship mechanically, much like some Catholics today who attend Mass on a weekend merely out of a sense of obligation. Jesus would run into heated conflict with such people. The primary point is that, if we are to better understand Jesus, we must recognize him as one who from his birth on was immersed in the rich prayer life of his people.

The Works of the Jews

Finally, let's briefly look at what we can call the *works* of the biblical Jews, the ways in which their religious faith was lived out in their behavior and in their everyday decisions.

This discussion calls for a note of caution. Christians tend to stereotype the relationship between Jewish and Christian religious and moral life. For example, Christians commonly claim to follow a *law of love* while suggesting that the Jews of the Bible followed a *law of fear*. In a similar way, Christians often claim to have a moral code that is based on forgiveness while accusing the Jews of Jesus' time of practicing a morality based on revenge, summed up with the saying "an eye for an eye." Such stereotypes are either completely wrong or based on a kernel of truth that is greatly exaggerated. We must strive to be unbiased, accurate, and fair in this discussion.

The fact is that the Jews of Jesus' time were identified by the neighboring cultures as a particularly caring people. Their covenant with Yahweh called them to love. Of the Ten Commandments, for example, seven deal directly with moral principles that govern relationships between people.

Some *rabbis*—that is, Jewish teachers—felt that faithful Jews should view these commandments as only a minimum, that they should go far beyond the letter of the Law to live out its spirit. According to some rabbis, for example, the giving of alms to the poor was a requirement of the Law, not merely an option for those who cared to do so.

Jewish history also reveals a profound commitment to justice as a guiding moral principle. Whenever the Jewish people began to lose sight of justice, the prophets called them back to their primary values. Listen to the prophet Amos, for example, as he speaks of Yahweh's words of judgment against the rich people who were exploiting the poor:

> I hate, I scorn your festivals,
> I take no pleasure in your solemn assemblies.
>
> . . . .
>
> but let justice flow like water,
> and uprightness like a never-failing stream!
> (Amos 5:21,24)

Remember that the Jews of the Bible, like all human beings, lived out their values and beliefs in a complex and difficult cultural setting. Although deeply grounded in Jewish history, justice was an ideal that was extraordinarily difficult to live out. As a result, Jesus would later condemn his society on many levels. Yet how would Jesus react if he were to evaluate *our* society and its values?

Adherence to the Law

We have seen that Jewish life in later biblical times was governed by the Law. The difficulty many Jews experienced was one of interpreting how the Law should be applied to daily life situations. For instance:

- Some groups held very rigidly to living the many laws of Judaism strictly by the letter, and they rejected any attempts to add to or interpret the Law as written in the Jewish Scriptures. This view was particularly strong among the group known as the **Sadducees**. This priestly caste of the Jews was also committed to proper worship in the Temple in Jerusalem.
- Another faction of Jews believed that the Law could be interpreted and expanded to better direct the lives of people in every detail. The emphasis by these **Pharisees** on the Law would cause conflicts with Jesus.

Social Classes at the Time of Jesus

Every society eventually develops social classes or groups: the haves and the have-nots, the rich people and the poor people, the politically powerful and the oppressed. The world of the Jews of Jesus' day was no different.

First of all, a great imbalance existed between the rights of men and those of women. This inequality was found in every culture of the time and still exists in our own society. In Jewish society the husband and father was recognized as the head of the household, with both his wife and his children subject to his will. A law mandated that women wait on men but not eat with them. Women were also restricted to worshiping in only certain areas of the Temple in Jerusalem. Such practices help us to understand why in the Gospels the willingness of Jesus to talk and relate with women was the cause of so much controversy.

As in our own society, social standing in Jewish culture was based to a great extent on wealth. A wide gap separated the relatively few rich people from the many people who were desperately poor. Virtually no middle class developed, and the vast majority of people lived in dire poverty. During his ministry, Jesus would have much to say about this situation of wealth and poverty.

Some groups of Jews were clearly identified as social outcasts. For example, the Samaritans traced their origins back to the northern tribes of Israel and to those Jews who were not

For each of the social groups identified under "Social Classes at the Time of Jesus," identify a group in our modern society with similar needs and concerns. Write a brief description of how Jesus might respond to the needs of each group if he were to come among us today.

sent into exile. Although they worshiped Yahweh, the Samaritans were not accepted as true Israelites. In fact, they were detested even more than pagans.

Other social outcasts included lepers and those suffering from other diseases. To us this behavior may seem to be terribly cruel, which, of course, it is. Again we must remember the unique characteristics of the time. For example, disease and poverty were seen as signs of the presence of sin and as punishments by God. A physically sick or mentally ill person was believed to be possessed by a demon. So fear, rather than outright cruelty, led many Jews to reject or avoid the sick people who were frequently encountered on their roads.

With our modern knowledge of illness, we might look down upon the Jews' fearful superstition. Yet think about this: with less reason we still fear illness and sick people. More to the point, these hardhearted attitudes described in Jewish society are everywhere in evidence today.

The Promises of Yahweh Are Fulfilled

The Jews of Jesus' day were a people who staked their lives as individuals and their history as a nation on the experience of waiting—waiting for the promises of their God to be fulfilled. The Jewish Scriptures record the tension and occasional trauma that all waiting seems to carry with it: the rising hopes and the shattering failures, the tremendous sense of expectations, and the seemingly endless disappointment. The Jews kept waiting, hoping for the Messiah who would set them free, who would fulfill all their dreams, who would end their long history of waiting and give them total peace and justice.

Christians believe that the promises of God were fulfilled over twelve hundred years after Yahweh first entered into covenant with the Jewish people. Into the history of the Jews and, indeed, into the history of all people, came a man—a very different man. This man was hardly what anyone had expected, and his message was not easily accepted. To those who can say yes, to those who can follow this man, is given "fullness of life." The man was born of a Jewish woman two thousand years ago, and he changed the world as no other person has changed it. We turn now to his story and, in a very real way, to the story of all those who choose to follow him as Christians.

Review Questions

1. Why is a sense of personal history so significant in our lives? Relate this reason to the need for a sense of history within communities.
2. What is the meaning of the term *patriarch?* Identify the three patriarchs of the Israelites.
3. How did Joseph and his family end up living in Egypt?
4. What is the meaning of the name *Yahweh?*
5. Describe the origins of the Jewish feast of Passover.
6. Provide the needed information about the Sinai Covenant in response to the following questions:
   a. What is the basic meaning of a covenant?
   b. Who were the major characters involved in the biblical story of the Sinai Covenant?
   c. What was the Israelites' end of the bargain in their covenant with Yahweh?
   d. What is the cornerstone of the Law?
7. What are three of the various names now given to the land of Canaan?
8. What were the names of the northern and southern regions of the country occupied by the Israelites?
9. Under whose leadership did Israel become a recognized kingdom?
10. Explain the origins of the terms *Judaism* and *Jew.*
11. According to historical standards, why should the Jews never have survived?
12. How many books of the Jewish Scriptures do Roman Catholics include in their scriptures?
13. Give two reasons why the Jewish belief in one God caused conflicts for them throughout their history.
14. Compare the Sinai Covenant to a marriage relationship.

15. Compare our usual understanding of laws with that of the Jews.
16. What is meant by the statement that the Jews discovered that they were a people with a destiny?
17. What role did many Jews expect the Messiah to play in their history?
18. Name and describe the three major religious feasts of Judaism.
19. What are two common stereotypes of the morality of biblical Jews that many Christians hold? What is wrong with these stereotypes?
20. Give three examples of how Jesus responded to the various social classes of his day.

Key Terms
salvation history
Law
Jewish Scriptures
Christian Scriptures
Christian Testament
polytheism
monotheism
Sinai Covenant
Messiah

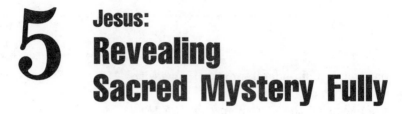

5 Jesus: Revealing Sacred Mystery Fully

The Search for Understanding: Who Is This Man?

Saint John's gospel account of the life and message of Jesus concludes with this note: "There was much else that Jesus did; if it were written down in detail, I do not suppose the world itself would hold all the books that would be written" (John 21:25).

As John suggests, what can possibly be said about Jesus in the brief space that we have available? How can anyone choose the points to highlight without at the same time ignoring other elements of Jesus' message that have tremendous significance? The approach of this course has been to paint with broad strokes, to make sweeping statements about key points of discussion. This tactic allowed a summary of adolescent development in only a few pages and a condensation of the complex history of the Jewish people. In this chapter and in the next we will stand back and take a wide-angle look at who Jesus was and is, at the message that he preached, and at the way he fits into the total historical plan of God. The hope is that the material will sharpen your appetite for searching out more about this incredible person and that you will look forward to the opportunities afforded you for that search in your religion classes during the coming years. The following is what one person wrote about Jesus as a kind of summary statement of what we might call his career:

> Here is a man who was born of Jewish parents, the child of a peasant woman. He never wrote a book. He never held an office. He never owned a home. He never had a family. He never went to college. He never put foot inside a big city. He never traveled two hundred miles from the place where he was born.

In one sentence try to sum up the major point of the reading on Jesus.

While still a young man, the tide of popular opinion turned against him. His friends ran away. One of them denied him. He was nailed to a cross between two thieves. His executioners gambled for the only piece of property he had on earth—his coat. When he was dead, he was taken down and laid in a borrowed grave through the pity of a friend.

Nineteen long centuries have come and gone, and he is the centerpiece of the human race and the leader of the column of progress. I am well within the mark when I say that all the armies that ever marched and all the navies that were ever built have not affected the life of man upon earth as powerfully as has that one solitary life.

Learning About Jesus All Our Lives

Throughout your life you have been hearing about Jesus. When you were just a child, your parents told you stories about him. You saw paintings of Jesus in which artists depicted their ideas of what he may have looked like. Through the years you have heard the Gospels that were written about him proclaimed from church pulpits. For years you have attended classes that attempted in a variety of ways to share this man and his message with you. Yet after all these years you may still be asking: Who is he? Was he truly God or just a good man? Did his message make sense only for the old days? Or does it say something truly significant for my life today?

The fact that you will probably be asking such questions for the rest of your life may not be much consolation. Your continued questioning, however, will constantly deepen your understanding of Jesus. The particular difficulty that you may be encountering now is the one faced by each of us as we seek deeper insights into our religious faith. Consider this: Few of us had the experience of many converts to Christianity. These people received an intense, short course on faith—a course that gave the entire Christian message a sense of unity, a sense of fitting together logically. For most of us, however, our religious heritage has been handed down to us bit by bit. We normally learn one thing about Jesus and his message as first graders, then something more in third grade. In sixth grade we may perhaps learn something contradictory to our previous learning. Thus, the years of religious education pass. What often results is the feeling that we know a lot of things *about* Jesus, but we do not truly know *him*.

The approach here will be to give a sense of Jesus in his totality:

- how he fits into the Jewish history that we have just reviewed
- how he reveals our God to us and shows us who that God is
- how his message can make so much sense even while demanding so much of those who choose to accept it

In other words, let's try to discover the very unique faith in God revealed in and through the person and message of Jesus.

Teaching About Jesus Through Parables

To share insights into the reality of God, Jesus often used parables. **Parables** are brief, easily remembered stories, which are usually about very common events in our lives but which also speak of great truths in uncommon ways. The most familiar example is probably the parable of the prodigal son. This simple story tells about a boy who turned his back on his home and family and then headed immediately for the wrong side of town. When the son almost literally came crawling back, his father welcomed him home in dignity and joy. Jesus told this story to depict the tremendous, unrestrained love that God has for each of us. This well-known parable, like all the parables Jesus told, allows us to achieve deep insights with a simpleness and clarity that is often startling.

So, in discussing Jesus, let's start with a modern-day parable, a simple story that contains some insights into the entire plan of God. Read the following parable carefully, seeking a sense of both the broad images as well as the details provided. Then we will discuss the wisdom contained within the parable.

A Modern Parable

This story is about a six-year-old boy named Manuel. Manuel was a Puerto Rican boy living in Spanish Harlem, in New York City. His family was poor, so Manuel had few toys. Many times he was forced to go out into the alleys behind the apartment buildings to bounce a ball off the brick walls or to pick through the garbage to find something to play with.

One day when Manuel was scavenging, he found a glass bowl, dirty and covered with grime. Because he had so few things, Manuel saw a beauty in that bowl that we would probably miss. He was very excited. He took his discovery gently in his hands and carefully climbed the steps up to the apartment his family lived in. Then Manuel carried the bowl to the kitchen sink and began to clean it. When he was finished, Manuel was delighted because he discovered that his bowl was perfect. No scratch or chip marred its beauty. Manuel gingerly carried the bowl to the kitchen table, sat down, and admired the bowl. Manuel was happy.

After a short time, however, the thrill of discovery began to wear off, and Manuel started to get bored. Then he had an idea. He would decorate his bowl! So Manuel went down into the streets and picked up a handful of shiny pebbles and pieces of wire and sticks. He took what he had collected back to his apartment, sat again by his bowl, and set to work. Manuel placed the pebbles on the bottom of the bowl and pretended that they formed a roadway. Next he placed the wire and sticks among the pebbles and pretended that they were bushes and trees. Then Manuel had another idea. He got an old tin can, cut it in half lengthwise, placed it over the roadway, and pretended it was a tunnel. When Manuel was finished, he looked upon his bowl with great pride—it was beautiful! Manuel was happy again.

Once more, however, the wonder and charm of the bowl began to fade for Manuel, and he began to lose that special thrill he had felt. Finally, Manuel realized what he was missing; he had no one with whom to share his bowl, no one to enjoy what he had created. So Manuel went to his mother. "Mama," he said, "can I buy a goldfish to put in my bowl?" Manuel's mother thought for a long time, knowing that they had very little money. When she looked into Manuel's eyes, however, she did what all mothers seem to do. She said, "All right, Manuel," and went to the cupboard and found a quarter. She placed it into Manuel's hand.

Manuel's feet seemed to fly above the sidewalk as he ran to the store on the corner. He bought a beautiful goldfish, ran back to his apartment, filled his new bowl with water, and gently dropped the fish into it. Then Manuel began to talk to his fish. "Swim along the roadway, fish! That's why I put it there—to make you happy." The fish merely swam around and around in the bowl, blind to Manuel's handiwork. "Hey, why don't you swim among the trees I made for you? That's why I put them there—to make you happy." The fish just kept swimming in circles, deaf to Manuel's pleas. Finally Manuel became so frustrated that he began to pound on the side of the bowl, demanding

that his fish swim through the tunnel. Again no response. The fish kept swimming around and around.

Manuel ran to his mother in tears. "Mama, why doesn't my fish listen to me? I keep telling him what's going to make him happy, but he won't do what I say. Why?" Manuel's mother was very wise and had been watching what was going on. Gently she took Manuel on her lap and said, "Manuel, the trouble is that you and the fish speak different languages. He doesn't understand what you're trying to tell him. The only way he could understand would be if you could become a fish, jump into the bowl, and swim along the roadway, among the trees, and through the tunnel. Then maybe the fish would watch you, see how you live in the bowl and follow you."

So Manuel spent a lot of time wishing that he could be a fish.

Write a brief interpretation of each of the following symbols:
- Manuel
- The fishbowl
- The fish
- Manuel's desire to become a fish

End of story—a kid's story, a fairy tale. Yet, if you read the first chapter of the Book of Genesis in the Bible, you will find that the story of the Creation, on which our parable is partly based, is not much more complicated. Moreover, the message of Jesus may be just as simple. Perhaps that is why he said that we must become like little children if we are to understand him and enter his Kingdom. Perhaps adults are like climbers who have gotten so far up the mountain that they can see only footholds and the next ledge. We must stand back if we wish to see God as a new climber would see the mountain—in its entirety and majesty. Let's take another look at the story of Manuel and see what it has to tell us of the big picture, of the great workings of God.

The Freedom and the Failure to Love

The Gift of Grace

We live in this great goldfish bowl that we call the world. God created it and decorated it beautifully. God, like Manuel, wanted to share this creation, this goodness. Out of that great longing to share, God created people—you and me. God's wish was that we would live together, sharing the wonders of creation in harmony and love. With this gift, God was sharing not just the world, but love itself. In traditional language, we call this great gift of love **grace.**

A remarkable trait about God that we so often miss is one that the Jewish people discovered in their experience at Sinai and told about in their scriptures. This quality is that God never stops loving us. In other words, God's grace is boundless and unconditional.

We often talk about God as a judge, whose sole intent is to watch our every move and to punish us when we make a mistake. This God, however, is not the God whom the Jews discovered in their experience of Yahweh. On the contrary, Yahweh is continually trying to reestablish communication with the Jewish people throughout their history. In fact, the history of this attempt at renewed communication takes up much of the Jewish Scriptures.

Remember Manuel and his fish? Like Manuel, God tried

Out of a great longing, God created people to share the wonders of creation.

"talking" to people by finding new ways to communicate love for them. Occasionally great events in nature, called *miracles,* demonstrated God's love. God sent great prophets—people who remind us of Manuel pounding on the side of the bowl in frustration as he tries to get the fish to follow his commands. In a similar way, the prophets jarred the consciences of people and called them back to an awareness of God's grace, only to see these people erect new monuments to other gods and to their own greeds. Like the fish in our story, people could not understand what God was trying to say. So they kept wandering around blindly, completely deaf to the directions that would set them on the road to happiness.

The Gift of Freedom

At this point, the history of salvation becomes more complicated than Manuel's story. For God realized that something is not fully a gift just because it is freely given; it must also be freely received. A gift that is forced on us is no gift at all. We do not say, "Take this gift and enjoy it—or else!" The gift offered in love must be freely accepted in love to be completely satisfying.

This concept of **free will**—that is, the ability to choose—is critical to the Christian understanding of life. Often people look at a tortured world and wonder: Why can't God stop the car before it kills in an accident? Why doesn't God destroy the weapons that people carry to war? Why won't God keep me from saying the things that hurt others so deeply?

No simple solutions exist to these kinds of questions. The mystery of pain and suffering in life has challenged people's minds and faith since the beginning of history. We can get a hint of an answer, however, from our own experience. Consider this: If you want a person to be your friend, you cannot merely walk up and say, "Be my friend or I'll beat you to a pulp!" That might convince the other person to be your follower but hardly your friend. Nor can you go to the person and say, "If you'll be my friend, I'll give you a hundred dollars." Even if the person accepted the offer, you would have to doubt his or her motives.

The mystery of love is that it is only present when the freedom to reject it is also present. Love cannot be forced, and it cannot be bought. So, if God wanted people to be able to give love, God had to give total freedom. Implied in all this is the belief that free will is sacred and must be protected—even though it so often seems to lead to pain and heartache.

Jot down three examples of how young people might try to buy or force the love of another. Why do such efforts fail?

Love is present only when the freedom to reject it is also present.

The Nature of Sin

If people are created in freedom, naturally some will choose to reject God's grace. In fact, at times we all choose selfishness rather than the sharing that love demands. Our world is scarred by the results of that selfishness that we call *sin*.

Just what is sin? Where does it come from? What does it do to people? Many of us have the false impression that sin is simply a decision to break laws or a refusal to live up to society's rules of behavior. In fact, sin is more than our committing forbidden actions and getting punished. Rather, sin begins with our unwillingness to share our time, talents, and possessions when they are needed by others. More precisely, **sin** is the breaking of relationships through personal selfishness; its effects are greed, cruelty, and injustice.

Sin weakens our self-respect, harms the lives of others, and undermines our faith relationship with God. Sin strains the harmony that God wills for all people, the harmony in human relationships, the harmony in nature itself, and thus, the harmony between people and God. Although sin strains that harmony, it is never fully destroyed because our God is a wondrous God.

God Becomes One with People

Through the wisdom of his mother, Manuel was given a great dream, the dream of becoming a fish in order to show his little fish how to enjoy the wonders of his bowl. God had a similar dream, the dream of totally communicating with people by becoming one with them. The basic difference between Manuel's story and the story of God's loving action in history is that Manuel could only dream his dream. For Christians, however, the dream of God became reality, for God became human in the person of Jesus.

God took on humanity in Jesus in order to walk along the roadways, among the trees, and through the tunnels of life *just as we do,* so that we might look at Jesus, see how he lived, and then follow him in living the kind of lives God wants of us.

Jesus: Both a Human Being and God

Let's pause here to ask the question posed today by so many people, young and old alike: "Isn't it a bit much to believe that Jesus was God? I can buy him as a good man, even as a great prophet. But this God-stuff, that's going too far!" We will discuss this question more fully later, but for now consider this: *if* one accepts belief in a God and *if* one accepts the belief that God is good and loving—as apparently most people do—is the idea of Jesus as God reasonable?

Recall your own experience of friendships. When we like someone, we like to be with that person. We try to communicate with him or her in as many ways as possible. When we are separated, we feel lonely and think about getting together again. This drive for togetherness is true of all love relationships.

Now consider this: If God loves us, that love would be total, infinite, and unconditional. Would not God then want to be with us? Would not God also strive to communicate with us, just as we do with our friends? What better way—in fact, what other way—for God to be *with* us than by becoming one *of* us?

Naturally many people have difficulty accepting a human being as God. What is interesting is the fact that probably just as many have a hard time accepting God as human. We often push God off into the heavens. We will say that Jesus was human, but in the same breath we want to qualify that statement:

> Jesus was human, perhaps, but certainly not like me! Certainly he didn't feel down in the dumps as I do so often. He didn't have the doubts about God that I do. After all, he had inside information on that question! Certainly he didn't get as frustrated and angry as I do. He was always sweet and kind and understanding. Certainly he never suffered the loneliness that I do. I mean, he was God, right? So how could he be like me?

Accepting Jesus as fully human is every bit as important as accepting him as God. If we do not accept Jesus as one who experienced life *as we do,* how can we possibly identify with him and try to live as he did? If we do not believe that Jesus suffered the pain of doubt or loneliness, how can we possibly look to him for ways to live with those sorts of pain? If we do not recognize that he loved people while experiencing the human difficulties involved in doing so, how can we possibly expect to love others as Jesus asks us to?

Saint Paul says that Jesus became one with us in all things but sin.

> Who, being in the form of God,
> did not count equality with God
> something to be grasped.
>
> But he emptied himself,
> taking the form of a slave,
> becoming as human beings are.
>
> (Philippians 2:6–7)

Paul's having said this does not make Jesus' identity any less mysterious. Over the centuries of Christian history, the greatest issue for believers has been accepting Jesus as having both a divine and human nature.

Complete the following sentence in one paragraph: "I find this explanation of God becoming human in the man Jesus convincing (or unconvincing) because . . ."

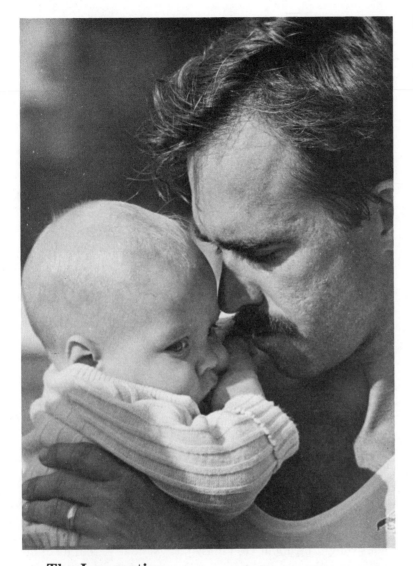

In the Incarnation, God's love took on flesh in a way similar to the love reflected in the birth of an infant.

The Incarnation

As mentioned earlier, we need to clearly define the concepts that we deal with in discussing religion. We need to discover a common vocabulary in order to communicate effectively. The word traditionally used for the mystery of Jesus being both God and man is the **Incarnation.** The word means literally "in flesh," referring to the belief that God took on flesh in becoming one with us. Using one word like this to identify a belief that is so central to Christian faith is helpful for discussions. At the same time, however, we must readily admit that one word can hardly capture the infinite dimensions of this incredible mystery.

Mary, the Mother of God

A special mention can be made here of Mary, the mother of Jesus. Christians have always held Mary in high esteem because of her call to participate in such a special way in the plan of God. Because of her sensitivity to the workings of the Spirit of God in her life and because of her courageous willingness to live according to the promptings of that Spirit, she has been honored as a model of perfect faith.

The elevated title that Mary holds in Catholic history—**Mother of God**—deserves special mention in the context of our present discussion on the identity of Jesus. Not until the year A.D. 431—some four hundred years after the death of Jesus—was Mary officially given this title by the Church. In response to several attacks against its teachings on Jesus' identity, the Church wished to reassert its belief in both Jesus' humanity and divinity. By officially recognizing Mary as the Mother of God, both of these teachings about Jesus were reinforced: By recognizing Mary as a human mother, the humanity of Jesus was affirmed. By calling her the Mother of God, Jesus' divinity was asserted.

Protestant denominations of Christians have had some difficulty with the Catholic teaching on Mary, fearing that her role has been given too much significance. Yet the Catholic Church has remained firm in its teachings on and affection for this most remarkable and faith-filled woman.

Mary's special role has been depicted in many ways by artists throughout Christian history.

The Wisdom of Jesus: Disclosing Sacred Mystery

Jesus taught us about God in two ways: he first told us of incredible truths and realities, and then he lived out those realities in the actions and attitudes of his daily life. Using the framework established for this course, we might say that Jesus shared profound wisdom and then affirmed that message through his works, through his ministry. Let's look at both Jesus' wisdom and works, beginning with the former.

Jesus said some powerful and beautiful things that the world had never heard before. The fact that what he said was truly new to people is something that often escapes us today. That lack of newness causes us to sometimes view his message with boredom. Our problem is that we have heard the Good News of Jesus so often that we may take it for granted.

So try again to hear the message of Jesus as if you had never heard it before. Put yourself in the place of the Jews into whose history Jesus so simply yet so dramatically entered. Try to imagine yourself oppressed, yearning for freedom, and waiting for the fulfillment of a dream that has so often seemed out of reach.

In fact, are these feelings so completely foreign? Have you never experienced oppression? Have you never yearned for freedom? Have you never sensed your grandest dreams becoming mere fantasies, never to be fulfilled? Jesus' message touched the hearts of people and rocked history back on its heels. It can touch us as well. Listen.

"In your prayers do not babble as the gentiles do, for they think that by using many words they will make themselves heard. Do not be like them; your Father knows what you need before you ask him. So you should pray like this:

Our Father in heaven,
may your name be held holy,
your kingdom come,
   your will be done,
   on earth as in heaven.
   Give us today our daily bread.
And forgive us our debts,
as we have forgiven those who are in debt to us.
And do not put us to the test,
but save us from the Evil One.

Yes, if you forgive others their failings, your heavenly Father will forgive you yours; but if you do not forgive others, your Father will not forgive your failings either." (Matthew 6:7–15)

Jesus' vision is summed up in the marvelous prayer that he left us. This biblical version of the Our Father, or Lord's Prayer, provides a fresh sense of the power of his words.

The Love of God

What did Jesus, first of all, have to tell us about God? He spoke of God with a sense of intimacy and affection that was astounding. He called God *Father*—his Father and our Father. Just what did he mean by that? For Jesus called God not just Father but *"Abba*, Father" (Mark 14:36). Saint Paul tells us that we, too, can call God by this name: "All who are guided by the Spirit of God are sons of God; for what you received was not the spirit of slavery to bring you back into fear; you received the spirit of adoption, enabling us to cry out, '*Abba*, Father!' " (Romans 8:14–15). Why is this title for God so significant?

Abba in English is best translated "daddy," "papa," or even the more childlike name given fathers by infants, "dada." This Jewish word might be used by a little child as she sits on her father's knee, playfully tugging at his beard. The attitude that we are to have toward God, then, is that of a child who is secure in the arms of a parent who loves him or her totally and unconditionally.

The Jews of biblical times, of course, had a sense of God as a caring, loving Father. Listen to this marvelous passage from the book of Hosea in the Bible:

The name that Jesus used for God is best translated into English as "dada" or "papa."

> When Israel was a child I loved him,
> and I called my son out of Egypt.
>
> . . . .
>
> I myself taught [Israel] to walk,
> I myself took them by the arm,
> but they did not know that I was the one caring for them,
> that I was leading them with human ties,
> with leading-strings of love,
> that, with them, I was like someone lifting an infant
>   to his cheek,
> and that I bent down to feed him.
>
> (Hosea 11:1–4)

Yet the Jews have long held the name of God to be sacred and unspeakable, preferring to use the title *Lord* in praying directly to God. So Jesus' addressing God as *Abba* was simply without precedent. In Jesus, God was seen to be as close, real, and reachable as a father to an infant.

The Limitations of Language

As noted several times already in this course, words are very limited—especially when used to attempt a description of the limitless God. Christians rightly hold a special reverence for the name *Father* as a reference for God. After all, this name for God was given us by Jesus in the treasured prayer that he shared with us, the Our Father. This title is not the only one, however, that we have available to use for God.

For instance, the Scriptures offer us many other images of God, among them God as Mother. In the book of Isaiah, the love of God is compared to that of a mother:

> [Israel] was saying, "Yahweh has abandoned me,
> the Lord has forgotten me."
> Can a woman forget her baby at the breast,
> feel no pity for the child she has borne?
>
> (Isaiah 49:14–15)

Jesus himself used a wonderfully maternal image in describing his affection for Jerusalem: "How often have I longed to gather your children together, as a hen gathers her chicks under her wings . . ." (Matthew 23:37). We might, then, more accurately speak of God as a loving Parent rather than only as Father or Mother. At the same time, the image of fatherhood is central to the life and message of Jesus. So when we speak of Jesus' relationship to his Father, we must be true to the imagery that Jesus used—the image of God as our Father.

A related concern is that our images of God can become so masculine, so dominated by male characteristics, that we not only misrepresent God but also risk offending or excluding women. Our culture is making great strides in recognizing this difficulty, and this course tries to reflect that sensitivity. If you have been reading this textbook very carefully, you may have noticed that at no time, other than when quoting from the Bible, have masculine pronouns, such as *he* or *him*, been used in referring to God. Occasionally clumsy wording results from this practice, but the commitment to inclusive language is important. You might wish to reflect on your own images of God. Strive to think of God in ways that include, rather than exclude, other people.

Change the prayer Our Father to Our Mother and then reflect on the meaning of each phrase. Write a brief summary of your reactions. What insights about God does this shift in language produce?

The Scriptures offer us many images of God, among them God as Mother.

Jesus Reveals That We Are Lovable

In his own very special experience of the loving God, Jesus underlined the most freeing message of all: each one of us is totally, perfectly, and unconditionally lovable.

No matter who we are, we are loved. No matter what we look like, we are loved. No matter what our race or ethnic background, we are loved. No matter how we have acted or will act, we are loved. Absolutely nothing can separate us from the love of God—the God who is love.

We do not have to earn this love by the way we behave; this love is purely and simply a gift. We cannot lose this love by the way we behave; it is freely given and cannot be withdrawn.

The God whom Jesus revealed does not make mistakes— no matter how much we might feel that God made one on our birthday! God's message, the most important message that Jesus wanted to share with us, is simply that God loves us just the way we are!

Why is this belief in God's grace and in our own lovableness so significant? Several answers come to mind. First, modern psychology is just beginning to understand that we are only capable of reaching out to others in love if we first experience ourselves as loved. When the unconditional, freely given love of God is showered upon us, we are freed to celebrate and share that love with others. We then see ourselves as persons of worth, persons with something to offer to others. As a result, we can begin to reach out in love and service to others.

Second, the love of God for all people is the great equalizer, destroying all the reasons that people have drummed up for separating themselves from others by thinking themselves superior or inferior. We are all equal in the eyes of God.

Third, God's grace is central for this reason: If God is my Parent and if God is your Parent as well, then, as brothers and sisters, we ought to take care of one another. The central message of Jesus is ultimately just that simple, yet no truth is more profound.

A New Commandment

The sure knowledge of God's love for us, then, frees us to engage in the nearly overwhelming challenge that Jesus presents to

Respond in a paragraph to the following questions:
- If we are in fact loved by God, why do we often not *feel* or experience that love?
- What is required if we are to personally experience the love of God in our lives?

us: we must love one another. "I give you a new commandment," Jesus said, "love one another; you must love one another just as I have loved you" (John 13:34). We have heard that passage many times before. What does it actually mean? Listen again to the message of Jesus. Listen not only to the words but to their full meaning.

For example, consider the great prayer that Jesus taught us, the Our Father. At Mass we often recite the prayer as if we are on a mad dash with the priest to see who can get to the finish first. Yet we say some shocking things in that prayer. We say, for example, "forgive us our trespasses as we forgive those who trespass against us." Exactly what are we saying? "Dear God, please, forgive me only to the degree that I am willing to forgive other people. Love me only as much as I love others—no more, no less. Judge me exactly the way that I judge others." Sounds a bit different put that way, doesn't it? A little less appealing, perhaps? A little less safe? We have to listen with a new attentiveness to the words of Jesus if we wish to get to the heart of what he is trying to tell us.

Loving Enemies

At first glance, Jesus' challenge to love others is tough enough. Yet he went even further. Imagine Jesus on a hillside, speaking to the people gathered about him. You are there also. He looks out at the crowd, you among them, and says:

> You've heard it said many times that you're supposed to love other people. And I know some of you do. But look at the people you choose to love. Look about you. See the people here whom you love. You love your parents if they love you. Husbands, you love your wives who love you in return. You love your best friend sitting next to you. You parents love your little kids who are cute and lovable without even trying to be. What's so unusual about that kind of love?
>
> But here is what I mean when I speak of the love you must have: love your enemies. Do good to those who can't stand you, who hate you. Pray for those who make fun of you, who laugh at you, who reject you. Love your enemies!
> (Based on Matthew 5:43–48)

Imagine that Jesus, instead of speaking about love to a crowd gathered on a hillside, tries to share these same thoughts while speaking in the school cafeteria at noon or during halftime of a basketball game.
- Rewrite the two paragraphs from Matthew 5 with either of these two settings in mind.
- Then comment on how the modern-day people would likely react to him.

Jesus spoke about a tough kind of love that can reach out to others with courage and kindness.

Recall and write a brief reflection on an incident in your life when doing something painful made you feel truly happy.

Many of those present shake their heads as if to say "These are the words of an insane person!" and wander away. What do you do?

When Jesus spoke of love, in other words, he did not mean merely the sweet, nice, warm kind of love. He also meant the kind of love that is tough, that is hard work, and that is more action than passion. He meant the kind of love that rises above feelings of anger or repulsion and reaches out to others despite what we might be experiencing. Consider these examples:

- A wife remains hopeful and loving despite an alcoholic husband who has disappointed her and threatened to take the joy out of her life.
- A man loses his job because of illness but refuses to despair. He remains a patient and amusing parent to his four children.
- A teenage boy pauses to talk to an unattractive girl, even though he aches inside knowing that he will suffer the ridicule of his friends.
- A ninth-grade girl listens patiently to the rambling conversation of an aging grandparent, frustrated that she can't be somewhere else with her friends.

What is loving, in fact downright heroic, about these people is that they choose to care *despite the way they feel inside.* Jesus said that loving is easy when doing so makes us feel great, but he called us to a greater kind of love.

Within this idea of love, however, is an interesting puzzle. Ask yourself: How does the boy feel when he walks away from the ridicule of his friends? How does the girl feel when her grandmother hugs her good-bye at the end of their conversation? Very likely they feel good about themselves, true to themselves, whole, and in a word, happy. Maybe they did not seek those feelings. The good feelings were a result or spin-off of the love that they had freely given. The puzzle is that doing things that hurt can somehow bring us happiness. How can that be?

Unconditional Love

The answer to this puzzle of hurt and happiness is found in Jesus' message. Jesus realized better than any other person in history the power of love. He discovered that love—if it is unconditional, if no strings are attached—can free people.

Much of what we call *love* has all kinds of conditions attached. Although we may not say any of the following statements out loud or even consciously think them, many of us condition our love in these ways:

- I will love my parents if I can stay out as long as I want to and if my allowance goes up with inflation.
- I will love my best friend if she calls me so I don't have to call her or if she will go where I want to go when we go out.
- If you love me, you'll let me!

As soon as we put conditions on our relationships, love is no longer possible. Instead, the relationship becomes an economic one, based on payoffs. If the conditions are not met, we submit a withdrawal slip for our love. In such cases, the question is whether love was ever there.

All genuine love is, in fact, unconditional love. Only unconditional love can free people to be fully themselves, unafraid of having to meet the expectations of others. This kind of love can also empower people to reach out to others with courage and kindness. This love is the kind of love that God has for us, as revealed in Jesus.

Only unconditional love can free people to be fully themselves.

The Works of Jesus: A Man of Loving Actions

Jesus spoke beautifully of God and of God's love. No doubt he must have been a tremendous orator, holding people captive with the content of his message and with the way in which he expressed his convictions. Jesus not only talked about love; he also lived it. Every action, every attitude, every contact with people was a demonstration of love in action and a lesson to us about what genuine love is.

Love Can Be Gentle

Jesus showed, for example, that at times love must be kind and tender. The gospel image of Jesus gathering little children about him demonstrates the wonderful capacity he had for making people comfortable in his presence (Mark 10:13–16). The point of that scene is not simply that Jesus loved kids. More significant is that little children loved him. Children can usually see through people's masks, and they keep away from adults who offer even the slightest threat. The fact that the children so desperately wanted to be near Jesus is a sign of how warm, open, and honest he must have been.

Love Can Demand Courage

Jot down the names of five television or movie actors who have an image of being consistently courageous. Then compare the notion of courage reflected in these characters with the kind of courage demonstrated by Jesus.

Jesus also showed us that at times love must be courageous. The powerful scene with the woman caught in adultery depicts this (John 8:3–11). The law of the land demanded that a woman caught in the act of adultery had to be taken out and executed by having people throw stones at her until she was dead. When Jesus was asked for his response to the order to kill this particular woman, he confronted the people with their own sins. "Let the one among you who is guiltless be the first to throw a stone at her," he said. Do you think he was afraid when he did that? Would you be scared if you had to protect someone from an attack by a mob? Of course. Courage is *not* the absence of fear. Courage is the willingness to rise above the fear that we feel and to follow our convictions despite our terror. Jesus had that capacity, a necessary quality of unconditional love.

Love Can Be Angry

Jesus showed us that at times love must be angry. Recall or read the scene in the Temple when Jesus witnessed the fraud and deceit of the money changers in the house of God (Matthew 21:12–13). Unable to stomach such hypocrisy, Jesus started turning over the tables and driving out the sellers. Was this the action of a weak-willed, sappy person? Hardly! Love can be as strong as it is gentle. People who love are softhearted but also hardheaded, willing to stand up and be counted.

The examples go on and on. Very likely you have never had the opportunity to read one of the four Gospels reflectively and privately. Do it sometime. Read imaginatively, placing yourself at the scenes, watching Jesus deal with people, trying to sense the depth of his message. You will meet a person you will never forget, just as the world has been unable to forget him for nearly two thousand years. You will realize as well that an encounter with Jesus demands a response of some kind. Not to take him seriously is impossible once you really look at him.

The Kingdom of God

The totality of Jesus' message of love is summed up with a phrase that he used often—the *Kingdom of God.* In Matthew's Gospel, the phrase used is the *Kingdom of heaven.* Just what is this Kingdom?

The Beatitudes

Jesus' proclamation of the Beatitudes, found within the Sermon on the Mount in Matthew's Gospel, summarizes the qualities of those who hope to enter the Kingdom of God.

Seeing the crowds, he went onto the mountain. And when he was seated his disciples came to him. Then he began to speak. This is what he taught them:

How blessed are the poor in spirit:
the kingdom of Heaven is theirs.
Blessed are the gentle:
they shall have the earth as inheritance.
Blessed are those who mourn:
they shall be comforted.
Blessed are those who hunger and thirst for
uprightness:
they shall have their fill.
Blessed are the merciful:
they shall have mercy shown them.
Blessed are the pure in heart:
they shall see God.
Blessed are the peacemakers:
they shall be recognized as children of God.
Blessed are those who are persecuted in the cause of
uprightness:
the kingdom of Heaven is theirs.

(Matthew 5:1–10)

In our minds a kingdom is a geographical reality—a place or even a nation. Some Jews had this same concept in mind: many expected the long-awaited Kingdom to be a return to political power that would be realized in the military conquest of the world.

Jesus taught about a Kingdom of God that is based on love and peace.

In the sense that Jesus uses the term, however, *Kingdom of God* means the rule or reign of God over the hearts of people and a new social order based on unconditional love of God and other people. Jesus was saying that the Kingdom of God was to be realized only when people responded to his message of unconditional love. When people lived as brothers and sisters, when they learned to live in peace, the Kingdom of God would be established. We pray for this Kingdom in the Lord's Prayer when we say "thy kingdom come."

Jesus not only announces the Kingdom but actually possesses it: "the kingdom of God is among you" (Luke 17:21). As we will see later, the Church is called to announce this Kingdom, to proclaim the coming of the Kingdom by proclaiming Jesus of Nazareth.

The World's Response to Jesus

When a remarkable and loving figure passes through history— the kind of person who demands a response from those who encounter him or her—two things can happen.

First of all, many people take notice of and cling to the person. Some people reacted to Jesus in this way. He came among a people, remember, who were at the time under the thumb of the Romans. The Jews' long and difficult history had led them to a passionate yearning for the one who would save them, the one who would relieve them of their suffering—the Messiah.

Jesus was hardly what the Jews expected. They were looking for a take-charge military leader; Jesus told them to turn the other cheek. They wanted to become masters of their destiny; Jesus told them to humble themselves and to serve. They wanted wealth; Jesus told them to give everything to the poor.

Despite all this, the Jews found Jesus irresistible. For they knew that he offered them the kind of freedom that could not be gained from wealth and war. Surely many people listened, found Jesus' message impossible to accept, and walked away. Many others, however, followed and staked their lives on this man and his message. The world is so hungry for love that, when a loving person is finally met, we find that person especially attractive. So Jesus came upon the scene, and in a dramatic fashion, people began following him in vast numbers.

A second thing seems to happen when this kind of leader emerges in history. The powers that be—that is, the political, social, and religious leaders of the time—are threatened by the new leader and new ideas that they cannot control. Many Jewish leaders refused to accept Jesus as the Messiah whom they awaited. They were also irate about Jesus' criticisms of those who twisted the Jewish heritage, which he loved so deeply. Those who resented Jesus included the legalists who taught a spiritless form of the Law and the pompous leaders who felt themselves superior to the poor and the powerless. For their part, the Romans also feared Jesus. He threatened their base of power by stirring up the people's desire for freedom and equality. No doubt about it—this fellow had to be gotten rid of permanently.

So the authorities plotted against Jesus. The religious leaders clearly wanted Jesus dead, but they did not have the authority to carry out the death penalty. They needed the help of the Roman political authorities. The charges brought against Jesus and the details of his arrest and trial are complex and difficult to fully understand. Apparently the Jewish leaders accused him of *blasphemy*, suggesting that Jesus was claiming a personal dignity reserved for God alone. This accusation, a purely religious one, held no political significance. Therefore, the political charge against Jesus was that of inciting among the Jews a

Define or describe in twenty-five words or less the kind of freedom that cannot be gained from wealth and war.

revolt against the Romans. Jesus was arrested on these charges, led away as his followers fled in fear, and condemned to scourging and to death on the cross. Romans crucified only foreigners because death by crucifixion was considered too harsh a punishment for Roman citizens.

The Crucifixion

A true sense cannot be given of the awesome agony suffered by Jesus during his scourging and Crucifixion. His scourging alone was terribly brutal, consisting of several beatings. Sometimes the soldiers whipped Jesus with long pieces of rawhide. Attached to the ends of the whip were small bones or pieces of metal that would literally tear the flesh from his body.

Jesus was then given a crown of thorns to further mock him as "King of the Jews." This crown was formed from a plant that grows much like our ivy but that has thorns about one-half to three-quarters of an inch in length. After pressing the crown onto his head, the soldiers pounded the thorns into his skull.

Finally Jesus was given the cross. It was not in the shape of a † as we normally imagine. Rather, Jesus carried one wooden beam weighing about 150 pounds. He carried the beam, which was tied to his wrists, over his shoulders. Jesus fell several times during the quarter-mile walk to the hill where he was to be crucified. When he fell on the gravel streets—without hands free to break the fall and with 150 pounds coming down on top of him—the stones gashed his body.

Jesus reached the bottom of the small hill on which he was to be executed. Probably the soldiers had to drag him to the top of the hill. Jesus was placed on his back, his arms outstretched along the beam. The soldiers drove spikes through his wrists into the beam that he had carried. (If the nails had been driven into his palms, they would have torn through when he was lifted up.) After Jesus was nailed to the beam, the soldiers lifted it and lashed it to an upright beam that was permanently set in the ground. So that his suffering could be prolonged, the soldiers nailed Jesus' feet to the stationary beam to give support to his body.

Jesus writhed on the cross for several hours of agony. He could not hang limply, with his body slumped down, for his diaphragm would pinch his lungs and strangle him. So he had to stretch on the cross constantly, lifting his tortured body up so that he could gasp for air, then falling again in pain and exhaustion.

Finally, in the midst of a physical agony that we cannot begin to comprehend, in the midst of the emotional trauma of hanging near death while those who professed to love him ran away, in the midst of the mental turmoil of wondering even if the God on whom he staked his life was real—in the midst of all that, he looked out at those who were killing him and said,

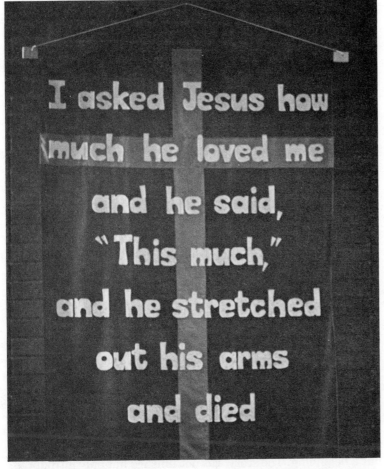

The death of Jesus was the consequence of a life lived in total dedication to people and to God.

"Father, forgive them; they do not know what they are doing" (Luke 23:34). As death neared, he made a final act of trust in the God whom he called *Abba:* "Father, *into your hands I commit my spirit*" (Luke 23:46). Then, as Saint John's Gospel states, Jesus said " 'It [the work of his Father] is fulfilled'; and, bowing his head he gave up his spirit" (John 19:30). In the ultimate act of a love that knows no limits, Jesus gave his life.

Write a brief poem or prayer in response to the description of the Crucifixion of Jesus on pages 152–153.

The world has never known greater love. "No one can have greater love than to lay down his life for his friends" (John 15:13). The death of Jesus was the consequence of a life lived in total dedication to people and to the God whom he called *Abba*. Jesus gave nothing less than all he had.

Jesus' execution was also the result of the crippling effects of sin, of the blindness of people who could not recognize God in their very midst. Yet the monumental challenge of Jesus' command to all people—to love as he did—is clear when seen against the backdrop of the cross. No one but Jesus ever attained an entire life of unconditional love, but all are called to strive for it. In the struggle to achieve that goal, we will discover what being truly human, as fully human as Jesus, means.

Does Life End with Death?

Does the story end here—at the cross? Imagine Jesus' followers cowering in fear as the man whom they loved was brutally executed as a common criminal. What must the Apostles and other disciples of Jesus have thought and felt? Here was the man on whom they had placed all their hope. They thought he was the Messiah—the one who would give them fullness of life and unrestrained joy. Surely his death was the most dismal failure of that dream. Along with suffering their grief and depression, the disciples feared for their own safety. If identified as Jesus' followers, they might face the same end. So they ran away in fear and hid.

Two thousand years later we are still talking about these events—two thousand years after Jesus died the death of a criminal, two thousand years after his few followers scattered in terror, denying they had ever known him. Why do people still remember a man who died as such an apparent failure? What could possibly explain this? How can we logically account for the fact that one out of four people living in the world today is a Christian? The answer is simple: The cross was not an end but a beginning. The story was not finished but only introduced, and the next chapter of that story would turn a scene of despair and fear into a triumph of joy and new life.

Review Questions

1. How can a person know a lot of things about Jesus but not truly know him?
2. What needs to happen for his fish to be able to understand Manuel? What might this idea symbolize in terms of the discussion of Jesus and his role?
3. How can Manuel's attempt to communicate with his fish be related to the role of prophets in Jewish history?
4. Explain how the concept of free will can account in part for the presence of evil in the world.
5. What are the effects of sin?
6. What explanation does the text offer for the belief that God became a man in the person of Jesus?
7. Why do Christians need to accept the humanity of Jesus as well as his identity as God?
8. What does the Church teach by proclaiming Mary as the Mother of God?
9. In what two ways did Jesus teach us about God?
10. What is the significance of the name *Abba* given God by Jesus? Why would his use of this term disturb loyal Jews?
11. What is the difficulty with relying on totally masculine images for God?
12. Give three reasons that the belief in God's love for us is so significant.
13. What does loving without conditions mean? Give an example.
14. Give three characteristics of love demonstrated by the actions of Jesus. For each characteristic, indicate a gospel story that illustrates it.
15. In what sense was Jesus not what the Jews had been expecting in their Messiah?
16. Why did the religious and political leaders of his day view Jesus as a threat?
17. On what religious and political charges was Jesus arrested and finally executed?

Key Terms
grace
free will
sin
Incarnation
Kingdom of God

6 The Resurrection and Pentecost:
Conquering Death and Beginning a Church

The Resurrection of Jesus

A man hung dead on a cross. His followers hid in fear, at times denying that they even knew him. The dream of the coming of the Messiah was shattered, and the rising hopes of people for an age of justice and peace were destroyed in the brutal execution of a man who preached and lived those ideals to the full. Feelings of joy and expectancy suddenly were overwhelmed with despair, grief, and fear. What happened after the death of Jesus that possibly could have led the first Christians to profess love, justice, and peace?

The Resurrection in the Scriptures

The New, or Christian, Testament—the development of which we will discuss in a later chapter—gives us several accounts of what happened following the death of Jesus. After Jesus died, a man named Joseph of Arimathea went to Pilate to ask if he could take the body and give it a decent burial. (The common practice would have been to simply throw the corpse into a pit with others who had been executed.) Pilate, the Roman official who had condemned Jesus to death on the cross, granted the request. Joseph took the body of Jesus from the cross, wrapped it in a burial cloth called a shroud, and laid it in a tomb hewn out of stone. A large stone was then rolled in front of the entrance to the tomb. Matthew's Gospel clearly states that Roman soldiers were ordered to guard the tomb to prevent the theft of the body by followers of Jesus. Apparently officials were concerned that Jesus' followers would claim that he had risen

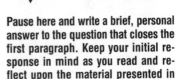

Pause here and write a brief, personal answer to the question that closes the first paragraph. Keep your initial response in mind as you read and reflect upon the material presented in this chapter.

from the dead as he had predicted when alive. Let's now read an account of what followed:

> After the Sabbath, and towards dawn on the first day of the week [Sunday], Mary of Magdala and the other Mary went to visit the sepulchre. And suddenly there was a violent earthquake, for an angel of the Lord, descending from heaven, came and rolled away the stone and sat on it. His face was like lightning, his robe white as snow. The guards were so shaken by fear of him that they were like dead men. But the angel spoke; and he said to the women, "There is no need for you to be afraid. I know you are looking for Jesus, who was crucified. He is not here, for he has risen, as he said he would. Come and see the place where he lay, then go quickly and tell his disciples, 'He has risen from the dead and now is going ahead of you to Galilee; that is where you will see him.' Look! I have told you."

"Mary of Magdala and the other Mary went to visit the sepulchre."

> Filled with awe and great joy the women came quickly away from the tomb and ran to tell his disciples.
>
> And suddenly, coming to meet them, was Jesus. "Greetings," he said. And the women came up to him and, clasping his feet, they did him homage. Then Jesus said

to them, "Do not be afraid; go and tell my brothers that they must leave for Galilee; there they will see me."

Now while they were on their way, some of the guards went off into the city to tell the chief priests all that had happened. These held a meeting with the elders and, after some discussion, handed a considerable sum of money to the soldiers with these instructions, "This is what you must say, 'His disciples came during the night and stole him away while we were asleep.' And should the governor come to hear of this, we undertake to put things right with him ourselves and to see that you do not get into trouble." So they took the money and carried out their instructions, and to this day that is the story among the Jews.

Meanwhile the eleven disciples set out for Galilee, to the mountain where Jesus had arranged to meet them. When they saw him they fell down before him, though some hesitated. Jesus came up and spoke to them. He said, "All authority in heaven and on earth has been given to me. Go, therefore, make disciples of all nations; baptise them in the name of the Father and of the Son and of the Holy Spirit, and teach them to observe all the commands I gave you. And look, I am with you always; yes, to the end of time." (Matthew 28:1-20)

This event—what we call the **Resurrection** of Jesus—is central to the entire meaning of Christian faith. Saint Paul tells us, "If Christ has not been raised, then our preaching is without substance, and so is your faith. . . . If our hope in Christ has been for this life only, we are of all people the most pitiable" (1 Corinthians 15:14,19). If the message of love that Jesus preached leads only to incredible suffering and death, if it all ends with Jesus dead on the cross, why would anyone want to believe in him and his message? The Resurrection—if it actually happened—says in effect, "It's all worth it." The Resurrection—if it occurred—tells us that death cannot conquer us as individuals, that we, too, will overcome death and experience new life, resurrected life. This astoundingly Good News is the news of eternal life and the guarantee of immortality. If, in fact, the Resurrection happened, then we can join with Saint Paul in exulting, "Death is swallowed up in victory. Death, where is your victory? Death, where is your sting?" (1 Corinthians 15:55). On the other hand, if the Resurrection did not happen, we are fools.

Choose a pro or con position on the following statement and write a paragraph defending your position: Living according to Christian values and the teachings of Jesus would be reasonable even if we could prove that he was never raised from the dead.

How Can We Believe in the Resurrection?

To say that the Resurrection was an astounding event and to admit that many people have difficulty accepting it are understatements to the extreme. We are not asked, however, to accept the teachings of Christianity totally on faith, if by that we mean that we are to blindly accept teachings that make no rational sense. As stated earlier, faith always requires trust and always involves a risk. Yet the trust need not be blind, and the risk need not be foolhardy. So the legitimate question remains, Why believe?

The Bible: Sometimes More Questions Than Answers

Some believers tell us that our faith in the Resurrection of Jesus is based totally on a literal reading of the Scriptures. These believers say that we should simply accept as truth whatever the Bible states about this event. The difficulty with this position arises when one looks carefully at the accounts of the Resurrection of Jesus in each of the Gospels. You have already read the account given in Matthew's Gospel. Take a few minutes to read the Resurrection accounts given in Mark 15:42—16:20, Luke 24:1-12, and John 19:38—20:29. The similarities are obvious—Joseph of Arimathea burying the body in the tomb, the discovery of the empty tomb, startling appearances of Jesus, and so on. Yet disturbing inconsistencies (that is, differences

in the accounts) are confusing and can lead the objective reader to some degree of doubt if not disbelief.

The differing biblical accounts make clear that the authors had no intention of giving us a strictly historical portrait of the Resurrection. Too many apparent contradictions exist. For example:

- In Luke's account, several women are the first to arrive at the tomb. In John's Gospel, the only person mentioned is Mary Magdalene.
- In Luke's account, Peter runs to see the tomb, apparently alone. In John, the "other disciple" (John himself?) gets to the tomb first.
- In Matthew's Gospel, one angel descends from heaven, rolls away the stone, sits on it, and announces that Jesus has risen. In Mark's Gospel, on the other hand, a "young man in a white robe" is met *inside* the tomb, where he makes a similar announcement. Furthermore, in Luke's account, "two men in brilliant clothes" are depicted, and in John a far more elaborate scene is described.
- In John's Gospel, Mary Magdalene meets Jesus, whom she mistakenly believes to be a gardener, while in Luke the incident is not even mentioned.

The point is clear: those who base their belief in the Resurrection solely on a literal reading of the Scriptures are forced to live with some confusing contradictions.

At the same time, some people refuse to believe in the Resurrection precisely because of this problem. They point to the apparent errors of the Bible as a basis for rejecting Christian faith. However, the believer can legitimately counter this with another argument: If the authors of the Scriptures were trying to deceive or fool us, why would they allow such glaring inconsistencies in the accounts? If they were trying to trick us, would they not make sure that all the details agreed so that the accounts would be more acceptable? One major lesson to be learned about the Resurrection from the Scriptures may be that the little details are not essential to the truth of the event or to our faith. The number of angels, the dimensions of the stone, and the number of guards at the tomb are interesting but not terribly significant.

What *is* significant, then, about the gospel accounts of the Resurrection? More importantly, if the Bible cannot be used as absolute proof, how can we believe in the Resurrection—the event upon which Christian faith stands or falls?

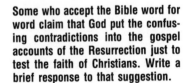

Some who accept the Bible word for word claim that God put the confusing contradictions into the gospel accounts of the Resurrection just to test the faith of Christians. Write a brief response to that suggestion.

What Kind of Evidence Do We Need?

The answer to these questions lies in our understanding of evidence, in the kind of proof that we seek for our belief. Let's pretend to be detectives for a moment. Consider the following case:

- A car accident has taken place. The car in question has a flat front tire with a gaping hole in it. The car is discovered pinned against a tree, its hood crushed in, and the driver unconscious. What happened?

Imagine yourself as the investigator of this accident. How would you go about determining what had actually happened? If you have watched many detective stories on television or in the movies, you have seen investigators seek and interpret the following kinds of evidence:

The Physical Evidence

The first thing many investigators do in a case is assess all the available physical evidence. In the case of this accident, for example, after attending to the victim's needs, the investigators would likely take detailed photos, making sure that nothing is changed or moved. By looking for and measuring tire tracks, they might investigate to see if the driver had attempted to stop before hitting the tree. They might order tests to determine the speed at which the car was moving when it hit the tree. This gathering of physical evidence is often tedious and painstaking, but avid viewers or readers of detective stories know that the clues found at this stage of an investigation are often crucial in determining the outcome of a case.

The Accounts of Eyewitnesses

Along with assessing physical evidence, investigators often quickly seek out and interview any eyewitnesses to the event in question. In a case like our imaginary accident, this might be a comparatively easy task. In more complicated cases, such as murder cases, the discovery and interrogation of eyewitnesses can make up the most interesting part of the investigation. Good investigators look for several qualities or characteristics in their work with eyewitnesses.

Credibility: If the eyewitnesses are not personally involved in the incident, their testimony may be more believable than that of a witness who has something to gain by lying. Also, the mental condition of individual witnesses is often called into question. For example, the testimony of someone who was sober would be more reliable than that of someone whose judgment was impaired by drugs or alcohol.

Support of testimony: Often the number of eyewitnesses available is significant. For example, the fact that only one passerby, rather than one hundred passersby, witnessed the mishap would make a considerable difference in the investigation of our car accident.

The testimony of eyewitnesses can make up the most interesting part of an investigation.

Consistency: More important than the number of eyewitnesses, however, is their agreement or disagreement about what happened. Also significant is whether their accounts are consistent with the physical evidence.

The Personal Experience of the Investigator

Besides collecting and examining physical evidence and the testimony of eyewitnesses, a good investigator will often draw upon a great deal of past experience with similar cases. How many times, for instance, have we seen the heroic detective in a story simply refuse to accept both the physical evidence and the testimony of eyewitnesses because "something just doesn't feel right" about the case? We are dealing here with the factor called *intuition,* which is a kind of sixth sense that our favorite fictional detectives often possess. Even in real life we often experience this way of knowing or perceiving reality. Many times we have to trust our hearts more than our heads when deciding what is real and what is not.

The Compatibility of the Evidence

Finally, good investigators will weigh all the available evidence and then arrive at a conclusion. Do all the pieces of the puzzle fit together—that is, are the facts compatible? Or is the case filled with contradictions and conflicting evidence? If the evidence does not fit neatly together, what do the investigators do? Do they give more weight to the physical evidence? to eyewitnesses? to their own intuitions?

Let's return to our example of the car accident. If the driver recovers and explains what happened in a way that is supported both by the available eyewitnesses and by the physical evidence, the case will quickly come to a close. Not much material for a good detective story here. Yet what if the driver is left in a coma, the car tire shows evidence of tampering, no witnesses come forth, and the driver's husband has just taken out a million dollar insurance policy? Now we have enough material for a month of soap opera episodes!

The point here is that, to get to the historical truth of the Resurrection of Jesus, we have to do some investigative work. Certainly we can accept the Resurrection as truth simply because the Bible and other believers claim it to be. In fact, the acceptance of the Resurrection by the Church worldwide and throughout history can be weighted heavily in our decision. Some people may find that such general acceptance satisfies their own need for evidence. They may have little difficulty accepting the truth of the Resurrection.

Yet many adolescents are seeking more grounding and explanation for their beliefs than they were able to grasp as children. This detailed discussion of the Resurrection is intended for all those who seek such explanations.

So let's continue our investigation of the Resurrection of Jesus, a central element in the faith of Christians. How much evidence can we gather to demonstrate beyond a reasonable doubt that Jesus was truly raised from the dead?

The Evidence for Accepting the Resurrection

In this discussion we will approach the question of the Resurrection from the perspective of the four kinds of evidence identified above. The questions that we therefore must ask ourselves are the following:

- What, if any, physical evidence do we have to support belief in the Resurrection?
- Were there eyewitnesses to the Resurrection, and if so, is their testimony credible, supportable, and consistent?
- As investigators ourselves, what are our own intuitions about the truth of the Resurrection?
- Finally, after weighing all the available evidence, what do we conclude? Do we believe in the historical reality of the Resurrection, or don't we?

Naturally, the last two of our four questions are very personal. Each of us must come to some personal decision about this pivotal event both in the ministry of Jesus and in our response to him and his message. When discussing those two questions, therefore, you will be offered more questions to help you reflect on your conclusion at this point in your life.

Imagine that you are a detective. Before reading on, briefly list whatever physical evidence you can think of to support belief in the Resurrection of Jesus. Then compare your response to the ideas presented in this section.

The Physical Evidence for Accepting the Resurrection

Our discussion of this dimension of the question will be, for some, disturbingly brief. For the plain and simple fact is this: we have no physical evidence either to support or to disprove the Resurrection of Jesus. The only decisive physical evidence nonbelievers could hope to produce to prove that Jesus was *not* raised from the dead would be the physical remains of the crucified Jesus, that is, his corpse. Clearly no one was ever able to produce such evidence.

For a curious insight on this point, reread the third paragraph of the passage taken from Matthew's Gospel on page 159. Note that the chief priests and elders, after hearing the news of the Resurrection from the guards, pay the guards to claim that the disciples of Jesus had stolen the corpse. This claim was a way for the nonbelievers to explain the absence of physical evidence. As the Scriptures state, "To this day that is the story among the Jews."

Believers might argue that the lack of a corpse can be considered physical evidence that Jesus was in fact raised from the dead. Would you as an investigator find this argument convincing? Certainly one possibility may be that the followers of Jesus hid his body.

Other believers might suggest that some of the other details from the scriptural accounts of the Resurrection could serve as physical evidence of the Resurrection—the stone that had been moved, for example, or the empty tomb. We have already noted, however, that the gospel stories cannot be relied upon in these details. We must look elsewhere.

The Testimony of Eyewitnesses to the Resurrection

Of all the possible sources of evidence regarding the Resurrection, this one deserves our greatest attention. Were there eyewitnesses? If so, was their testimony reliable, substantiated by others, and consistent with everything else we know? Let's look at the evidence.

The records kept by non-Christian historians, who would have no reason to lie about such facts, demonstrate the following:

- A historical figure named Jesus existed.
- He preached the message that Christians claim he preached.
- He alienated the Jewish and Roman officials.
- He was executed by the method of crucifixion.

That these last two events would frighten Jesus' followers and drive them into hiding for fear of their own lives is completely reasonable.

These sources also clearly demonstrate that those same men and women who fled in fear suddenly emerged from their hiding places and boldly and joyfully professed that they had experienced that same Jesus alive in their midst. So deep was their conviction that many would ultimately go to their own deaths as martyrs rather than deny that belief. All of this we know from nonbiblical historical records.

Can we trust the witnesses to the Resurrection? Were these the kind of witnesses on whom to base our own faith? No doubt they were sincere and personally believed in the Risen Jesus whom they professed. Only sincere faith can explain the insults, injuries, and often death that these people willingly accepted in defense of that belief. Yet could they perhaps have been mistaken? Could the early eyewitnesses—the Apostles and others—have been in such a state of shock over the death of their beloved leader that they lost touch with reality? Did they hallucinate? Could they have simply imagined a Risen Lord?

This explanation might be acceptable if the witnesses were few in number. The Scriptures note, however, that Jesus appeared to hundreds of people after the Resurrection. Granted, we have said that the Scriptures cannot be used as absolute proof. Yet the gospel accounts of the Resurrection were composed while witnesses to these events were still alive. A claim

Reread the account of the Resurrection at the beginning of this chapter as well as those referred to on page 160. While you read, list any eyewitnesses to the Resurrection that are mentioned. Then, next to each name, evaluate the reliability of each eyewitness by using the following code:
− = not reliable
? = not sure
+ = very reliable

of hundreds of witnesses could not reasonably be made unless literally hundreds verified the claim at the time.

The clarity with which the Resurrection is professed by the early Church is also significant. The Church made no attempt to *explain* the Resurrection; instead, the Gospels simply and powerfully *proclaim* it. Belief in the Resurrection, which was apparently accepted without doubt, was clearly unanimous in the early Church.

Note also that nothing in Jewish tradition—and most of the early eyewitnesses were devout Jews—would have led them

Non-Christian historians testify to the fact that Jesus was executed by crucifixion.

in their wildest imagination to create such a story. In Jewish thinking, as we saw earlier, the Messiah was to be a great military leader who could destroy the Jews' enemies and elevate the Jewish people to nationhood. Jesus' death and Resurrection contradicted everything that the Jews expected. No wonder the disciples were amazed and bewildered by their master's appearance: they simply would not have considered such a possibility. The disciples' belief and the depth of that belief seem most reasonably explained by an actual, not an imagined, Resurrection.

Finally, in assessing the reliability of the eyewitnesses to the Resurrection, we should consider the long-term effects of this experience on the disciples. Many were totally transformed and were actually compelled to preach the Good News to the whole world. If the disciples were simply trying to ease their sense of loss by imagining Jesus as resurrected, they might more reasonably be expected to do so quietly, content with their own illusions, and even protective of them.

Remember that one issue regarding the reliability of eyewitnesses is whether they have anything to gain by lying. The early Christians could gain nothing but pain by claiming belief in a Resurrection that did not happen. They faced the ridicule and rejection of friends, relatives, and the Jewish community. In many cases they gladly accepted death at the hands of the Romans. In short, the disciples endured much to make known the glorious message that Jesus of Nazareth, who was crucified, had been raised from the dead by God and now lived!

The Intuitions of the Investigator and the Lack of Proof

Millions of people throughout history have weighed the available evidence regarding the Resurrection, and they have come to various conclusions. Many have been highly educated; others have trusted their hearts more than their heads. Literally hundreds of millions of people have opted to believe in the Risen Jesus. On the other hand, we have no way of knowing how many have evaluated all the evidence and have decided not to believe. In deciding about the historical reality of the Resurrection, however, one thing is clear: no such thing as absolute proof either for or against belief is available.

This lack of absolute proof should not surprise us—even though it may occasionally frustrate us. After all, can we absolutely prove *anything* that has happened in history? To a greater or lesser extent we are always dependent upon eyewitnesses. Even when we seem to come to agreement about the facts of an event, some will still disagree. Some people, for example, simply refuse to believe the verdict that Lee Harvey Oswald was the sole assassin of President Kennedy. Others claim that the Nazi death camps never existed. Still other people believe that the landing on the moon was a hoax. Therefore, virtually everything we choose to believe about history implies an act of trust or a leap of faith on our part.

As you weigh the evidence about the Resurrection, what does your heart tell you to believe? To use a more graphic phrase, what do you believe about the Resurrection in your gut, in the pit of your stomach? To what decision do your investigative intuitions lead you?

Complete the following sentence in one paragraph: "I find the discussion of the Resurrection convincing (or unconvincing) because . . ." Be prepared to compare your response to those of your classmates.

Weighing the Evidence: The Choice Is Yours

Several times this course has said that ultimately all decisions regarding faith include a risk. The degree of risk that we assume in our everyday decisions is directly related to the importance of a particular decision. When we choose peppermint-bubblegum ice cream for the first time over our favorite chocolate-chip-cookie flavor, we risk not liking the choice. Yet the risk involved is not of much consequence. By contrast, the implications of deciding to believe or not to believe in the Resurrection of Jesus are far-reaching. For, if we believe in the Resurrection, then everything that Jesus stood for deserves our commitment—even if that commitment should lead us to pain and suffering. If we judge that the Resurrection is a lie or a fairy tale, then we must question everything that Jesus preached, practiced, and ultimately died for.

Before leaving this important part of this discussion, let's remember that believers spend their lifetimes deepening their decision about the truth of Christian faith, making their commitment over and over and over again. So you need not feel pressured into finally deciding about your own beliefs at this point. Youth is a better time for raising questions than for making definite decisions. The purpose of this discussion of the Resurrection has been partly to provoke your questions so that the answers that you eventually arrive at will have more substance, depth, and maturity. If you now experience doubt about some dimensions of Christian faith, embrace the doubt as an invitation to grow, to stretch, and to mature. By the same token, if you feel convinced of the truth of your present beliefs,

The degree of risk that we assume in our everyday decisions is directly related to the importance of a particular decision.

be grateful for the peace that such conviction can bring. Realize also that in the future you will likely encounter moments of doubt. The right to question and the doubt that often accompanies questioning are themselves signs of one of the greatest gifts offered by God—the gift of personal freedom.

A discussion of Catholic Christianity clearly revolves around belief in the Resurrection of Jesus. Given that conviction, we are confronted with the following logical questions: What happened to Jesus after he was raised? What is resurrected life like? Where is Jesus now? We turn now to a discussion of these challenging issues.

The Apparitions of Jesus

▼

Imagine that you are a reporter for your school newspaper. Write an imaginary account of an appearance by the Risen Jesus to your class. Be as specific and descriptive as possible.

The appearances of the Risen Jesus to various people following the Resurrection are called **apparitions**. They give us fascinating insights into the nature of resurrected life—that is, life after death. The apparitions also offer us an important understanding of the nature of Jesus' presence in the world today.

An Extraordinary God Is Revealed in Ordinary Ways

The Gospels do not record that blazing trumpets, magical signs, or roaring crowds accompanied Jesus' apparitions. On the contrary, he appeared simply and humanly. As noted earlier in this chapter, Mary Magdalene at first thought that Jesus was a simple gardener. Yet when he called her name, she suddenly recognized him. In a beautiful scene recorded in Luke's Gospel (24:13–35), Jesus took a long walk with two terrified and hopeless disciples who were totally shattered by the Crucifixion. Jesus slowly revealed to them the meaning of the events, and in the simple gesture of breaking bread together, they finally recognized him as their Lord and Master. Jesus also appeared to some totally shocked and frightened disciples who felt at first that they were seeing a ghost. He told them that they had nothing to fear, then asked simply if they had anything to eat. Again, Jesus shared a simple breakfast of fish by a lakeshore with Peter and others.

In all these apparitions the people were shattered by what had happened in the Crucifixion, were totally unprepared for the Resurrection, and were stunned by the one who was now present among them. In all cases Jesus brought overwhelming peace and joy.

The Resurrected Jesus: Present in a New Way

Some researchers have proposed the idea that Jesus actually survived the Crucifixion and that the later appearances were simply made when he recovered. However, Jesus' appearances began within days of the Crucifixion, and the brutal tortures that Jesus suffered from his scourging and execution would normally have required lengthy recovery.

Jesus' resurrected body, admittedly, was not his physical body simply recovered to health. Jesus had changed. In many of the apparitions Jesus was not easily recognized. Only people with faith or with at least an openness to faith recognized him. Jesus had entered into an entirely new form of existence. He appeared and then suddenly disappeared. Closed doors could not keep him out. He was still definitely Jesus, but at the same time, he was considerably different from the Jesus who had walked among the people for so many years.

The apparitions offer us an important insight because they are transitional moments. That is, the apparitions reveal the change from Jesus' earthly presence two thousand years ago to his presence as we experience it today. After the Resurrection, Jesus is no longer present among us in a physical way—that is, we can no longer see him with our eyes or hear him with our ears or touch him with our hands. Nevertheless, Jesus is truly present among us. As he promised, Jesus is present through his Spirit, a Spirit who continually brings back to our minds all that Jesus taught us and gives us the courage and insight to live out that message.

The apparitions offer another, related insight about Jesus' risen life: present through his Spirit in our midst, Jesus can only be recognized with eyes of faith. Even the disciples who experienced the apparitions had to have faith. The wonderfully touching story of Thomas the Doubter illustrates this point:

> Thomas, called the Twin, who was one of the Twelve, was not with them when Jesus came. So the other disciples said to him, "We have seen the Lord," but he answered, "Unless I can see the holes that the nails made in his hands and can put my finger into the holes they made, and unless I can put my hand into his side, I refuse to believe." Eight

Write a brief response to these questions:
- Should Thomas have been embarrassed by his lack of faith?
- Was Jesus reprimanding Thomas for his attitude?

days later the disciples were in the house again and Thomas was with them. The doors were closed, but Jesus came in and stood among them. "Peace be with you," he said. Then he spoke to Thomas, "Put your finger here; look, here are my hands. Give me your hand; put it into my side. Do not be unbelieving any more but believe." Thomas replied, "My Lord and my God!" Jesus said to him: "You believe because you can see me. Blessed are those who have not seen and yet believe." (John 20:24–29)

To be fair to Thomas, we should remember that earlier he had indicated his willingness to die with Jesus (John 11:16).

The greatly encouraging fact here is that even eyewitnesses sometimes had difficulty recognizing and accepting Jesus. Today we often seem to think that—if only we could see him, if only Jesus appeared directly to us, if only we could walk with him, touch him, hear his voice—faith would then follow. The apparitions demonstrate that faith was required even of those who were present at those marvelous moments, that only in faith were they able to recognize Jesus in their midst. We too can recognize him clearly through the eyes of faith.

The Ascension of Jesus

What happened after the Resurrection and the apparitions? Where is Jesus now? If Jesus is present among us today, just how is he present? For some insights into these questions, listen to Luke's description of the event referred to as the **Ascension,** as found in the Acts of the Apostles:

Now having met together, [the disciples] asked him, "Lord, has the time come for you to restore the kingdom to Israel?" He replied, "It is not for you to know the times or dates that the Father has decided by his own authority, but you will receive the power of the Holy Spirit which will come on you, and then you will be my witnesses not only in Jerusalem but throughout Judaea and Samaria, and indeed to earth's remotest end."

As he said this he was lifted up while they looked on, and a cloud took him from their sight. They were still staring into the sky as he went when suddenly two men in white were standing beside them and they said, "Why are you Galileans standing here looking into the sky? This Jesus who has been taken up from you into heaven will come back in the same way as you have seen him go to heaven." (Acts 1:6–11)

Again we see here the same kind of direct declaration of events that we found in the Resurrection accounts. The Scriptures give no lengthy explanations, no philosophical arguments, no involved discussions between the disciples and the two men in white. Scholars who have studied the Bible very carefully recognize certain features in Luke's account of the Ascension of Jesus that indicate the account may not be strictly historical. For instance, we see again the presence of the two men in white who were present in Luke's gospel account of the Resurrection and who may symbolize the holiness and presence of God. Also, the cloud that hid Jesus from the disciples is mentioned throughout the Jewish Scriptures as a symbol of the presence of God. If Luke's account is not strictly historical, however, what deeper truths was he trying to convey about the event? Let's find out.

The Meaning of the Ascension

Through his Resurrection and Ascension into heaven, Jesus broke free from the earthly limitations that we experience. Yet grasping such powerful truths is difficult for us because words normally convey a sense of time or place. When we say the word *heaven*, for example, we tend automatically to think of a place "up there." In the Scriptures, however, heaven appears to be more than a place; it is a state of being in the presence of God—who exists everywhere, not just "up there."

So in heaven Jesus was no longer tied to one place, to one time, talking about one thing to one particular group of people. Jesus was now free to be everywhere, with everyone, for all time, loving and caring and calling us back to his Father.

Resurrection, Ascension, heaven—these are difficult concepts to understand. We are limited, finite people trying to comprehend an unlimited, infinite God. Yet Jesus came to help us understand God. To do that, Christians search for a constantly deeper understanding of Jesus and the marvelous events of his life.

For example, insights into the kinds of presence that we experience with one another can give us some hint of how Jesus can be just as present to us now as he was when he walked the roads of Palestine nearly two thousand years ago. This insight can also help a great deal in understanding such difficult concepts as the presence of Jesus in the Mass and in other sacraments. Consider first the ways in which you are present to the world about you:

> Imagine that you are sitting in a classroom as you read this. First of all, you are physically present in the room itself, a room that might not be exactly where you want to be at this time. We even talk at times about being "a million miles away in our thoughts." You are most physically present to the chair in which you are sitting. You are also physically present to the rest of the students in the class. You are, however, more conscious of some students—close friends, for example—than you are of others.
>
> If you are in a class that you enjoy, you feel even more present. You may even feel that you and the teacher are on the same wavelength, meaning that you think alike and get along well.
>
> Now imagine that you begin thinking about someone whom you love. All of a sudden the chair and the room and the people seem to disappear. You lose yourself in your

Imagine that you are writing a letter to a seven-year-old relative who has asked you to explain what heaven is. What would you write?

daydream, and the teacher may as well be talking to the wall or to that chair on which you are sitting!

Think now about all the levels of presence evident in this apparently simple classroom scene. The lowest and least intimate level of presence is the mere physical presence of your chair or of the people who just happen to be in the room at the same time you are. When you are involved more personally— for example, when you and the teacher are communicating— you experience a deeper level of presence. Finally, when you are thinking about someone whom you love, you are fully present, experiencing a level of presence in which you seem to be almost totally absorbed. Yet that person is not physically present at all!

Pro and con: List three reasons that you would like Jesus to reveal himself physically to you right now. Then list three reasons that you think such an appearance by him would not be helpful for you.

How Is Jesus Present to Us Today?

Now let's return to our consideration of the presence of Jesus in our lives today. Many of us wish that we could see Jesus physically present. "If he's real, why doesn't he just come back and show himself to us once in a while?" we ask. Yet that physical, bodily presence is the lowest form of presence possible. That is why even some of those who saw the Risen Jesus did not always recognize him. Jesus was only present to them physically, so they could not hear or see him fully.

Now apply this same thinking to Jesus' presence in the consecrated hosts at Mass. His presence is not of the limited, physical kind. Instead, the presence that we experience today can be the personal presence of a loved one, the presence of a God who loves us totally. Because God's love for us is perfect and unlimited, the Risen Jesus can be much more than just physically present to those who believe in him. As Jesus himself said, "For where two or three meet in my name, I am there among them" (Matthew 18:20). "And look, I am with you always; yes, to the end of time" (Matthew 28:20). The wonderful fact is that he is!

Pentecost:
The Gift of the Holy Spirit

Shortly after describing the Ascension of Jesus, Saint Luke describes another marvelous event that occurred as the Apostles gathered together in a room on the Jewish feast of Pentecost. This particular celebration of the feast of Pentecost occurred fifty days after Easter, that is, after the Resurrection of Jesus. Luke gives the following account:

> When Pentecost day came round, they had all met together, when suddenly there came from heaven a sound as of a violent wind which filled the entire house in which they were sitting; and there appeared to them tongues as of fire; these separated and came to rest on the head of each of them. They were all filled with the Holy Spirit and began to speak different languages as the Spirit gave them power to express themselves.
>
> Now there were devout men living in Jerusalem from every nation under heaven, and at this sound they all assembled, and each one was bewildered to hear these men speaking his own language. They were amazed and astonished. "Surely," they said, "all these men speaking are Galileans? How does it happen that each of us hears them in his own native language? . . . We hear them preaching in our own language about the marvels of God." Everyone was amazed and perplexed; they asked one another what it all meant. Some, however, laughed it off. "They have been drinking too much new wine," they said. (Acts 2:1–8,11–13)

Christians refer to this wondrous event as **Pentecost**.

Jesus Fully Present in His Spirit

Jesus had promised his followers that he would send his Spirit—also referred to as the Helper, Comforter, and Advocate. His Spirit would remain with them and help them lead the lives to which he was calling them. As Jesus says in John's Gospel, "Still, I am telling you the truth: it is for your own good that I am going, because unless I go, the Paraclete [Advocate] will not come to you; but if I go, I will send him to you" (John 16:7). Jesus' bodily presence, as experienced by the Apostles, was to be replaced by the presence of the Spirit, and through the Spirit, Jesus would be profoundly and truly present today.

The Spirit in Jewish History

The belief in the Spirit did not begin with Jesus. As a devout Jew, Jesus was very conscious of a long history of waiting for the Spirit of God to be sent by Yahweh to the Jews. The Jewish Scriptures refer to the Spirit many times, mentioning the activity of the Spirit in Creation, in the history of the Jewish people, and in a special way in the lives and words of the great prophets. The dream of the Jewish people was that the Spirit would someday dwell in each of them. Immediately following the Pentecost event, the Acts of the Apostles shows Peter trying to explain the incredible event by recalling the prophecy of the prophet Joel:

> In the last days—the Lord declares—
> I shall pour out my Spirit on all humanity.
> Your sons and daughters shall prophesy,
> your young people shall see visions,
> your old people dream dreams.
> Even on the slaves, men and women,
> shall I pour out my Spirit.
> I will show portents in the sky above
> and signs on earth below.
> The sun will be turned into darkness
> and the moon into blood
> before the day of the Lord comes,
> that great and terrible Day.
> And all who call on the name of the Lord will be saved.
>
> (Acts 2:17–21)

This strong imagery is typical of the preaching style of the prophets and indeed of much of the Scriptures. Apparently the biblical authors wished to speak of realities that were simply too great to be conveyed through ordinary language. For example, the Hebrew word for *spirit* also means "breath" or "breath of wind." Water and fire are also used as scriptural images for the Spirit of God. We must be sensitive to this use of vivid language if we are to fully understand the true intent of the Scriptures.

A New Covenant Revealed

Something very special happened to the Apostles on the day of Pentecost. Many other examples of the outpouring of the Spirit occurred in the days of the early Church, but this one event on the feastday of the Sinai Covenant was particularly significant. Christians believe that on this day God established an entirely New Covenant with people. In the minds of Christians, this covenant was promised in the Jewish Scriptures. For instance, the prophet Ezekiel had said,

> I shall give you a new heart, and put a new spirit in you; I shall remove the heart of stone from your bodies and give you a heart of flesh instead. (Ezekiel 36:26)

The prophet Jeremiah had spoken in a similar way:

> I shall make a new covenant with the House of Israel . . . but not like the covenant I made with their ancestors the day I took them by the hand to bring them out of Egypt. . . . Within them I shall plant my Law, writing it on their hearts. Then I shall be their God and they will be my people. (Jeremiah 31:31–33)

This New Covenant between God and all people was established through the life, death, and Resurrection of Jesus and continues through the presence of the Spirit.

The Strange Events Surrounding Pentecost

The description of Pentecost is filled with marvelous imagery. Did all this actually happen? Did tongues of fire truly appear, did strong winds blow, did people speak in a marvelous language that all could understand? We simply do not know for sure. Regarding the marvelous language, the biblical writer may be

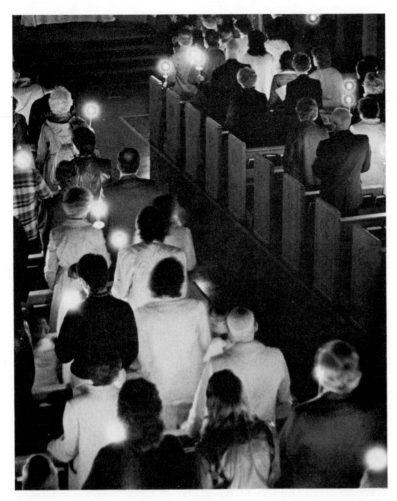

"I shall give you a new heart, and put a new spirit in you. . . ."

reminding us of the story of the tower of Babel in the Book of Genesis. In that story, human languages were multiplied and communication destroyed. On Pentecost, by contrast, the Spirit brought unity and understanding.

What we can be certain of is that the Apostles shared an incredibly intense experience, an experience that changed them radically and permanently. The immediate result of the presence of the Spirit was unbridled joy, so much so that bystanders thought the Apostles must be drunk. Peter quickly reminded them that it was only 9:00 in the morning (Acts 2:15)!

As with the Resurrection and the apparitions of Jesus, we must be careful not to lose sight of the meaning of Pentecost in our concern about the marvel-filled details of Luke's account. If we concentrate too much on the descriptive images, we may be led to believe that the event is completely foreign to our experience, and consequently not significant.

Some people might, in fact, experience Jesus' presence in spectacular and astounding ways. In his apparitions, however, Jesus revealed that he was also encountered in the everyday experiences of life—for example, in the sharing of a meal, in greeting a friend, or while engaging in a conversation. Similarly, we can encounter Jesus' Spirit in the common events of our lives. Saint Paul's letter to the Galatians describes the effects of the Spirit's presence as love, joy, peace, patience, goodness, among other qualities (Galatians 5:22–23). In other words, the Spirit is revealed most effectively and most commonly in lives filled with these simple qualities, not with the kind of special effects that we find in Hollywood films.

The Seven Gifts of the Holy Spirit

The Bible offers another insight into the workings of the Spirit—an insight drawn from a passage from the Jewish Scriptures:

> A shoot will spring from the stock of Jesse,
> a new shoot will grow from his roots.
> On him will rest the spirit of Yahweh,
> the spirit of wisdom and insight,
> the spirit of counsel and power,
> the spirit of knowledge and fear of Yahweh.
>
> (Isaiah 11:1–3)

On a piece of paper, list the seven gifts of the Holy Spirit. Next to each gift, write a word or phrase that would suggest an opposite meaning or antonym for each gift. (This list could serve as a guide for determining when the Spirit is *not* present in situations.)

Christians think that this passage refers to Jesus, who descended from the line of King David, Jesse's son. Christians understand that Jesus fully possessed the qualities described above and that believers are now invited to share in them through the power of the Spirit. These **seven gifts of the Holy Spirit** include wisdom, understanding, right judgment, knowledge, courage, love, and reverence. These gifts are often referred to in the theology and celebration of Confirmation. In that sacrament, the bishop mentions them as the qualities that characterize Christians' daily lives. As noted above, they are also rich and powerful signs of the presence of the Spirit.

The Birthday of the Church

For many people the word *church* refers to the building in which Christians worship or, less often, to those who take particular leadership in the Church—bishops, the pope, and so on. The fact is that the Church is most clearly understood in light of Pentecost. The **Church** is, simply yet profoundly, the gathering of those people who profess faith in the Risen Jesus and his message and who, through the power of the Spirit, live their lives in loving service to all people. The Church officially began with the experience of a chosen few in that small room on the feast of Pentecost nearly two thousand years ago. What occurred to those few has been repeated again and again throughout history—with less drama and with fewer wondrous displays, but just as truly.

From the time of Jesus' death and Resurrection, people have been touched by his Spirit, and so they have gathered in communities of faith.

From the time of Jesus' death and Resurrection until today, people have been touched by his Spirit, and so they have gathered in communities of faith. In and through these communities, believers constantly grow in their understanding of Jesus' message. They also support one another as they try to live out the demands of their faith in their daily lives. These believers pray together, share their concerns and their gifts, and constantly call to mind and celebrate the powerful presence of the Lord in their midst. In so doing, the Church stands as a herald of the coming Kingdom of God, a messenger to the larger world of the coming reign of God that was announced by Jesus. We turn now to a more thorough discussion of this very special community of Christian believers that we call the Church.

Understanding the Church

After his description of the presence of Jesus' Spirit on Pentecost and of Saint Peter's address to the crowds that witnessed that event, Luke continues his writing in the Acts of the Apostles with the following description of the earliest days in the Church:

> [The people were convinced by Peter's arguments, and they] accepted what he said and were baptised. That very day about three thousand were added to their number.
>
> These remained faithful to the teaching of the apostles, to the brotherhood, to the breaking of bread and to the prayers.
>
> And everyone was filled with awe; the apostles worked many signs and miracles.
>
> And all who shared the faith owned everything in common; they sold their goods and possessions and distributed the proceeds among themselves according to what each one needed.
>
> Each day, with one heart, they regularly went to the Temple but met in their houses for the breaking of bread; they shared their food gladly and generously; they praised God and were looked up to by everyone. Day by day the Lord added to their community those destined to be saved. (Acts 2:41–47)

To Christians today this scriptural passage contains some familiar ideas and actions. For example:

- The notion of gathering for prayer is a common experience for Christians today, as is the joining for the "breaking of bread"—which we now call Eucharist or the Mass.
- This passage also describes a sense of tremendous generosity, a willingness to share one's goods. Many Christians have witnessed similar generosity in weekly offertory collections at Mass, in the gathering of food and clothing for the poor, in the building of churches and hospitals and schools—in many uplifting experiences in the Church today.
- The sense of shared purpose and vision in Luke's description is so much a part of the experience of the Church that at times its members take that sense for granted. Many practicing Catholics are struck by their Catholic identity, for instance, only when experiencing the religious expressions of other Christian denominations or of other faiths.

Reading the description of the early Church in Acts, we might also feel that we are eavesdropping at someone else's party. We are witnessing the activities of an entirely new religious movement that may seem foreign to our experience of the Church. The members of that ancient community, for example,

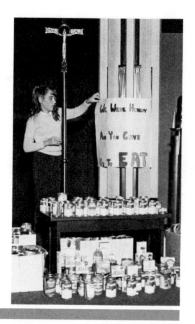

Many Christians have witnessed generosity in the gathering of food and clothing for poor people.

Recall an incident in your life or in the news in which you were suddenly made aware of the uniqueness of Catholic Christianity. Write a brief description of this occurrence.

not only celebrated their common faith but also owned everything in common. Likewise they went to homes, not to churches, to worship. Finally, that first community grew at a rapid rate, with new members joining day by day.

The early Church, which gathered immediately after Pentecost to proclaim and celebrate the life, death, and Resurrection of Jesus, is the bedrock upon which the contemporary Church is founded. In fact, the early Church and the modern Church are one and the same: today's Church *is* that same Christian community with some two thousand years of history behind it. Yet much has happened to the Church during those many years.

The Present Is Based on the Past

Christians are bearers of a message that is almost literally out of this world. Yet they are attempting to live out that message very much *in* this world. Because the Church is a community of people, it is affected directly by the world—that is, by historical events, by cultural influences, by social movements, and by contact with new ideas and new philosophies. The constant challenge to the Church has been to maintain its roots while growing new shoots. In other words, the Church, while striving to remain true to Jesus' message, also struggles to explain that message to new and changing cultures.

In trying to achieve these twin goals—of fidelity and flexibility—the Church has acted like the very human community that it is. That is to say, the Church, in acts of courage, dignity, creativity, and loving service, has demonstrated throughout its history the presence of God's grace. Yet the Church has also demonstrated occasional small-mindedness, selfishness, brutality, and the constant presence of sin.

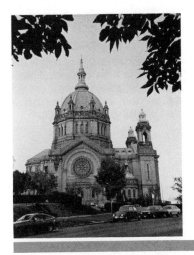

Looking at the Big Picture

Dozens of questions may concern you about the Church, and these certainly should not be avoided. The continual attempt in this course, however, has been to take a rather brief, broad view of each topic. In this discussion that means the following:

The Church strives to remain true to Jesus' message and also struggles to explain that message to new and changing cultures.

- In the remainder of this chapter, we will discuss the nature of the Church.
- In chapter 7 we will explore the Church's wisdom, particularly as it is expressed in the Christian Testament and the Tradition of the Catholic Church.

- The Catholic Church's worship will be the focus of chapter 8, in which we will discuss the seven Catholic sacraments and the annual cycle of religious seasons and feasts known as the liturgical year.

- In chapter 9, then, we will reflect on the works of Catholic Christians, with brief treatments of such themes as conversion, Christian morality, and the Christian lifestyle of commitment to social justice and the pursuit of a peaceful world.

A final comment by way of introduction to our discussion of the Church: Catholics are often inclined to think of Catholic Christianity as *the* Church and to think of Protestant denominations as *other* churches. The reality is that *the* Church includes *all* those who profess faith in Jesus Christ and are committed to seeking the Kingdom of God by living out their faith in loving service.

This shared faith finds varying religious expressions in the many different Christian churches. This is not to say that all Christian churches are equally accurate in living out the message of Jesus. If there is one Jesus who proclaimed one message, then some churches must more closely respond to and adhere to that message than do others.

The Church means the entire Christian Church. In 1967, Pope Paul VI and Athenagoras I, the ecumenical patriarch of Constantinople, met to end the ancient split between the Roman Catholic and Orthodox churches.

Not surprisingly, each Christian church believes itself to be most fully in possession of the truth that Jesus proclaimed. One of your challenges as a maturing adult is to evaluate these traditions and occasionally to make some difficult decisions about them.

The major point here is that, in general, Christians of various traditions are much more alike than they are different from each other. Roman Catholics have been leaders in the effort to reunite Christian churches, at least to the point that all churches can respect one another. In an effort to support that attitude in this course, the following clarification is necessary: In this textbook, the term *the Church* means the entire Christian Church, Catholic and Protestant alike. In those cases when the text discusses religious expressions that are uniquely Catholic—for example, the seven Catholic sacraments or the pope—the terms *Catholic Christianity* or *the Catholic Church* will be used. The term *Protestant* will be used to refer to all the non-Catholic Christian churches. All this may seem a little confusing, but this language reflects a desirable attitude.

On a separate piece of paper, break the definition of the Church into its individual phrases as demonstrated in the discussion under "The Church as a People of Faith." For *each* phrase, give a personal example of how you have experienced in your life that dimension of the Church.

The Church as a People of Faith

The previous section on Pentecost offered a definition of *the Church*. That definition seemed perhaps a bit complex, but it summed up a reality that is obviously full of mystery and wonder. The Church is the gathering of those people who profess faith in the Risen Jesus and his message and who, through the power of the Holy Spirit, live their lives in loving service to all people. Let's take a closer look at this definition.

A Gathering of People

By nature we are communal. That is, we gather in communities for self-preservation, for the sharing of goods and services, and for many other human needs. The experience of God also seems to be communal: as individual persons we discover God through our contact with other people, through our human relationships, and most directly, through our contact with formal religious communities. Once God is discovered by individuals, the desire to share that discovery with others is natural, almost necessary. So that is one facet of the Church—people coming together to share a common experience.

A People Professing Faith in Jesus and in His Message

Professing faith in Jesus is far more than simply assenting to a series of statements of beliefs or following a pattern of certain religious rituals and practices. Earlier in this course faith was defined in a very general way as the sense of trust we have in a power beyond ourselves, in a supreme being or the creator of the universe, and in the one whom we name God. That definition of faith makes sense when speaking of world religions generally. For Christians, however, faith is seen to be much more.

Christian faith can be understood as the human response to the unconditional love of God as revealed in Jesus. That response, an intellectual assent to the truth of Jesus' message, is also a response of the heart and ultimately of the total person. The Christian, quite simply, has fallen in love with God as revealed in the life, death, and Resurrection of Jesus. The Church, then, is the gathering of those people who have experienced that love relationship with Jesus and who have joined together to celebrate that love and to support one another in living out that love. The Church will therefore be only as strong and loving as the personal faith of its individual members.

A People Gathered
Through the Power of the Holy Spirit

Jesus said, "I am with you always; yes, to the end of time" (Matthew 28:20). The gift of his Spirit at Pentecost was the fulfillment of that promise. As such, the Church is not merely a community of people who are trying to live with fond memories of the past. Rather, we are a people who live very much in the present, experiencing and celebrating and growing in our understanding of a God who is here, among us, right now.

The conviction of Christians is that the Spirit is continually guiding the Church, constantly reminding its members of the powerful message of Jesus, and giving them the insight and strength to live according to that message. Granted, the Church does not always do a good job of responding to that Spirit. At times the Church makes mistakes, and it stumbles around in ignorance and selfishness. In other words, the Church remains human with all the strengths and weaknesses of human beings. Perhaps the fact that the Church has survived for two thousand years despite its often embarrassing shortcomings is the best evidence that God is definitely with it.

A People Gathered to Serve Others

No dimension of Jesus' message comes through more clearly and directly than his command to love as he loved. In his first Epistle, Saint John described that command this way:

God is love,
and whoever remains in love remains in God
and God in him.
(1 John 4:16)

John also says,

Children,
our love must not be just words or mere talk,
but something active and genuine.
This will be the proof that we belong to the truth.
(1 John 3:18–19)

And again,

Let us love, then,
because [God] first loved us.
Anyone who says "I love God"
and hates his brother,
is a liar,
since whoever does not love the brother whom he can see
cannot love God whom he has not seen.
Indeed this is the commandment we have received from
[Jesus],
that whoever loves God, must also love his brother.
(1 John 4:19–21)

As individuals, we are often overwhelmed by the problems of the world. If we join with others, however, we find enormous strength.

The implication of these statements both for the individual Christian and for the Church as a community of believers is almost frighteningly clear: we can discover and respond to God only in our love for others.

Earlier we discussed what this means for the individual in terms of growing in the capacity to love others unconditionally. For the Church as a whole the implication is basically the same. The Church is only a true gathering of Christian people when its members are reaching out in love to a suffering world. To remain true to its calling by Christ, the Church must strive constantly to lessen and eliminate poverty, racism, war, disease, pollution—all those social evils that threaten and destroy so many lives. As noted, we will discuss this point in more depth in chapter 9.

This call to battle against social injustice is a very powerful reason for gathering in community. As individuals we are often overwhelmed by the problems of the world. We are painfully aware of how little power individuals possess. If we gather

Love is the dream, the vision, and the prayer of all Christians.

our forces by joining with others, however, we find enormous strength. The Catholic Church alone has over 800 million members today—that is, three times the total population of the United States! Imagine what a tremendous power for good the Catholic Church could be if all Catholics became what they are called to be—people professing faith in the Risen Jesus and committed to living lives of loving service through his Spirit. That force for love could change the world! That love force is the dream, the vision, and the prayer of all Christians—and ultimately it is the reason for the existence of the Church. If the Church avoids that responsibility or loses that incredible vision, it will forfeit its reason to exist.

A Community of Faith Seeking Religious Expression

Recall our treatment of the distinction between faith and religion in chapter 3. In fact, take a few minutes and look back to that chapter now for a quick review of these essential ideas.

Chapter 3 said that people throughout history have apparently shared the need to express their understanding of God in outward, physical, concrete ways. Religion was then defined as the attempt by communities of people to express their shared faith through outward signs—including symbols, celebrations, statements of belief, and codes of behavior. The way in which these outward signs develop is very much affected by the kinds of symbols and expressions that are available in given cultures and readily understood by the people using them.

The faith revealed by Jesus is incredibly profound and exciting:

- the wonderful mystery of a totally loving God who enters into our human history as a man
- a message of unconditional love for each of us, which in turn frees us to reach out in love to others
- death conquered and a God who is present, among and within us, for all time
- people called to a community of love, a gathering of people committed to justice and peace

How are such profound ideas and realities to be shared? How can they be celebrated? How are people to pass on to future generations that marvelous vision that is the message of Jesus? These questions confronted that early community of faith that we read about in the passage from the Acts of the

Apostles. What does Luke tell us? That the followers of Jesus "remained faithful to the teaching of the apostles, to the brotherhood, to the breaking of bread and to the prayers ... [that] they regularly went to the Temple but met in their houses for the breaking of bread ... [that] they praised God" (Acts 2:42,46). In other words, they gradually developed religious expressions for the faith that had virtually overwhelmed them with love, joy, and peace and with the need to share that faith with others.

The Religious Expressions of Christian Faith

The attempt by the Church to discover religious expressions for Christian faith led to the development of the Christian Scriptures, to the formal teachings of the Church, and to the Church's sacraments and other liturgical expressions. These signs of Christian faith often touch those of us who have been raised in the Catholic tradition. So we need to gain an understanding of them in order to live our Catholic faith consciously and enthusiastically.

On at least a weekly basis, for instance, Catholics gather for the sacrament of the Eucharist, during which they also hear the Scriptures proclaimed. They also attend Catholic weddings, Baptisms, Confirmations. During each of these experiences, they hear Jesus' message proclaimed in the reading of the Scriptures. Many Catholics take these commonplace experiences for granted. Many Catholics stop asking vital questions such as the following: If the Scriptures were written thousands of years ago, why are the Scriptures so important today? Why do we have all these sacraments when our Protestant friends do not? To live their faith maturely, Catholic Christians need to seek sound answers to these and other such questions.

The Church's attempt to express Christian faith led to the development of the Christian Scriptures, formal teachings, and the sacraments.

Let's turn now to a discussion of these important aspects of our experience of the Church. As we do so, try to imagine yourself as a member of the early Church, that small community of people so recently touched by the awesome mystery of God. Try to see the world as they saw it. Try to sense their need for sharing the message of Jesus as well as their struggle to find the best ways in which to do that.

In the next chapter, we will discuss the development of the Christian Testament that is held in reverence by all Christians. Then we will discuss a particularly Catholic dimension of the wisdom of the Church, what is known as the Tradition of Catholic Christianity.

Review Questions

1. Why is the reality of the Resurrection of Jesus so central to the faith of Christians?
2. Why does the Bible itself not serve as convincing proof of the historical truth of the Resurrection?
3. List the four kinds of evidence sought by detectives as they attempt to solve a case.
4. What are three criteria used by investigators to determine the reliability of eyewitnesses? Briefly define each criterion.
5. What physical evidence exists to support belief in the Resurrection?
6. On what grounds can we accept the eyewitnesses to the Resurrection as reliable witnesses?
7. Why should we not be surprised to learn that absolute proof for or against the Resurrection is not available?
8. What consistent effects did the apparitions of the Risen Jesus have upon people?
9. How can we say that Jesus after the Resurrection is still truly present among us?
10. What is required before one can experience the risen presence of Jesus?
11. Why is the story of Thomas the Doubter encouraging to believers?
12. What do we mean when we say that Jesus is now in heaven?
13. What do Christians believe is the significance of Pentecost in relation to the Sinai Covenant?
14. What is the danger of concentrating too much on the wondrous events that surround Pentecost and other biblical events?
15. What is the relationship between the Church and the Kingdom of God?

16. Identify the twin goals of the Church as it moves through history. Briefly define each one.
17. How is Christian faith distinct from religious faith in general?
18. On what grounds, according to this chapter, could the Church forfeit its reason to exist?
19. What have been the general results of the Church's attempt to find religious expressions for its shared faith?

Key Terms
Resurrection
Pentecost
Church
Christian faith

7

The Scriptures and Tradition:
Passing on
the Living Word of God

The Scriptures:
This Is the Word of the Lord

A marvelous scene in the Book of Ezekiel from the Jewish Scriptures suggests the role that the Scriptures can play in the lives of believers. In the midst of a profound personal encounter with Yahweh, Ezekiel experienced the call to be a prophet to the people of Israel. Ezekiel clearly did not relish the assignment. He knew that great hardship was in store for any prophet. Nor did Yahweh soft-pedal the difficulties involved. Yet Yahweh gave Ezekiel the help he needed to fulfill his prophetic role. Ezekiel is the narrator in this passage, and Yahweh refers to him as the "son of man." Listen:

> I looked and fell to the ground, and I heard the voice of someone speaking to me.
>
> [Yahweh] said, "Son of man, get to your feet; I will speak to you." As he said these words the spirit came into me and put me on my feet, and I heard him speaking to me. He said, "Son of man, I am sending you to the Israelites, to the rebels who have rebelled against me. They and their ancestors have been in revolt against me up to the present day. Because they are stubborn and obstinate children, I am sending you to them, to say, 'Lord Yahweh says this.' Whether they listen or not, this tribe of rebels will know there is a prophet among them. And you, son of man, do not be afraid of them or of what they say, though you find yourself surrounded with brambles and sitting on scorpions. . . . Open your mouth and eat what I am about to give you."

In preparation for discussing the material that follows, write a response to this sentence: "When I hear people say that the Bible is 'the word of God,' I think they mean that . . ."

> When I looked, there was a hand stretching out to me, holding a scroll. He unrolled it in front of me; it was written on, front and back. . . . He then said, "Son of man, eat what you see; eat this scroll, then go speak to the House of Israel." I opened my mouth; he gave me the scroll to eat and then said, "Son of man, feed on this scroll which I am giving you and eat your fill." So I ate it, and it tasted sweet as honey. (Ezekiel 1:28—2:6; 2:8-10; 3:1-3)

To this day, a scroll with a drop of honey on it is often given to Jewish young people when they are initiated as adult members of their faith. They prayerfully lick the honey from the scroll as a sign of the spiritual nourishment that the sacred Scriptures can provide those who seek to grow in their relationship with God.

The challenge that confronts all people of faith is to help heal a selfish and suffering world. In that sense, all believers are called to be prophets—living witnesses to God's love for the world. To fulfill this prophetic role, believers need continual personal encouragement. As the passage from Ezekiel suggests, the Bible is one major source of that nourishment.

In this chapter we are going to look at the Scriptures as the first of two dimensions of what we have called the *wisdom* of Catholic Christianity. In the second half of this chapter, then, we will explore the unique role of what is called the Tradition of Catholic Christianity.

The Jewish Scriptures in the Early Church

In chapter 4 of this course, we discussed the place of the Jewish Scriptures—what Christians commonly call the Old Testament—in the lives of the Jewish people.

- Devout Jews viewed these sacred writings as the very word of God in their midst.
- The Scriptures were central to the worship of the Jews as well as to their daily lives.
- Within the Jewish community, groups such as the scribes and the Pharisees were concerned with the understanding and interpretation of the Scriptures, particularly as they revealed the Law of Yahweh.

The early Church had to struggle with many questions about the relationship between itself and Judaism. Actually, to speak of Christianity in its earliest stages of development as a new or as a different religion is not accurate. At first Christianity was more like a new sect, or branch, of Judaism. As a devout Jew, Jesus himself appeared to seek a renewal of the Jewish faith rather than to start a whole new religion. Most of the first Christians, moreover, were practicing Jews who continued for a time to attend services at the Temple in Jerusalem. So the many questions confronting them were very personal. For example, did Jews have to give up their faith to become Christian? Did those in the Christian community have to follow Jewish laws and traditions?

On the other hand, the value of the Jewish Scriptures was not debated in the early Church. These scriptures were the only ones available to the early Christian community. Consequently, the Church prized the Jewish Scriptures highly. In fact, Christians believed that the Jewish Scriptures helped to explain the meaning behind Jesus' life, death, and Resurrection. Christians came to believe that Jesus fulfilled many of the passages and prophecies of these scriptures and that he was the Messiah of whom so many key passages spoke. For example:

- We have heard about Adam, the first man in creation. Jesus was now understood as the New Adam, as the founder of a whole new age and a whole new people.
- We discussed earlier the Jewish understanding of the Law. Jesus was now seen as the giver of a New Law. In Saint Paul's writings especially, the Law of Moses is reduced to the commandment to love.
- We talked about the Sinai Covenant, the very special relationship between God and the Jewish people. Christians now recognized that in Jesus' life, death, and Resurrection a New Covenant had been established between God and all people.

The Church today continues to recognize the Jewish Scriptures as the inspired word of God, and readings from it are shared in much of Christian worship.

Who Is This Man?

How did our Christian Testament, what we have traditionally called the New Testament, develop? For persons who have been raised in the Church, this question may seem a strange one. They may feel that the whole Bible (the word *bible* means "book") was always there. As with all religious expressions, however, the Bible grew gradually out of the life experiences of people as they explored their relationship with God.

Try to imagine the members of the early Church drawn together and inspired through the experience of Pentecost. Certainly they were stunned by all that had transpired. They lived with an incredible mixture of joy, confusion, excitement, and fear. What did all these events mean? Jesus was their teacher, but he was obviously more than that—much more. Who was this Jesus who had died and been resurrected?

Although some of the members of the early Christian community were eyewitnesses to the astounding events of faith that were part of Jesus' ministry, only gradually did they arrive at an understanding of who he truly was. As devout Jews they simply could not conceive, as he walked among them, that Jesus was God. This idea would have seemed not only logically impossible to them but religiously intolerable.

In that case, just who did the first Christians think Jesus was? Their perceptions of Jesus probably changed and grew gradually as the disciples experienced his life and message. Certainly he was a very special person who spoke with great authority and truth. Only slowly did they recognize and accept him as the Messiah, as the one who was to be sent by Yahweh. Remember, though, that the Jewish concept of the Messiah never included the notion that the Messiah was God. The Messiah was expected, rather, to be a kind of special messenger from God.

When did the disciples, then, recognize Jesus as God? Only after the experience of the Resurrection and after their awakening at Pentecost. Only then were many of the things that Jesus said and did understood clearly for the first time. Only after the Resurrection and Pentecost could the early Christians proclaim, "Jesus is Lord!"

A Time of Reflection

Events of great magnitude require time to assess. In our own lives we may spend years trying to comprehend the meaning of marvelous or tragic occurrences. Similarly, the early Christians could not immediately commit their experiences to writing. They needed many years to work through the significance of Jesus' life, death, and Resurrection. So the first Christians gathered regularly to pray and to share stories about the person who had transformed their understanding of life. They tried to remember all that Jesus had said. In doing this, they recognized, often for the first time, the depth of some of Jesus' sayings.

This sharing of intimate memories was not simply a matter of gratification and enjoyment. Rather, the early Christians needed to reassure and to support one another constantly as they proclaimed Jesus' message to an indifferent and sometimes hostile world. The first Christians felt driven to proclaim this message—almost literally to shout from the rooftops that, through the Resurrection, "the Lord and Christ whom God has made is this Jesus whom you crucified" (Acts 2:36).

We need time to assess the meaning of great events in our lives.

The Composition of the Christian Testament

How was this message to be preserved and handed on to future generations? For the eyewitnesses themselves, the recalling of Jesus' life and teaching through the discussions and storytelling that we today call the oral tradition was enough. Would this method, however, serve their children or those people in faraway lands who had not yet heard the name of Jesus? Out of this need to preserve the message of Jesus intact, the Christian Testament gradually came to be written. The Christian Testament, as we know it today, consists of the following:

Using any Bible, list all the books of the Christian Testament. Next to each book, identify the number of pages each includes. Then determine what percentage of the total Christian Testament is devoted to the four Gospels.

The Gospels: The word *gospel* means "good news." These four accounts of the life, death, and Resurrection of Jesus bear the names of the men traditionally accepted as their authors or editors. Some scholars question whether these men actually wrote the Gospels. They think that other persons may have written or edited the works and then dedicated them to these men. In any case, tradition holds that these men were the four gospel writers:

The Christian Testament

The twenty-seven books of the Christian Testament are listed here in the order in which they appear in the Bible:

The Gospels
  Matthew
  Mark
  Luke
  John

The Acts of the Apostles

The Epistles
  Romans
  1 Corinthians
  2 Corinthians
  Galatians
  Ephesians
  Philippians
  Colossians
  1 Thessalonians
  2 Thessalonians
  1 Timothy
  2 Timothy
  Titus
  Philemon
  Hebrews
  James
  1 Peter
  2 Peter
  1 John
  2 John
  3 John
  Jude

The Book of Revelation

- Matthew, a tax collector who became one of the Apostles
- Mark, a young disciple from Jerusalem
- Luke, often referred to as "the beloved physician," an educated non-Jew and companion of Saint Paul
- John the Apostle, often called "the disciple whom Jesus loved," who was a teenager when he walked with Jesus and who wrote his very profound Gospel as an old man, after many years of reflection and prayer

The Acts of the Apostles: This extension of Luke's Gospel depicts life in the early Christian community and the spread of the Christian faith through the travels and preaching of Saint Paul and others.

The Epistles: This collection contains twenty-one letters that were written to various Christian communities or individuals in response to a wide variety of problems and needs. The Epistles are organized in the following sequence and are traditionally attributed to the following authors:

- thirteen Epistles written by Paul to various communities
- one Epistle, the Letter to the Hebrews, whose author is unknown
- one Epistle by James
- two Epistles by Peter
- three Epistles by John
- one Epistle by Jude

The Book of Revelation, or the Apocalypse: This visionary and highly symbolic work, which concludes the Bible, is also attributed to John.

Thus the Christian Testament contains twenty-seven small, unique books that were written by different authors and collected together by the Church as its scriptures. The first of these books to be written were the Epistles of Paul, which he began composing in the early part of the decade of the fifties. The last book of the Christian Testament, the Book of Revelation, was written by John during the decade of the nineties. The first firm decision about which books to include in the Christian Testament was not made until about the year A.D. 200, over one hundred and fifty years after the death of Jesus. In fact, not until this time was the term *New Testament* used for these writings. Nearly eighteen hundred years later, these same scriptures continue to be the most popular and influential writings in the history of humanity.

At some point in your high school education, you may be able to study in some depth the Christian Testament or even the entire Bible. Given the wide scope of this course, however, we must concentrate on the four Gospels—those very special books that deal most directly with the person and message of Jesus.

The Gospels: The Early Church Proclaims the Good News

Our news-hungry society expects the communications media to supply information quickly. If a famous rock music star died tomorrow, we would find around-the-clock coverage on television and radio and a book on the market in a matter of weeks.

Obviously, in Jesus' day these media were not available. So when the disciples experienced the Resurrection, they could not immediately broadcast or publish their reactions. Instead, they began a walking campaign to spread the Good News by word of mouth. Among those who listened, some chose to believe in the message and to gather in small groups to remember Jesus, to share stories about him, to pray together, and to try to interpret the meaning of all that had happened. These beginnings of the Church were described at the beginning of this chapter. These small communities, then, gradually evolved an oral tradition that included such elements as prayers that the believers liked to share again and again and stories about Jesus that would be told repeatedly.

Our society expects news to be published or broadcasted immediately.

A Spoken Message Committed to Writing

The Gospels, then, were originally committed to memory, not to parchment. They were written down only gradually through a process of collecting and editing the material of the oral tradition. The Gospels as we have them today were not actually written until anywhere from thirty-five to seventy years after the death of Jesus. Even when they were written, they were not intended to be newsy, day-by-day accounts of the life and message of Jesus. Rather, the Gospels were proclamations of the Good News of Jesus by communities of believers.

Belief, by the way, is a critical factor in our own understanding of the Scriptures. Remember that only people of faith could

Develop an outline of the section "A Spoken Message Committed to Writing" by summarizing in short statements the stages involved in the development of the Gospels.

recognize Jesus in his apparitions. Those who did not believe simply could not see him. The same holds for the recognition of the true meaning of the Scriptures: only a believer will find these writings fully understandable and exciting.

Also note that each of the Gospels, and each of the Epistles as well, was preached to or written for a particular audience in response to particular needs. Matthew, for example, was writing for the Jewish community, and his Gospel recognizes Jesus as the giver of a New Law that fulfills the Law given to Moses. Luke, on the other hand, wrote for cultured Greeks with their own special perspectives and concerns. As a result, if we are to fully understand the meaning of the Gospels, we need to learn as much as possible about the cultural setting in which each was written.

What Is *Not* in the Gospels

The need to understand the historical settings brings us to the major difficulty that we confront when trying to read the Scriptures: we are unprepared for the way in which they are written, and we expect something completely different from what we find. Simply put, the Scriptures are a collection of Middle Eastern religious writings that we read with Western scientific mindsets.

The implications of this tension are very important. Consider, for example, what you would do if you were to write an account of the life and message of Jesus today. What would you write about? What would you include in your book? Because you operate out of a Western mentality, you would likely develop something along the lines of a biography or a dramatic novel. Specifically, how many of the following items would you include?

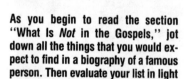

As you begin to read the section "What Is *Not* in the Gospels," jot down all the things that you would expect to find in a biography of a famous person. Then evaluate your list in light of the information provided here.

- information about Jesus' ancestors and immediate family and the date, location, and circumstances surrounding his birth
- stories about Jesus' youth—the community that he was raised in, activities in which he partook, and information about his physical development and appearance
- a detailed account of Jesus' adult ministry, possibly with a week-by-week commentary on where he went and what he did and said
- in-depth character portrayals of those people closest to Jesus—certainly of his mother and probably of the Apostles

■ evidence supporting his claims, his miracles, and the teachings of those who believed in him following his Resurrection and Ascension

You might decide to include most or all of the above items in your gospel account. Yet the fact is that the Gospels offer very little of this kind of information. We do not know, for example, the exact dates of any of the major events of Jesus' life—namely, his birth, the years of his ministry, or his death. We also know virtually nothing about his years as a child. In a similar vein, nowhere are we given even a hint of what Jesus looked like. We have common impressions of his physical appearance, but these are all based on artists' imaginative renderings. We are not even totally sure what Jesus said when he preached. Although we believe that the Gospels give a reliable understanding of his message, we are not sure when they contain Jesus' exact words. Can you imagine writing a biography that avoided this essential information? Imagine a news reporter interpreting the words of all the people interviewed rather than quoting them exactly! The point is that our Christian Testament is a very special kind of writing, and our approach to it must take into account its unique character.

Important Reflections on the Bible

Given all that we have said so far, several points must be made before closing this brief treatment of the Christian Testament.

Not Just a Book About the Past

Because the entire Bible was written long ago and in a faraway land, we often feel out of touch with its style and its tone. At times we may think that the Bible simply does not relate to us, that it is not relevant. A common complaint among young people, for example, is that the Bible is outdated, that it does not speak to their own needs as they experience them today.

Yet consider the fact that the Scriptures deal with the revelation of a God whose love is always available. That revelation can never be outdated. Moreover, people today seek responses to the same questions and fears that confronted our ancestors—questions about the meaning of life, the fear of loneliness, and the fear of death itself. The Bible speaks directly to these dimensions of human experience.

People today seek responses to the same questions and fears that confronted our ancestors.

Inspired by God

Christians recognize and accept both the Jewish and the Christian Testaments as products of a loving God revealing sacred Mystery through the words of human authors. The Bible is commonly said to be "God's book" or "written by God." Often these expressions give the false impression that in the composition of the Bible, God worked independently of people. We can get the feeling at times that the Bible was written in heaven and then simply plunked down on someone's writing desk by a divine delivery service. Actually the biblical authors interpreted their experiences of God in ways influenced by their own personalities and by their cultures. Yet Christians believe that these authors also wrote with the constant **inspiration** of the Spirit whom Jesus promised. What does the inspiration of the Scriptures mean?

The question of inspiration is both complex and crucial. Its importance becomes clear if you have occasion to meet *fundamentalist Christians*—Christians who believe that every word in the Bible is literally true. Fundamentalists, for example, believe that the world was created in just six days, as the Book of Genesis states. How do other Christians respond to such a belief if, for instance, they find the evidence for the evolution of the universe over millions of years to be persuasive? Does that mean that they disagree with the Bible and, therefore, that they are living contrary to the teachings of the Church?

The perhaps unnerving response to this question is yes and no. Yes, we may hold some views that are seemingly in disagreement with what is in the Bible, but no, we are not necessarily living contrary to what the Church teaches. The basic understanding of the composition of the Scriptures held by Catholic Christians is that the Bible is inspired by God and is therefore true—here comes the crucial part—in all those things that are necessary for our salvation. What does that last part mean? To some degree, we can trust our common sense on the question of which things are necessary for salvation.

For instance, which of the following stories and teachings taken from the Bible do you consider so central to the revelation of God and to the life and message of Jesus that they would be considered necessary for us to be truly Christian?

- All humans are descended from just two people, Adam and Eve.
- The Jewish belief in one God is more truthful than either atheism or the belief in many gods.

- In the Jewish Scriptures, a man named Methuselah lived for 969 years.
- Jesus fully revealed to people the nature and will of God.
- Jesus cursed a fig tree and made it wither and die.
- Jesus' message of unconditional love, even of one's enemies, is a basic moral principle.
- The Church is guided by the presence of the Holy Spirit to remain true to the essential message of Jesus.

Obviously some things in the Bible are written in the form of poetry or of legends and folktales. Such writings have insights to offer into the wonderful workings of God, but their kernels of truth are in husks or shells that are not essential. You might recall our story of Manuel and his fish in chapter 5 as an example of this kind of writing. That story's message, or moral, remains true even though the story itself is fictional. The Catholic Church holds that, in such cases, catching hold of the truth being expressed through the story is more important than believing in every detail involved in its telling.

In other instances in the Scriptures, the truth is being revealed with such directness, authority, and certainty that little or no room exists for indecision or rejection by the reader. For example, in the Scriptures Jesus clearly calls us to care for our brothers and sisters. We ultimately will be judged by God on the basis of our loving response to the needs of the poor and outcasts. Jesus' call and our response is central to the entire Christian message and to the Church that follows that message.

The examples from the Scriptures that we have chosen to use in this discussion of inspiration are simple ones. What about all those passages in the Scriptures where the meaning is unclear, where a variety of interpretations are possible? How do we decide what to believe about such passages? Of the two responses to this question, the first deals with the need to study the Scriptures with guidance. The second response deals with the teaching authority of the Church, a point we will discuss at some length in the next major section of this chapter.

Proceed with Caution

A major factor in the historic splits between Christian denominations involved scriptural issues—deciding the meaning of certain passages, for instance, or determining who had the authority to settle arguments over these meanings. Because of the tremendous importance of the Scriptures, the Catholic Church has always counseled caution regarding the use of the

Identify four stories from the Bible that you have always had a difficult time accepting as historical events. For each story, briefly explain what you think might be the value or lesson of the story even if it did not actually happen.

The Catholic Church has always counseled caution regarding the use of the Bible—out of a concern that it could be interpreted wrongly.

Imagine that you are on a committee of students assigned to develop a course on the Bible to be taught in your high school. Your task is to list four questions about the Bible to which you would like the course to respond.

Many Catholics today are joining Bible study groups—a tremendous change from past practice.

Bible. The disagreements with Protestants, unfortunately, caused the Catholic Church to become overly protective of the Scriptures, and for a long time individual Catholics were afraid to read the Bible privately. We have recently seen a tremendous change in this regard, however, and many Catholics today are reading the Bible for the first time, joining Bible study groups, and so on.

This increased interest in the Bible among Catholics is to be applauded and encouraged, but the tone of caution so long associated with the Catholic Church is still valid and necessary. At times throughout Catholic history the Scriptures have been used to justify the most unchristian actions. Those who choose to read the Scriptures for personal growth and enjoyment, therefore, should be encouraged to do so with the help of sound study manuals and perhaps in the company of persons who have knowledge and background in the Scriptures. The more central to Christian faith a particular scriptural passage appears to be, the more it deserves thorough study and discussion. The Scriptures are simply too important to be taken lightly or to be interpreted without appropriate guidance.

A Valuable Foundation

Finally, a fully developed understanding of the Christian faith is impossible without an adequate background in the Scriptures. For this reason, throughout your high school career you will likely be required to take various courses related to the

Bible. These courses will not always be easy, nor will you always feel that what is being taught and discussed relates directly to your personal life. However, in the study of the Scriptures you will discover a valuable foundation for knowing and appreciating Christian faith. Try to be open to that possibility and supportive of the teachers who will be attempting to share this information with you.

We turn now to a discussion of the second major component of what we have called the *wisdom* of Catholicism—the Tradition of the Catholic Church.

The Catholic Church and Tradition

In our earlier discussion in chapter 3 of the relationship between faith and religion, we talked about the fact that the inner, personal experience of faith demands the outward, public expressions offered by religion. Certainly the Scriptures reflect this fact. The authors of the Scriptures, guided by God, found powerful and lasting expressions of their faith in the words of the Bible.

In this next part of our discussion, we will explore other expressions of the *wisdom* of Catholic Christianity, namely, its official teachings. Earlier, when reflecting on the rich meanings in the Scriptures, we discussed the importance of understanding the nature of the sacred writings, their origins, and their intended audiences. Let's approach our discussion of church teachings with a similar caution. A brief story will help make the point:

> The devil once went for a walk with a friend. After a while they saw a man ahead of them stoop down and pick up something from the street.
>
> "What did that man find?" asked the friend.
>
> "A piece of the truth," said the devil.
>
> "Doesn't that disturb you?" asked the friend.
>
> "Not at all," said the devil. "I shall let him think that piece is all the truth that there is."

As with most good stories, we had best not analyze or comment at length on this one. Let's simply say this about its message: People struggle to find words for the infinite sacred Mystery whom we call God. Those words reflect or express the truth, but they do not capture it fully. The words are only like sign-posts on the way, not the destination. When the words or statements of belief become the goal or object of our worship, they become hindrances on our path to God. Conversely, when our formal statements of belief point us toward and even lead us to an encounter with God, then they are great gifts worthy of our deepest respect.

With this caution about the limitations of words in mind, let's continue our discussion of the wisdom of Catholic Christianity.

A Definition of Tradition

Recall for a moment the definition of the Church that we have been using in this course: the Church is the gathering of those people who profess faith in the Risen Jesus and his message and who, through the power of the Spirit, live their lives in loving service to all people. We also discussed the reference to the Spirit of Jesus in this definition: the Catholic Church believes that the Spirit is continually guiding the Church, constantly reminding its members of the powerful message of Jesus, and giving them the insight and courage to live according to that message.

This strong conviction in the constant presence of the Spirit in the Church throughout its history has led the Roman Catholic Church to the belief known as *Tradition*. The term itself is based on a Latin word that literally means "to hand on." So Tradition deals with the handing on of Christian faith from generation to generation throughout the ages.

Throughout nearly two thousand years of history, the Spirit of Jesus has been with the Church as it has evolved. Over those years the Church has had to grapple with challenges against virtually every belief that it holds regarding Jesus and the Good News that he proclaimed. In response to each challenge, the Church has clarified its understanding of the meaning and implications of that message. In addition, communal prayers and forms of worship have emerged, ultimately having as their primary expression in the Catholic Church the seven sacraments that we will explore a bit later in this course. The Catholic Church has developed other religious expressions as well—for example, gestures such as the sign of the cross, forms of government for the community, a variety of leadership roles, and so on.

The Catholic Church teaches that, whenever these gradual developments have resulted in teachings or practices that can be regarded as central to the faithful living out of the message of Jesus, those teachings and practices are then as much a part of God's revelation as are the Scriptures. The essential teachings and practices that have emerged from the ongoing, lived faith of the Christian community are what is known in the Catholic Church as **Tradition** with a capital *T.* Furthermore, the Catholic Church believes that the Truth of God revealed fully in Jesus is expressed most completely through both the Bible and Tradition taken together.

In the strictest sense, we probably should not speak of the Scriptures and Tradition as if they were two distinct sources of God's revelation in the Church. In fact, the Scriptures are themselves one part of the total Tradition of the Church. Within the Catholic Church, however, the Scriptures and Tradition are customarily spoken of as two sources of revelation. This distinction helps to clarify the Catholic position on revelation in relation to that of Protestant churches.

Imagine that you are approached by someone who claims that you are not going to be saved because you do not understand the true meaning of the Scriptures. How would you feel? How would you respond to that person?

The Spirit of Jesus has been with the Church through the nearly two thousand years of its history.

Catholic and Protestant: An Essential Difference

Many young people as well as adults raise the question, What is so different about Catholics and Protestants? The reality is that many differences exist among all Christian denominations. If that were not the case, we would not have so many denominations! Yet this issue of Tradition is certainly a major characteristic that identifies Catholicism as distinct from most Protestant churches. So the topic of Tradition is vital to this course, the main objective of which is to clearly define Catholic Christianity.

Simply put, a major difference between Catholics and Protestants is that Protestant churches place a central importance upon the Scriptures, treating the Bible as the sole foundation of all their teachings and practices. Often Protestants say, "If it isn't in the Bible, it isn't part of Protestant Christian faith." For this reason, Protestant churches generally recognize only two sacraments—Baptism and Eucharist—because these two are the most clearly identified Christian religious celebrations in the Scriptures. This biblical foundation also explains why Protestant young people are often much more familiar with the Bible than are their Catholic peers: religious education in Protestant churches places great emphasis on the learning of biblical stories, the ability to locate certain important passages in the Bible, and so on.

Catholics, on the other hand, accept not only the Scriptures but also Tradition as the foundation for their teachings and practices. Catholics believe that, as the Church moves through history, the Spirit of Jesus guides the Church to create particular teachings and practices. On that basis, Catholics accept as parts of God's revelation certain elements other than those explicitly mentioned in the Scriptures. For example, in addition to Baptism and Eucharist, Catholics accept five sacraments that have developed over the years—Confirmation, Penance, Matrimony, Holy Orders, and the Anointing of the Sick. Furthermore, along with the Scriptures, Catholics emphasize in their religious education the understanding of the basic teachings and practices of the Church. As noted earlier, however, Catholics are only recently recovering a strong sense of the importance of the Scriptures, so young Catholics today often feel ill equipped to discuss the Bible with their Protestant friends.

Catholics believe that the Spirit of Jesus continues to guide the Church in developing its teachings and practices.

Tradition and Traditions

Our normal use of the word *tradition* is so familiar that we might confuse it with the very special meaning of the word in the Catholic Church. So a useful distinction can be made here between the Church's Tradition and its traditions.

Every community, not only the religious sort, develops customary routines that help to keep the community together but that have little other significance. Both Catholic and Protestant churches have many such customs. For instance, if your parents were raised as Catholics, they may remember that as children they were not allowed to eat meat on Friday. Another past practice was that of using only the Latin language in the Mass. Such customs can, quite obviously, change over time because they are not considered essential to religious faith in the same sense as are more profound teachings and practices such as the sacraments.

The important distinction is this: A teaching or practice that if rejected or lost would distort the essential message of the Gospel is automatically considered to be part of Catholic Tradition. But a teaching or practice that cannot be found in the Scriptures or is not recognized by church leaders as essential to Christian faith is merely a custom that can be changed or eliminated.

This distinction, between Tradition and traditions, may at first seem trivial. Yet throughout the history of the Church, many conflicts between faithful Catholics have focused on whether or not a particular practice or teaching is essential to faith. Distinguishing between the Church's Tradition and church traditions is an ongoing process involving the teaching authority of the official Catholic Church, the work of theologians, and the lived experience of the entire faith community.

Who Decides What Is Tradition and What Is Merely a Custom?

Even adult, devout Roman Catholics can be surprised to learn that no single place lists all the teachings and practices that are officially accepted as part of the Church's Tradition. With a little reflection, however, the reason for this becomes clear. Despite all that people know about God through revelation, the fact is that God remains a mystery. We cannot hope to neatly or fully describe the infinite God with our words or symbols. We are always just scratching the surface of sacred Mystery and catching fleeting glimpses of the face of God. For this reason, in the Catholic Church's journey through history, its customs and even its Tradition must be open to growth, refinement, and clarification. To repeat the most important point, Catholic Christians believe that the Spirit is always with the Church on its journey, keeping the Church faithful to the Gospel of Jesus.

We might still ask: Who leads the Church on that journey

of faith? Who is to help the Church evolve a Tradition that is totally true to the message of Jesus? The Catholic Church identifies three factors that work together to guide the Church.

The community of faith: The Spirit of Jesus that ultimately guides the Church is present to the entire community of faith, not merely to select individuals within it. Therefore, decisions about which teachings and practices are to be officially recognized as part of the Church's Tradition must take into account the lived experience of the entire Church.

The theologians: Certain members of the community, by virtue of their education and training, are recognized as valuable sources of information and direction on what is and is not essential to faith. These persons include theologians, whose lifework is to study and reflect on the Church's teachings and practices in light of the Gospel.

The bishops and the pope: The Catholic Church has always reserved a special authority for all the bishops in the Church, and it gives ultimate authority to the bishop of Rome, that is, the pope.

In Catholic history, bishops have long been understood to be the primary religious authorities within dioceses.

The Bishops and the Pope Are Special Leaders

Besides its belief in Tradition, another characteristic of Catholicism that makes it distinct from many other Christian churches is its understanding of the roles of bishops and of the pope. Catholics and a few of the Protestant churches believe that bishops are successors of the Twelve Apostles—those special persons who were recruited and taught by Jesus himself. Originally the word *bishop* meant "overseer," and in Catholic history **bishops** have long been understood to be the primary religious authorities over all the individual churches within geographic regions called **dioceses**. Within their dioceses, bishops are responsible for the following:

- assuring that all teaching about the message of Jesus is done in a way that is true to the Gospel
- seeing that the sacraments of the Church are properly celebrated
- governing the churches by, among other things, serving as a final authority in disputes between particular groups or parishes

The Roman Catholic Church is unique among Christian

churches in its understanding of the role and authority of the pope. The Christian Testament repeatedly implies that Saint Peter had a special role in the mission of Jesus. After Jesus' death and Resurrection, Peter's role became clearer when he assumed a strong leadership position in the early Church—as reflected throughout the Acts of the Apostles. History suggests that later on Peter lived, died, and was buried in Rome, and Christians eventually came to believe that Peter served as the bishop of Rome when he lived there.

The Catholic Church gives ultimate authority to the bishop of Rome—the pope.

Catholic Tradition holds that the current pope is the successor of Peter in much the same way that the bishops are successors of the Apostles. Just as Peter held a primary and authoritative place among the Apostles, so the Catholic Church believes that today's pope holds a special role and authority among all bishops. Furthermore, because Peter is viewed as having been the bishop of Rome, the pope of today holds that title and authority as well.

What does this discussion of bishops and the pope have to do with our original question: Who decides what is central to Christian faith and therefore part of Catholic Tradition? The simple answer is that the bishops, under the leadership and authority of the pope, make these decisions. As indicated above, however, the pope and the bishops exercise that authority with a sensitivity to the lived experience of the entire faith community and with the information and advice supplied them by qualified theologians.

Do a brief report on the current bishop of your diocese, including the following information:
- his name
- his place of birth
- the date of his ordination
- the place that he served prior to being named your bishop

Until he was assassinated in 1980, Archbishop Oscar Romero preached justice for the poor people of San Salvador.

The responsibility of the bishops and the pope to make decisions about church teachings and practices is an important function, but not their chief one. First and foremost, the bishops and the pope are called to be signs of Christian unity among the many millions of Catholics and their diverse parish communities. Christian unity is symbolized in the following ways:

- Individual bishops serve as signs of unity among the parishes in their dioceses.
- The bishops as a group, then, join together as a sign of the unity of all dioceses.
- Finally, the pope stands as a symbol of unity for the entire, worldwide Catholic Church.

This sense of unity is one reason why the pope evokes such deep affection and such powerful emotions wherever he travels.

Doctrines and Dogmas Are Official Statements of Faith

We have stated that the Catholic Church's sense of Tradition includes many dimensions—the sacramental life of the Church, various religious gestures and practices, even the Scriptures themselves. In the minds of most people, however, Tradition is most closely associated with formal teachings about faith.

Throughout its history, the Church has been challenged repeatedly and sometimes attacked for its basic beliefs. Such conflicts are not surprising, for the message of Jesus is powerful and challenging. That message and the way he lived it ultimately brought Jesus to the cross. So, naturally, the Church, which professes faith in that man and his message, has also faced repeated conflicts with all the cultures in which it has found itself. For instance:

- From its earliest days, the Church has had its understanding of Jesus as both God and man challenged.
- The Church's positions on various moral issues, such as the morality of war, have often alienated people and rulers.
- Even practices that are now routinely accepted were heatedly argued at various times. Everything from Sunday worship to church architecture has been debated and discussed at times in the Church's history.

In many cases, conflict has helped the Church by forcing its members and leaders to rethink and refine their understanding of the Gospel in light of the evolving needs of people.

At times the challenges confronting the Church have been

of such seriousness that they have demanded an official response by church leaders. Whenever a stated belief receives the official approval of the Catholic Church, it is called a **doctrine**. A doctrine is approved as an official church teaching by the bishops and the pope. Furthermore, whenever a specific doctrine of the Church is considered to be so essential to the faith of Catholics that any rejection of it would imply a rejection of the faith as a whole, it is called a **dogma**. In light of all that we have discussed to this point about the Church's Tradition, most doctrines and, certainly, all dogmas of the Church are rooted in the Scriptures or in the ongoing experience of the Church as it has been guided throughout history by the Spirit.

In the early sixties, Pope John XXIII called for a worldwide meeting of bishops, the Second Vatican Council, to study issues relating to church practices and unity.

The Trinity
Is the Central Christian Dogma

We have already discussed many doctrines or dogmas of the Church, for example, the Incarnation of God in the person of Jesus and the Church's recognition of Mary as the Mother of God. As was mentioned above, however, no one list exists in which all the official teachings of Catholicism can be found. Even if that list were available, this course is intended to be an introduction to Catholic Christianity, not a thorough discussion of it. Yet we must discuss the major dogma of the Church, the one shared by virtually all Christian churches, and the one that in many ways is at the very center of all Christian understanding about God. That dogma is the Trinity.

You may remember a definition of the Trinity from your past religious education. The most familiar definition is this:

the doctrine of the **Trinity** is the belief that there are three divine Persons in one God—Father, Son, and Holy Spirit. You may have been asked to memorize this definition for a religion test. Perhaps you memorized it but did not understand its meaning. The clear fact is that the Trinity, the very nature of God, is an absolute mystery that we can never fully understand.

The dogma of the Trinity as it is stated above is not found in the Scriptures. Yet the Church's belief in this dogma as part of its Tradition goes back to the very early years of the Church as it struggled to make sense out of the meaning of Jesus' life after his Resurrection. In fact, the belief in the Trinity was officially declared a dogma more than sixteen hundred years ago! The actual meaning of the dogma of the Trinity has naturally been the object of much prayer, study, and debate.

For our purposes, the following insight into the meaning of the Trinity might prove helpful. In the last chapter we quoted Saint John, who said in his first Epistle that "God is love, and whoever remains in love remains in God and God in him" (1 John 4:16). In what sense can we say that "God *is* love"?

One way to understand God as love is this: Whenever we experience or witness a deep, honest love relationship, three elements seem to be present.

- One person initiates the love and is the active party reaching out in love to the other.
- One person responds to the love, receives that love, and offers his or her own love in return.
- The actual love shared by the two persons adds an entirely

The Trinity can be compared to the experience of a love relationship.

new dimension to the situation. Simply put, when two people love each other, something "extra" is added to the lives of both the lover and the beloved.

If God is love, then God must in some way reflect these three dimensions of all true love relationships. This is what the dogma of the Trinity hints at.

- God the Father is the Lover, the one who initiates the love relationship, who reaches out in unconditional love.
- Jesus is the one who totally receives the Father's love—the "Beloved," as the Scriptures speak of him.
- The Holy Spirit, then, is the Love shared between the Father and the Son—a Love so infinite and unrestrained that it is a power, a person unto itself.

In other words, the Christian understanding is that God is, in a sense, a community of perfect love. In prayerful reflection upon the Trinity, therefore, Christians catch glimpses of the kind of love that they are called to share with people, all of whom are born "in the image and likeness of God" (based on Genesis 1:26).

Creeds Are Special Statements of Faith

As noted already, Catholics will not find a complete, clearly stated listing of all the doctrines and dogmas that make up the Tradition of the Church. However, the Church has constantly sought religious expressions for its faith—often in the context of trying to pray and to worship God as a community. This effort has on occasion resulted in formalized statements of belief known as *creeds,* a term that comes from a Latin word meaning "to believe."

Creeds are not intended to be detailed summaries of every belief held by Christians. Rather, they are essentially communal prayers that attempt to express the believers' shared convictions about the nature of God. For this reason, we should not normally analyze creeds like a theologian or a lawyer who is trying to debate a point of law would. Rather, we should pray creeds solemnly, reverently, and sincerely.

The Nicene Creed

The creed most often shared by Catholics in Sunday worship is commonly known as the **Nicene Creed** because it was first developed in an official church council held in a city named Nicaea in the year A.D. 325. Think of it: For over sixteen hundred years Catholics and many of their Protestant brothers and sisters have been reciting this creed as a summary of their deepest convictions about God. As a prayerful ending to this discussion of the Church's wisdom, read this creed again yourself. Take the time to read it slowly and thoughtfully. Read it with an attempt to sense the profound mystery behind every phrase. The creed may never sound quite the same to you again.

We believe in one God,
    the Father, the Almighty,
    maker of heaven and earth,
    of all that is seen and unseen.

We believe in one Lord, Jesus Christ,
    the only Son of God,
    eternally begotten of the Father,
    God from God, Light from Light,
    true God from true God,
    begotten, not made, one in Being with the Father.
    Through him all things were made.
    For [us] and for our salvation
        he came down from heaven:

by the power of the Holy Spirit
    he was born of the Virgin Mary, and became man.

For our sake he was crucified under Pontius Pilate;
    he suffered, died, and was buried.
    On the third day he arose again
        in fulfillment of the Scriptures;
    he ascended into heaven
        and is seated at the right hand of the Father.
He will come again in glory to judge the living and the
        dead,
    and his kingdom will have no end.

We believe in the Holy Spirit, the Lord, the giver of life,
    who proceeds from the Father and the Son.
    With the Father and the Son he is worshiped and
        glorified.
    He has spoken through the Prophets.
    We believe in one holy catholic and apostolic Church.
    We acknowledge one baptism for the forgiveness of sins.
    We look for the resurrection of the dead,
        and the life of the world to come. Amen.

If the Trinity is considered the most central Christian dogma, what do you believe would be the *second* most central dogma of the Church? For possible responses, read the Nicene Creed to the right. Be prepared to support your choice.

Review Questions

1. Why do we not say that Christianity in its earliest stages was "a new religion"?
2. How did the early Christians interpret the Jewish Scriptures in light of their experience of Jesus? Give an example.
3. Describe the first Christians' growing understanding of the identity of Jesus, and identify what event eventually led them to recognize him as God.
4. What prompted the early Church to develop what we now know as the Christian Testament?
5. How many separate books are there in the Christian Testament? How many of those are Gospels? Name the Gospels.
6. Which book of the Christian Testament might be considered a sequel to Luke's Gospel?
7. During what time period were the Gospels written?
8. Why do we need to understand the cultural setting in which each Gospel was written?
9. Explain why the Gospels cannot be understood as biographies, or historical accounts, of the life of Jesus.
10. How do Catholic Christians understand the inspiration of the Bible by God?
11. Explain the difference between Catholics and Protestants on the role of Tradition.
12. Why do Protestants seem to know the Bible so much better than many Catholics?
13. What three factors work together to guide the Catholic Church through its history?
14. What are the chief responsibilities of a bishop?

15. The pope is considered the successor of what person who is mentioned frequently in the Christian Testament? Where did that person serve as bishop?
16. What is the primary function of both the bishops and the pope?
17. What is the central Christian dogma?
18. How does an understanding of the nature of love provide insights into the mystery of the Trinity?

Key Terms
Tradition
doctrine
dogma
Trinity
Nicene Creed

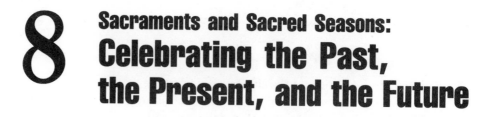

8 Sacraments and Sacred Seasons: Celebrating the Past, the Present, and the Future

Celebrations and Symbols

Let's begin this chapter with a word game. The question is this: What first comes to mind when you think about each of the following events?

birthday   homecoming
graduation   anniversary
Christmas   Easter
wedding

Remember your responses while answering these questions:

- For each event were your thoughts *directly* connected to the primary focus of the event? For example, when responding to the word *birthday* did you focus on the delivery of a baby into the world? For the word *wedding* was your focus on the personal commitment of a man and woman to love each other for life? For *Christmas* did you first think about the birth of Jesus?
- Or, were your thoughts *indirectly* connected to the meaning of the event? That is, instead of the actual focus did you instead identify the symbols, rituals, traditions, customs, and so on that often surround these events? In the case of Christmas did you think of a lighted tree, gifts, or special music? For *birthday* did you remember presents, a decorated cake, or the birthday song?

The point of this game is this: when we find ways to successfully share life's special moments, we hold on to these vital elements and make them customary parts of our celebrations. For example, at some point in the past, people recognized that the birthday cake was a fitting sign of celebration and so passed on that custom to the next generation. In the same vein, people long ago found that the circular shape of a ring was a fitting symbol of never-ending love. So the symbol of the wedding ring became a traditional part of the marriage celebration.

On a sheet of paper, complete the word game under "Celebration and Symbols" as directed. Be prepared to share your results with the class.

In a paragraph or two, respond to this statement: The biggest reason that young people are not enthused about the sacraments is that they do not understand what these religious celebrations are all about.

This chapter is about the need for celebrations and symbols in religion and particularly within Catholic Christianity. Perhaps the most frequent contact today between Catholics and the Church is centered around their attendance at and participation in the sacraments. Most familiar of all the sacraments, of course, is the celebration of the Eucharist, the Mass. Most Catholics, however, have also witnessed a number of Catholic Baptisms and weddings and have experienced the Sacrament of Reconciliation (also called Penance or Confession). Likewise, many Catholic young people have recently experienced their own Confirmation.

You might think that, with all this personal experience, Catholics would have a pretty clear notion of what the sacraments are all about. Yet the fact is that many adult Catholics have never reflected on the basic meaning of their sacramental experiences. Many Catholics simply inherited these experiences as part of their religious background and have never stopped to ask themselves why they attend these religious celebrations.

This chapter deals with two major facets of the life of the Catholic Church:

1. its seven sacraments, which are the special celebrations of the key values and special moments in Jesus' life and ministry
2. its annual cycle of religious seasons that is known as its liturgical year

Because in the future you will probably take an entire course on the sacraments, this chapter will not analyze each of them. Rather, we will once again step back and take a broad view so as to gain a sense of the general meaning of the sacraments and increase our appreciation of them. To do so, we must first reflect on the basic meaning of symbols and celebrations as we experience them in our lives as members of communities.

When Does a Sign Become a Symbol?

Signs, as we usually think of them, are a method of communicating simple messages.

We are all familiar with signs that use words. Our days are filled with word signs telling us to stop, to go, and to be careful. We have similar signs pointing out what directions in which to travel and signs urging us to buy certain products that are, in turn, sold inside stores that have blinking, neon signs out front. Word signs, as we usually think of them, are a method of communicating simple messages.

Certain other signs to which we are very accustomed do not use words. These signs speak to us in eloquent and powerful ways. For example:

- We eat cake routinely, but when we put some candles on a cake, sing a song, and share a joke, a celebration happens!
- With persons about whom we genuinely care, we share small inexpensive gifts that often have much more significance than the cash register can calculate.
- We have worn all kinds of jackets. Yet when we put a big letter on one, it becomes an object of pride and satisfaction.
- The sun sets every day. When we watch a sunset with a loved one, however, the moment is remembered forever.

These experiences in which apparently ordinary events and objects take on extraordinary meaning are what symbols are all about.

List three meaningful symbols that you have experienced in the last twenty-four hours. Briefly note the meaning for each symbol.

When we put a big letter on a jacket, it becomes an object of pride and satisfaction.

For conveying our more profound and complex messages, simple words will not do. For example, when we want to tell someone we love him or her, we often "can't find the words to say it." Likewise, when we feel great joy, we do not sit down and write about it, we jump up and shout.

This is where symbols come in. A **symbol** is a kind of sign that helps us give expression to experiences that are simply too big for words. Symbols can be either objects or actions. Rings are examples of symbolic objects, just as hugs are often symbolic actions. In either case, to be effective, our symbols must be similarly understood and valued by all those involved. For

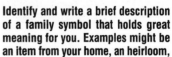

Identify and write a brief description of a family symbol that holds great meaning for you. Examples might be an item from your home, an heirloom, or a special tradition practiced in your family.

instance, a high school class ring found on the street by a grade school youngster may be viewed as valuable in terms of money but not as meaningful otherwise. On the other hand, a birthday cake is a symbol that can be understood and enjoyed by almost everyone.

Natural Events as Sacramental Moments

As the examples of rings and hugs suggest, often we use symbols in our relationships. Imagine, then, how much more this special language might be needed for expressing the wonderful but often mysterious relationship that people have with God.

For believers, all of nature is a symbol of God's power and love—an expression of who God is and what God wishes for us. So believers can glimpse something of God in even the smallest natural events: for example, a flower's perfume, sunlight on a forest floor, the cry of a baby, the touch of a loved one. No believer can honestly deny that we can touch and be touched by sacred Mystery when admiring a sunset or enjoying the view from a mountaintop. To deny this is to deny that all of creation is charged with the presence of its creator.

Rich religious symbols are found in the objects and events of the natural world.

Whenever sacred Mystery is revealed in the wondrous and heartfelt moments in life, we can legitimately call these sacramental moments. The word *sacramental* is based on a Latin word meaning "sacred." In other words, these moments are particularly God-charged and so can touch people profoundly, often changing their lives.

At the same time, believers in nearly all religions have recognized that some things in nature have particularly rich symbolic meanings—meanings that can be immediately sensed by almost everyone. Examples include fire, water, stone, bread, wine, and light. When religions use such things as symbols having religious significance, these objects are also said to be sacramental.

Within this context of the nature and power of symbols to convey religious meaning, we can begin to explore the meaning of those special ritual actions of the Church that we call the sacraments.

List five qualities or meanings that are conveyed by each of the following symbols of nature:
- fire
- water
- stone
- bread
- oil
- wine
- light

Sacraments: Celebrations of the Past, Present, and Future

We can easily recognize occasions in our lives that are so memorable and so profound that we feel an almost automatic need to see them as sacred. Some obvious examples are a birth of a child, a coming of age when individuals are granted adult freedoms and responsibilities, and marriage. These moments in our lives are not only special at the time that we first experience them but are so important that we often feel the need to recall and celebrate them.

Let's take a nonreligious event as an example. Each year we have birthday parties for ourselves and our loved ones. What are we celebrating?

- Certainly we are remembering a past event, perhaps our own birth. We hear the familiar stories surrounding this great moment—the time of day, what the weather was like, any unusual circumstances involved, and so on.
- Yet we are doing more than just remembering that past moment. We are also celebrating what we have become during the years since then. So we talk about how much we have grown—physically, of course, but also mentally and emotionally. In other words, we celebrate who we are now—today.
- We are also looking forward to what we will become or hope to become: "I wonder if I'll be on the team at this time next year." "Only a few more years and I'll be out of high school!"

So, along with the past and the present, we look to the future. All the memorable moments in our lives are celebrated with these three dimensions: We remember the past; we celebrate the present; and we point toward the future.

Some times in our lives are so special that we recall and celebrate them much later—in high school reunions, for example.

For each of the following events, identify the past, present, and future meanings being celebrated:
■ a wedding
■ a class reunion
■ the Fourth of July or Canada Day

As believers celebrate historic events of their religion, similarly citizens often celebrate the historic moments in the lives of their country's founders.

Historic Religious Events Relived Today

Most religious celebrations have been based on our human need to remember profound events from the past, to find ways to celebrate those moments in the present, and to give a sense of promise and hope to the future. Often the historic moments that are being recalled and celebrated occurred for the first time in the lives of the founders or of the early believers of the religion. These events, in turn, take on profound significance in the lives of later believers.

For example, in our previous discussion of Judaism we identified Passover and Pentecost as two of the Jews' major religious feasts. The historical basis of the feast of Passover was, of course, the escape from slavery in Egypt by the Israelite ancestors of the Jews. The celebration of Passover recalls that historical event, reminds Jews of their personal liberation through the saving acts of Yahweh, and gives the loyal Jew a sense of future hope that one day all the promises of Yahweh will be fulfilled. Similarly, Pentecost recalls the historical giving of the Law to Moses, helps the Jews celebrate their present gratitude for the Law, and enables them to renew their commitment to live out the statutes of the Law in the future.

To sum up the major point, **sacraments** are religious symbolic actions that have three purposes:
1. to recall profound religious events of the past
2. to allow current believers to realize and to celebrate the significance of those events in their own lives today
3. to provide the hope and direction that will sustain believers in the future

Jesus as the Primary Sacrament of the Church

For the early Christian believers—those who walked with Jesus, who lived and ate with him, and who experienced his death and Resurrection—the encounter with Jesus was the most powerful religious event that they had ever experienced. In meeting Jesus, believers gained a tremendous sense of having met God. Although many had already experienced God through nature and through human encounters, they had never experienced godliness as fully as they did in this person Jesus. Again, although many were devout Jews—that is, people who had their own rich history, religious traditions, and sacred memories—

they had never encountered God in such an astounding way as they did now.

The Scriptures make it clear that as Jesus taught, preached, and healed both broken hearts and crippled bodies, his impact on the disciples was powerful. Yet Jesus' effect on them was even more profound after they witnessed his death and then experienced him alive again and present among them after his Resurrection. In this experience of Jesus' death and Resurrection, the members of the early Church recognized Jesus for the first time for what he truly was: God fully present in a man. "Anyone who has seen me has seen the Father" (John 14:9).

So the believers of Jesus' time experienced him as the perfect sacrament of God. That is, Jesus served as the perfect physical, concrete symbol or image of the living God.

After Jesus' time on earth, however, he became present to people in a new way. Now Jesus was present through his Spirit, who continues to enliven and encourage the community of Christian believers. Just as Jesus is the sacrament of God, so the Church is the sacrament of Jesus—the outward, physical expression of the Risen Jesus.

Sacraments are symbolic actions that recall profound events, celebrate their significance, and provide hope and direction.

The Seven Catholic Sacraments

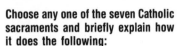

Choose any one of the seven Catholic sacraments and briefly explain how it does the following:
- recalls a past event
- celebrates something significant in the present
- provides believers with hope or direction for the future

The Church is most clearly recognized as the sacrament of Jesus in its sacramental life. Catholics believe that the sacraments of the Church are rooted historically in the life and teachings of Jesus. The sacraments celebrate the past, the present, and the future. That is, they allow Christians to recall Jesus, to re-present him—make Jesus present again—and to redirect our lives in the light of his presence. For example:

- Jesus gave an entirely new meaning to the Jewish Passover meal, which he shared with the Apostles at the Last Supper. In its sacrament of the **Eucharist**, the Catholic Church recalls that very special meal.
- The Eucharist is not just a remembrance of a historical event, however. In the Eucharist, the believers who are gathered together share fully in Jesus' presence by sharing the consecrated bread and wine.
- Finally, the Eucharist always points Christians to the future. Nourished by their sharing of the Lord's presence in the bread and the wine, the believers renew their commitment to work toward the unity required if the Kingdom of God is to be fully realized.

In the Eucharist, believers share fully in Jesus' presence by sharing the consecrated bread and wine.

Through the centuries, the Eucharist has been surrounded by additional symbols arising from various cultural influences. The basic sacramental action of the shared meal, however, remains unchanged.

In this course we have discussed the concept of grace, defined as the unconditional and undeserved love of God for people. Catholic Christians believe that the grace of God is nowhere more available and more recognizable than in the Church's celebration of its sacraments. Catholics believe that in their sacraments they encounter God in very special ways.

Given all that has been said to this point, we can now define sacraments as they are celebrated by the Catholic Church: *Catholic sacraments* are the religious celebrations shared by the community of faith

- in which it recalls the teachings and actions of Jesus,
- through which it experiences the grace of God within a personal encounter with the Risen Jesus,
- and from which it gains confidence and a sense of direction in its efforts to live out Jesus' vision of the future.

Identify the specific moments during the Mass when each of the three dimensions of a sacrament is most clearly stated or experienced.

The Number of Sacraments

As noted earlier, one of the historical disagreements between the various Christian churches has been the question of the number of valid sacraments. For example, the Protestant Reformer Martin Luther accepted only Baptism and Eucharist. He felt that only these two sacraments had very clear roots in the Scriptures. Many of the other Protestant churches followed this same line of thought. On the other hand, the Roman Catholic Church, relying on Tradition as well as on the Scriptures, gradually identified seven sacraments. Although noteworthy, these different Christian teachings and practices are not nearly as divisive as they once were. Current discussions between Catholics and Protestants display much agreement on sacramental issues.

In any case, the seven Catholic sacraments flow from the teachings and actions of Jesus as follows:

1. Jesus experienced a particular kind of baptism and later called all his followers to an even more special kind of rebirth. This event is recalled and celebrated in the Sacrament of Baptism.

2. Jesus sent his Spirit upon people and called them to witness through that Spirit the presence of a loving God in their midst. Catholics recall that event and celebrate it anew in the Sacrament of Confirmation.

3. Jesus broke bread and shared wine with those he loved and told them that this was his body and blood. In the Sacrament of the Eucharist, the Church celebrates Jesus' continuing presence.

4. Jesus valued marriage and prayed that nothing would destroy the union of love that Christian marriage celebrates.

Identify the Catholic sacrament that holds the most meaning and power for you. In a paragraph or two, explain why this sacrament is so meaningful for you.

The Catholic Church remembers that value and celebrates the permanent union of man and woman in the Sacrament of Matrimony.

5. Jesus recognized that some persons have a very particular role to play in the life of the community of faith, a role of leadership and of a particular kind of service. Catholics recall that value and celebrate it in the Sacrament of Holy Orders, the special anointing of the priesthood.

6. Jesus constantly forgave others and called all his followers to the same willingness to forgive and accept those who may fail in their efforts to love. In the Sacrament of Penance, the Catholic Church remembers that attitude, celebrates the liberation from sin of its members, and reaches out to others.

7. Finally, Jesus healed the sick and promised his followers that not even death could keep them from the fullness of life that he was offering. Catholics remember that promise and face their own sicknesses and death with the strength gained from the Sacrament of the Anointing of the Sick.

All these profound values and teachings are celebrated through the rich and powerful symbols of the sacraments. As a result, Catholics move into their futures as stronger, better Christians.

Catholics believe that the Risen Jesus is present more clearly in the sacraments than at any other time.

More Than Memories of the Past

An essential concept in the Catholic understanding of the sacraments is that they are not simply recollections of past events but rather re-presentations of those events in the lives of believers today. Jesus died nearly two thousand years ago, but he was also raised from the dead and he promised that he would be with us "always; yes, to the end of time" (Matthew 28:20). Jesus is present, here, among us.

Catholics believe that, in the sacraments and in the consecrated hosts at Mass, the Risen Jesus is present more clearly than at any other time. That is to say, the sacraments do what religious symbols are meant to do: they allow persons to reach to the depths of life rather than merely bob on its surface. Catholics believe that the seven sacraments help them reach to the depths of their faith experience of Jesus and, there, to meet God.

The Communal Experience of the Sacraments

Earlier we learned that symbols and celebrations can be truly effective only if they are understood and valued by those persons sharing them. Imagine, for example, a birthday party at which most of the partygoers are strangers who barely know the girl celebrating her birthday.

The same can be said of the sacraments: They are God-charged moments that can touch people and change their lives, but only if people have "the eyes to see and the ears to hear," as Jesus said. Those Catholics who experience the sacraments as empty and meaningless might check to see if their understanding of the sacraments is correct and complete.

We turn now from our concentration on the celebrations that make up the sacramental life of the Catholic Church to a discussion of the annual cycle of religious feasts and seasons that serves as the broad context of the communal worship of Catholics.

Write down three suggestions on how the Catholic Church might make the experience of the Mass more meaningful for young people.

Celebrating with Sacred Seasons

God Revealed in Nature

Imagine yourself as a cave dweller living tens of thousands of years ago. Put yourself in the place of a prehistoric hunter out alone at dusk, gazing in wonder at the moon's rising, yet having none of our modern scientific explanations for what is happening. As an early human, how would you explain the mysteries of creation?

We can begin to find an answer to that question by reflecting on how people typically react to natural events. When a snowfall blankets the earth, bringing with it incredible beauty and deep stillness, we will often hear people say, "God, how beautiful!" Similarly, when the springtime sun warms skin that has been covered for months by winter clothing, Northerners especially will sigh, "My God, how good it is to be alive!" When a long-awaited rainstorm eases the pain of a drought, farmers immediately want to shout, "Thank God!"

Even when nature seems to turn against humanity, people find the hand of God at work. A hurricane smashes into an island and kills thousands. A volcano spews forth molten lava, burning and crushing homes in its path. A tornado rips apart a neighborhood. An earthquake devastates whole sections of a city, leaving thousands dead or homeless. In response, people search their hearts and minds for answers to the haunting question, "Why? My God, why?"

If the workings of nature can put modern people in touch with God, we can begin to appreciate the religious response of prehistoric peoples to such events: our early ancestors saw gods at work behind every event in nature. In fact, most religions—early or modern—have been sensitive to the revelation of God within nature.

Developing a Sense of Time

As history progressed, people recognized nature's cycles. That is, they became increasingly conscious of the repeating seasons and of the predictable movements of the sun, moon, and stars. Based on their observations of natural cycles, people slowly developed the notion of time. The idea that ancient people did not know about time may seem impossible. In our society, we are so concerned about being "on time" that imagining a historical era in which no sense of time even existed is hard for us to do. Yet the whole notion of time only gradually developed out of people's growing awareness of natural cycles as well as out of their changing social needs. For example, when humans took up farming, they had to determine the best time to plant and to harvest crops to avoid the risk of damage by floods or frosts. Our familiar units of time developed along the following lines:

The day: Throughout history the notion of a twenty-four-hour day evolved, based on observations of the sun. For us moderns, the official start of a day is midnight, but this was not always the case. Originally the day was measured from one sunrise to another or from one sunset to another. We have seen,

The notion of time gradually developed out of an awareness of natural cycles as well as of changing social needs.

for example, that Jewish holy days last from one evening to the next. Then again, we often talk about the morning as "the start of a new day."

The week: Eventually early cultures began to think in terms of larger units of time than days. The concept of a seven-day week, for example, was based mainly on the Jewish story of creation, which is found in the Bible. According to this story in the Book of Genesis, God created the world in six days and then rested on the seventh. This led the Jews to establish the weekly holy day called the Sabbath, from the word for "rest." We will have more to say about the Sabbath a little later.

The month: The unit of time that we call a month was based on observations of the moon's changing phases. The lunar cycle lasts approximately twenty-nine and one-half days. So the earliest unit that we now call a month included either twenty-nine or thirty days. Throughout history, many religious observances have been linked to this monthly cycle. As we shall see later, our modern approach to determining the date of Easter is directly related to the lunar cycle.

The year: When people gradually recognized the need for a longer unit of time than the month, the answer seemed obvious. They could add up enough lunar months to make a year. The problem was that lunar cycles do not match the cycle of the seasons. Eventually the lunar calendar for a year would fall out of step with the growing seasons. Clearly, another natural cycle was needed that would be a more practical and predictable standard for figuring out when to plant or harvest crops. People eventually realized that the position of the earth in relation to the sun follows a constant pattern. Based on this predictable cycle, then, a period of 365 days became the unit of time that we call a solar year. Days were then added to the lunar months to fit them to a solar year.

Cultures outside of Europe developed solar calendars. For example, the Aztecs of Mexico had an agricultural calendar of 360 days, with five days added at the end.

Religions and the Passage of Time

Why discuss the cycles of nature, the changing seasons, and the evolving concept of time? The reason is that almost all religions have developed major religious celebrations centered on their central beliefs and on key moments in their histories. These celebrations are, in turn, often linked to the cycles of nature. The result is an annual cycle of religious celebrations that are considered sacred days or sacred seasons.

Occasionally a religion will take a nonreligious festival or the celebration of another religion and give it a new religious significance. For example, we have discussed the Jewish feast of the Pentecost. Before the Jews existed as a people, this was a springtime festival celebrating the harvest of the winter crop. Jewish rabbis then began to associate this celebration with the giving of the Law to Moses on Sinai. What was once a celebration with little religious significance thus became an important religious feast. As we will see in a moment, the Christian celebration of Christmas has a similar history.

The Liturgical Year of the Church

The Church has evolved a complex series of religious seasons and special feasts based on the life, death, Resurrection, and gospel message of Jesus. Although not organized on the basis of our modern solar calendar, these seasons and feasts do follow an annual cycle. The purpose of this cycle of worship is to help Christians to daily touch the very heart of their faith—the mystery of Jesus of Nazareth, risen and alive among us today. This annual cycle of religious feasts and seasons is known as the Church's **liturgical year.** The word *liturgy* is based on a Greek word meaning "public." So the term *liturgical* refers to the public or communal worship practiced by a religion.

As part of our discussion of the Church's worship, let's explore in a very general way how the liturgical seasons and holy days of the Catholic Church unfold throughout the course of the year. More specific information on each season will be provided later.

The Liturgical Year at a Glance

As we begin our discussion of the Catholic Church's liturgical year, take a moment to reflect on the chart of the annual cycle of seasons and major feasts provided on page 236. Doing so will give you a good sense of how the seasons and feastdays flow from one to another throughout the course of the year.

Just as our solar year is divided into units of time—that is, days, weeks, months, and seasons—so the liturgical year is also divided into recognizable units of time. The church year includes five major seasons that unfold in this order:

- Season of Advent
- Season of Christmas

Before reading on, try to list the names of all the religious seasons that occur during the Church's worship throughout the year. Which season is your favorite? Explain briefly.

Religious celebrations are often linked to the cycles of nature.

- Season of Ordinary Time, which is divided into two parts—the first part falls between 6 January and the start of Lent; the second part follows Pentecost
- Season of Lent
- Season of Easter

Within this annual cycle, many individual days celebrate particularly important events in the life and ministry of Jesus.

- Every Sunday is dedicated to Jesus and the memory of his death and Resurrection. We will discuss Sunday worship more fully later on.
- Certain Sundays are recognized as particularly significant, as are a few of the weekdays during the year.
- Most of the weekdays of the year are dedicated to the memory of saints who in special ways witnessed to the gospel values of Jesus.

Let's explore some insights into the specific days and seasons of the church year, insights that can make our experience of the Church's liturgy more rich and satisfying.

The Liturgical Year: A Closer Look

The Season of Advent

Keep in mind in our discussion of the Church's liturgical year that our normal calendar year and the liturgical year of the Church do not begin at the same time. We immediately think of the New Year as beginning on 1 January. The Church's liturgical year, however, begins with the Season of Advent, which starts four Sundays before Christmas. During these weeks the Church prepares to celebrate the coming of Jesus by focusing on scriptural themes related to the coming of the Messiah.

The Season of Christmas

The Season of Christmas begins, of course, with the joyous celebration of Christmas Day on 25 December. As a whole, this season continues the celebration of the early life of Jesus and the growing awareness by the early Church of his identity as the Son of God. As early as the fourth century, the Church recognized and celebrated Christmas as a special day. Remember the comment earlier that the Jewish feast of Pentecost had its roots in a relatively nonreligious celebration? Our celebration of Christmas also has borrowed some of its characteristics

Choose a religious symbol that is used during the Christmas Season. Using an encyclopedia, determine the origin of the symbol and its present meaning. Write a short report summarizing what you discover.

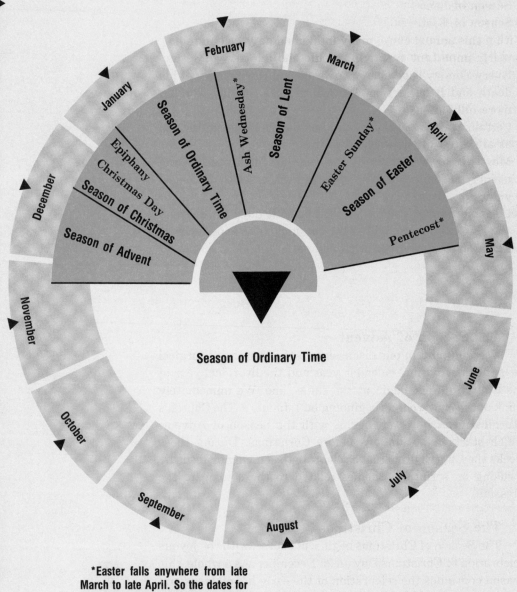

February

March

January

Ash Wednesday*

Season of Lent

April

Season of Ordinary Time

Easter Sunday*

Epiphany

Christmas Day

Season of Easter

Season of Christmas

April

Season of Advent

Pentecost*

December

May

November

Season of Ordinary Time

June

October

July

September

August

*Easter falls anywhere from late
March to late April. So the dates for
Ash Wednesday and Pentecost also
vary from year to year.

The Liturgical Year

from non-Christian customs. Perhaps by coincidence, the celebration of Christmas fell about the same time as the Roman feast of the "Invincible Sun" and some customary observances based on the position of the sun in the midwinter sky. Out of this mix of cultural and religious practices, Christians developed such customs as giving gifts, decorating homes with greenery and lights, and so on. Even the symbol of the Christmas tree has its roots in pagan custom.

The Christmas Season closes on 6 January with the feast of the Epiphany. The word *epiphany* is based on a Greek word meaning "manifestation." On this day and during the period immediately following it, the Church celebrates the first awakenings of people to the special identity of Jesus as God. In the Western Church—that is, the Christian Church of which most Christians of Western cultures are members—the Epiphany emphasizes the first recognition by non-Jewish people of Jesus' identity. This is represented by the gospel story of the Magi's visit to the infant Jesus.

The Season of Ordinary Time

At this point in the Church's liturgical year we have the first part of the Season of Ordinary Time. This lasts from the Epiphany to the beginning of Lent, and that length of time can vary depending on when Easter falls in a given year. During this season—which is also known as simply the Season of the Year—the Church concentrates on the life and teachings of Jesus rather than on the central events of his birth and Resurrection. During this season, individual Christians reflect on those qualities of Jesus that should characterize their daily lives.

The Season of Lent

The fourth major season of the Church's liturgical year is the Season of Lent. Lent begins with Ash Wednesday, which occurs forty days before Easter Sunday, not counting Sundays. This season reminds Christians of two events: the forty days Jesus spent in prayer in the desert following his baptism in the Jordan River and the forty years the Israelites wandered in the desert following their escape from slavery in Egypt. A solemn time during the Church's cycle of seasons, Lent helps Christians recall and reflect on all the events that led up to the world's rejection and ultimate execution of Jesus. As individuals, believers reflect as well on those areas in their lives where they

Even the symbol of the Christmas tree has its roots in pagan custom.

have failed to live out the values of Jesus. Yet Lent is not meant to be a totally sad time. Rather, the primary purpose of Lent is to help the Church and its individual members properly prepare for the celebration of the central Christian mystery--the Resurrection of Jesus. Lent, therefore, does not celebrate pain and suffering but rather the inevitable triumph of life and hope over death and despair.

The Season of Easter

Easter Sunday, the most important feast in the Church's cycle of worship, is the start of the fifth major season of the Church's liturgical year—the Easter Season. Just as the Jewish feast of the Passover is a great springtime feast for the Jews, so the central Christian feast of Easter is celebrated in the spring of the year, the time of new life. Easter does not fall on the same day each year as do Christmas and the Epiphany. For complicated historical reasons, Christians celebrate Easter on the first Sunday following the first full moon of springtime. This can fall anywhere from late March to late April. Curiously, a part of our worship is still linked to the changing phases of the moon. Churches in our day are attempting to arrive at a standard day of the year on which to celebrate Easter.

The Easter Season lasts for fifty days and is a period of great joy and hope. During this time, the readings at Mass focus on the disciples' encounters with Jesus following his Resurrection from the dead. The entire Church, it seems, is joined in spirit with Thomas, the Apostle who initially doubted that Jesus had been raised and who later joyfully exclaimed in meeting him, "My Lord and my God!" (John 20:28).

The Easter Season lasts until the feast of *Pentecost*, which is celebrated on the Sunday that falls on the fiftieth day after Easter. Pentecost, you will remember, celebrates the coming of the Spirit upon the group of frightened disciples who had gathered following the death and Resurrection of Jesus. The Church was born on that day, a Church that nearly two thousand years later continues to celebrate these marvelous events.

The Season of Ordinary Time—Revisited

The second phase of the Season of Ordinary Time begins the day after Pentecost and lasts until the beginning of Advent and the start of a new year in the Church. Several of these weeks of Ordinary Time focus on the divinity of Jesus. The last Sunday of the year, for instance, celebrates the feast of Christ the

King. During the closing weeks of Ordinary Time, the Church celebrates the belief that the Risen Jesus will one day come again in glory. In other words, Christians renew their sense of awaiting the coming of the Lord. The spirit of the Church's worship during this season is perhaps best summed up by the very last words of the Bible:

> The one who attests these things says: I [the Lord] am indeed coming soon.
>
> Amen; come, Lord Jesus.
>
> May the grace of the Lord Jesus be with you all. Amen. (Revelation 22:20–21)

So, at the close of the liturgical year, Christians renew their sense of awaiting the coming of the Lord and, in that spirit, enter into Advent. The marvelous cycles of the liturgical year begin anew.

The central Christian feast of Easter is celebrated in the spring of the year, the time of new life.

Sunday:
Christians Dedicate the Week to God

Special mention must be made of the central role of Sunday Eucharist in the Church's worship. Christians throughout the world and since the earliest days of the Church have recognized the obligation of believers to worship together on the first day of each week. Many Catholics are so accustomed to following this practice that they may not even know where it comes from. So let's briefly explore the origins of Sunday worship.

This course has made a strong point of recognizing the Jewish roots of Christianity. In our discussion of Jewish worship in chapter 4, we noted that the Jews consecrated their week to God through Sabbath worship. From early in their history, the Jews have regarded the Sabbath, which extended from sunset on Friday until nightfall on Saturday, as a sacred time. Absolutely no work of any kind was allowed on this day of rest. During their pre-Christian history, some Jews even allowed themselves to be slaughtered rather than break the Sabbath laws by taking up arms against their enemies. When we hear of the commandment to "keep holy the Sabbath," we must remember this history to gain a sense of the importance of this law in the minds of the Jews.

Many Catholics are so accustomed to Sunday worship that they may not even know where the practice comes from.

Most of the earliest Christians were, of course, Jews. After they had experienced the Resurrection of Jesus on the first day of the week—what we know as Sunday—they almost immediately began to gather on that day each week to celebrate the Resurrection and to prepare for what they expected to be the almost immediate return of the Risen Jesus. For a time, many of the Jewish converts continued to attend Sabbath worship with the Jews and then joined with Christians for worship on Sundays.

This Christian worship on Sunday was very simple compared to what Christians experience today. Believers gathered in small neighborhood communities for prayers and the breaking and sharing of bread. The worship would often take place very early in the morning because Sunday was an ordinary working day at that time and many Christians had jobs and because the act of gathering at the time of the rising sun to honor the Risen Son was a strong symbol in itself.

In the beginning, these weekly gatherings were celebrations of Easter. Only when Christians realized that the Risen Lord would not be returning soon did they set aside one Sunday of the year as a special celebration of the Resurrection. Naturally they associated the Resurrection with the Jewish feast of Passover. So, even today, these two religious holy days occur at nearly the same time every year.

Parts of the Jewish synagogue service were gradually incorporated into Sunday worship. Later, as the Christian Testament began to emerge, readings from it also became part of the worship. Throughout the centuries, of course, the celebration of the Mass has taken on ever greater complexity. Incidentally, in recent years Catholics have begun to consider Saturday evening through Sunday as the appropriate period for attending Mass. This change reflects the original Jewish understanding of a day lasting from one sundown to the next.

Right from the beginning of Christianity, Sunday worship was recognized by believers as a very special responsibility. Society did not acknowledge Sunday as a special day, however, until a Roman emperor, in the fourth century, accepted Christianity as the official religion of the state. At that time Sunday was established as an official day of rest for the entire Roman Empire. This practice remains somewhat true to this day, at least to the extent that most people do not work on Sundays.

Today Catholic Christians of all ages frequently question the value of Sunday worship. Many reasons are given for this attitude—among them a reluctance to attend Mass merely out of a sense of obligation. Rather than treating Mass as a question of duty, however, believers might be more in touch with the spirit of Sunday worship if they recalled its profound and beautiful history. For when Christians gather for worship now, they are in a very real and wonderful way gathering in spirit

When Christians worship, they are gathering in spirit with believers from the earliest days of the Church until the present.

For the following statement, give two reasons to support the pro position and two reasons to support the con position: Without pressure from the Church, Catholics should be allowed to decide on their own whether to attend Mass on the weekend.

with their fellow believers from the earliest days of the Church until the present. As always, they gather in the sure conviction that they do so not only in the name of the Lord, but also in the Lord's very presence. "For where two or three meet in my name," promised Jesus, "I am there among them" (Matthew 18:20).

The Church's sacramental and liturgical life was founded upon more than a thousand years of Jewish history and worship.

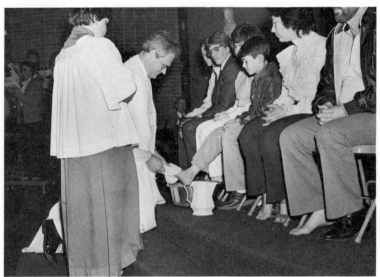

Community Worship and Personal Spirituality

The worship of Catholic Christianity is complex and occasionally confusing. This should not surprise us, growing as it does out of nearly two thousand years of complicated church history. Remember also that the Church's sacramental and liturgical life was founded upon more than a thousand years of Jewish history and worship. The point is, if you feel a bit overwhelmed by all the information contained in this chapter, relax. That just proves that you are normal!

In closing this discussion of Catholic worship, we must recall that the experience of faith and religion is both communal and deeply individual. On the one hand, Catholics share a very real bond with over 800 million other believers. Wherever they gather across the globe, they all share essentially the same beliefs, celebrate the same seven sacraments, and relive in the liturgy the life, death, and Resurrection of their Lord.

On the other hand, each believer experiences a unique journey of gradual conversion to the Lord. Often a Catholic person's sense of participation in the life of the community is directly affected by what she or he is experiencing in terms of personal faith development.

We have concentrated a great deal in the last three chapters on the communal dimensions of Catholic Christianity. We have discussed the nature of the Church, explored its Scriptures and Tradition, and reflected upon its worship. Hopefully your own understanding of the unique Catholic expression of Christian faith has been expanded and deepened through this discussion.

As we now move to bring this course to a close, we need to return to reflection upon the more individual dimension of Catholic Christianity. For if the Catholic faith is to have any true meaning for its members, it must speak to the hearts of believers as they grapple with the everyday issues of the Christian life:

- How can I grow in my own personal relationship with God?
- What does meeting God in prayer mean, and how can I do that in a way that satisfies me?
- What guidance can Catholic faith offer me as I confront the difficult issues of my daily life?

We will discuss these questions in the next and final chapter.

Review Questions

1. What is the relationship between words as signs and symbols as signs?
2. What is required if symbols are to be effective in communicating meaning?
3. What is the name given to symbols that are used by religions to convey religious meaning?
4. On what historical events are most religious celebrations based?
5. What three purposes do most religious celebrations have?
6. In what sense can we describe Jesus as the perfect sacrament of God?
7. How can the Church be described as the sacrament of Jesus?
8. Many Protestant churches accept only two sacraments. What are they? On what grounds does the Catholic Church accept seven sacraments?
9. Name the seven sacraments of the Catholic Church. Briefly describe the meaning of each.
10. The Catholic Church believes that the Risen Jesus is more clearly present in the sacraments than anywhere else. What does this mean?
11. Give one reason that the sacraments seem meaningless and empty to many Catholics.
12. Why would prehistoric people be more inclined than modern people to see God at work in nature?
13. Why do Jewish holy days last from one evening to the next, rather than from midnight to midnight as ours do?
14. In the order in which they occur, name the five seasons of the liturgical year.
15. On what theme does the Church focus during the Season of Advent?
16. What is the significance of the feast of the Epiphany?

17. What is the focus of the Church during the Season of Ordinary Time?

18. Of what do the forty days of Lent remind Christians? What does this season help Christians do? Why need this not be a sad time for believers?

19. What is the most important feast in the Church's liturgical calendar? Why?

20. What is the connecting theme between the close of the liturgical year and the beginning of the next liturgical year?

21. Out of what Jewish religious practice did Christian Sunday worship grow?

22. Why should we not be surprised that the worship of Catholic Christianity occasionally confuses us?

Key Terms
symbol
sacrament
Catholic sacraments
liturgical year

9

Spirituality and Morality:
Living by the Spirit
of Jesus

The discussions of Judaism and Catholicism in this course are organized according to each religion's *wisdom, worship,* and *works.* In chapter 7 we explored the Catholic Church's *wisdom* as it is found in the Scriptures and in Tradition. In chapter 8 we reflected on the *worship* of Catholicism as it is expressed both in the sacramental life of the Church and through its liturgical year.

In this last chapter, then, we turn to a discussion of the *works* of Catholic Christianity—the works by which Catholics live out their faith. Daily living is the true testing ground of religious faith. For within the tasks and challenges of day-by-day living, we discover how faith contributes to life. So this chapter, which may prove to be the most important one in the entire course, deals with this essential question: What difference can Catholic Christianity make in a person's everyday life?

Time to Turn Around

A delightful Jewish story will help us begin our reflection upon the personal significance of Catholic Christianity.

> Long, long ago a desperately poor man yearned to escape the agony of his wretched existence. He dreamed of a magical, heavenly city far away where all his pain would be dispelled and all his wishes fulfilled.
>
> One day, with some fear but also with great hope, the poor man decided to go in search of the magical city of his dreams. With little regret he left his miserable home, kissed his wife and children good-bye, and began his journey.

Summarize what the opening story means to you by creating a brief motto or moral of your own.

The man walked all morning and through the heat of midday. Near nightfall he decided to stop. He ate a crust of bread, said his prayers to Yahweh, and prepared to sleep. In his simple innocence he took off his shoes and placed them directly in the middle of the path on which he had been walking, carefully pointing the shoes in the direction that he had been traveling. In this way he felt sure that the next day he would begin his walk in the proper direction toward the magical city of his dreams.

While the poor man slept, a practical joker passed by the spot and came upon the shoes on the path. The joker turned the shoes around so that they were now pointing back toward the direction from which the poor man had come. When he awoke the next morning, the man thanked Yahweh for the gift of a new day, ate another crust of bread, stepped into his shoes, and resumed his trek to the heavenly city of his dreams.

The man walked throughout the morning and through the heat of midday. Finally, as evening fell, he looked off into the distance and his heart leapt as he saw the skyline of the magical city. The city was not nearly as large as he had expected. In fact, it seemed vaguely familiar. Yet with great expectation the man passed through the gates. As he walked through the city he came upon a street that looked strangely like the one on which he used to live. He walked down the street, and he came upon a house that looked very much like the one he had left. He knocked on the door of the home, rejoiced when the family that lived there greeted him with great affection, and lived happily ever after in the heavenly city of his dreams.

Like all great stories, this one has many layers of meaning. On one level, it suggests that we will find the deepest kind of happiness not in dreaming of faraway places but, rather, in accepting and treasuring life as we experience it each day. A popular poster expresses this message when it proclaims, "Bloom where you are planted."

A related theme is that each of us needs a joker in our life—that is, someone who can almost literally turn us around in our tracks when we stray in the wrong direction in our search for meaning and happiness.

For some people, Jesus has served as this "joker in the night" in that his life and message can turn people around and

"Bloom where you are planted."

head them in the direction of happiness. Two elements of Jesus' teachings are especially noteworthy.

1. The Kingdom of God Within

If Jesus were asked to sum up the meaning of the story of the man in search of the heavenly city, what would he say? In Luke's Gospel we hear Jesus telling the Pharisees that "the Kingdom of God is among you" (Luke 17:21). Some versions of the Bible translate this phrase as "the Kingdom of God is within you."

What did Jesus mean by this teaching? The kingdom theme in Jesus' preaching is very complex and rich in meaning, but this passage suggests that we will ultimately discover God by looking deep within our own hearts. When we stop trying to be what we are not and instead accept and embrace who we are, we will then discover not only our true selves but also God. As in our opening story, Jesus' teaching stresses that we must look at our present circumstances with new eyes.

2. A Change of Heart and Mind

In Mark's Gospel, we find a related insight into Jesus' understanding of the Kingdom of God. This insight is also connected to our opening story. In Mark, we find this statement: "After John [the Baptist] had been arrested, Jesus went into Galilee. There he proclaimed the gospel from God saying, 'The time is fulfilled, and the kingdom of God is close at hand. Repent, and believe the gospel'" (Mark 1:14–15).

The Greek word that Mark used for "repent" literally means to "turn around" or to change one's direction. This turning around refers to a deeply personal change of direction—that is, a change of heart or a change of mind. Jesus taught that, if people hope to fully experience the Kingdom of God, they must not only see God within themselves but also within others. In Christian theology, this change of heart and mind is called conversion.

Jesus' teaching stresses that we must look at our present circumstances with new eyes.

The Catholic Understanding of Conversion

Various Christian churches understand conversion in different ways. If you have watched some of the preachers on Sunday morning television programs, for example, you have heard conversion described as a dramatic, very emotional moment in believers' lives when they "accepted Jesus as their Lord and

Savior." Or perhaps at the door of your home or even in a public place, someone has asked you directly, "Have you been saved? Have you turned your life over to Jesus?" Some Christians can even provide a specific date and time when they asked Jesus into their hearts.

On some television programs, you may have heard conversion to Christian faith described as a dramatic, emotional moment.

▼

Watch a broadcast of a fundamentalist television program, noting especially any references to the experience of conversion. Then write a one-page essay explaining the meaning of conversion as described in that program. You may want to include reference to a personal conversion story if one was shared by someone on the show.

Certainly God can touch the minds and the hearts of people in dramatic and deeply moving personal experiences. Yet most Christians are rather uncomfortable with these understandings of conversion. The long-standing Catholic view of **conversion** is that it is a very gradual, lifelong process in which the person of faith turns to God as the center of his or her life. This process can be filled with many turns and twists, with hopeful leaps forward and fearful steps backward, with moments of intense closeness to God and times of deep loneliness and confusion.

In the Catholic tradition, therefore, conversion is understood as very similar to the process of human development on all other levels of life. That is, each of us must grow through childhood, adolescence, and years of adulthood before we can achieve full maturity. In the same way, only gradually can people choose, freely and consciously, to live out a faith in Jesus.

Christian Faith: A Love Relationship with God

In chapter 3, we discussed religious faith as the sense of trust people have in a power beyond themselves, in a supreme being or creator of the universe, whom we call God. We then went on to talk about religious faith as a deeply personal relationship between people and their God.

Later, in chapter 6, this broad understanding of religious faith was applied to the particular beliefs of Christians. We found that Christian faith can be defined as the human response of people to the unconditional love of God as revealed in Jesus. At that point the following statement was made: "That response, an intellectual assent to the truth of Jesus' message, is also a response of the heart and ultimately of the total person. The Christian, quite simply, has fallen in love with God as revealed in the life, death, and Resurrection of Jesus."

We can gain many insights into the process of conversion by reflecting on this notion of Christian faith as a love relationship between the believer and God. Love relationships—whether they are between parents and children, between good friends, or within couples—share common characteristics. By reflecting on the common characteristics of other love relationships, we can learn many things about conversion as a growing relationship with God. Let's explore some of these characteristics.

We can learn about conversion by reflecting on Christian faith as a love relationship.

Love Is a Developing Relationship

The word *love* has many meanings in our society. We use the word to describe our feelings about food ("I just love ice cream!"), clothes ("Don't you just love that outfit?"), music, sports, and pets. The list is endless. Coming to a thorough description of the meaning of love in terms of human relationships could therefore require another course! Yet our concern here is not to define love but to reflect on what it can teach us

Leaf through any popular magazine, taking notes on any advertising or article titles that make direct or indirect reference to love. Try to summarize the basic meaning of love as revealed in the magazine.

Choose one of your relationships—one that is characterized by caring and commitment. Then, for each of the four traits of love relationships listed to the right, offer one example of how that trait has been experienced or expressed in your relationship.

Love relationships often start with a special moment.

about faith. So let's simply assume for this discussion that we are speaking here of love as a relationship between persons that is based on caring and commitment.

Notice that this definition can include many more relationships than just the sexual or romantic ones that we usually associate with the idea of love. This use of the term *love relationship* includes most relationships within families or between friends of the same sex—all of which include caring and commitment.

Now let's get back to the characteristics mentioned above. Four traits seem to occur in the development of our love relationships:

1. The relationship often begins on a special note.
2. The persons then grow in knowledge of one another.
3. That knowledge leads to a commitment.
4. Finally, the commitment to love is continually renewed and deepened.

A Special Start

Think for a moment about a person about whom you care. This choice may be difficult—you may care about your parents very deeply in one way, a grandparent in another way, your best friend in still a different way. Any such choice is fine for this exercise.

Now think about the way in which that relationship developed. Obviously you began by somehow meeting the person. If the person about whom you are thinking is a parent that initial meeting is not one you can recall—you were a bit too young at the time! Nevertheless, that relationship had a beginning that may have seemed like a miracle to your parents.

If the person whom you are considering is now your best friend, you may be able to recall very clearly where you were when you met, what you were doing at the time, what you talked about, and so on.

In any event, the relationship started somewhere at some particular time, and very likely the first meeting set a special tone for the relationship. Married couples, for example, often look back at their first meeting as a case of love at first sight. Something clicked in their minds and hearts that made marriage later on seem a natural result.

A Growing Knowledge

In your relationship, you next went through a process of gradually getting to know that person. This aspect of all love relationships is delightful yet often difficult. With people like your parents, this growth in knowledge has been so gradual—so much a part of your daily life—that you may not even be conscious of it. Yet compare your knowledge of your parents now to what it was when you were four years old: you have learned much about them and they about you.

Compare your knowledge of your parents now to what it was when you were four years old.

Growth in knowledge has also taken place with your best friend. You may even now be experiencing long conversations with your friend in which you share all kinds of ideas and dreams. Perhaps you and your friend have had occasional arguments—followed by the wonderful experience of overcoming the problem and again becoming comfortable with each other. All love relationships include this kind of growing knowledge and understanding.

An Eventual Commitment

Another characteristic of all love relationships is that they require decisions and commitments. Even in family relationships this is true because simply living together is no guarantee of the presence of love. Parents have to demonstrate very clearly that they love their children. In the same way, children eventually arrive at a point when they must decide whether to respond to that love or to reject it.

Many people have found that the full experience of love for their parents is only possible when they themselves become independent adults. Possibly your parents never felt like friends with their own parents (your grandparents) until they were independent and experiencing the joys and trials of raising their own families. The reason is that love demands freely made decisions. That kind of freedom is difficult to experience when we are dependent on our parents for food, clothing, and shelter—much less our spending money!

So love relationships demand a freely made commitment. In the case of your relationship with your best friend, you may even be able to identify the time when that commitment became very clear to you. You may have said to yourself, "Hey, this is a great person, and I'm really lucky to have him or her for a friend!" The decision need not always be that conscious or that clear-cut, but it will always be present in a love relationship.

A Continual Growth

Finally, a love relationship continues to develop and grow. A marvelous characteristic of lasting love is that it can continually grow because the two people never stop growing themselves and never stop discovering new things about each other. The longer that we care for someone, the more aware we are that each human being is an infinite and changing mystery.

Perhaps you have grandparents who have been married forty or even sixty years and who still genuinely enjoy each other. They may have arguments, they certainly experience times when they do not feel close to each other, and they have confronted all kinds of difficulties in their lives. Nevertheless, they have repeatedly made the decision to love, and therefore they are able to continually deepen their relationship.

A love relationship grows because the two people never stop growing as individuals.

You have likely experienced ongoing growth in your own love relationships. Perhaps you have never felt closer to your parents than you do right now, for example. Or maybe you have found that you like your best friend even more today than you did a month ago. Love makes that kind of growth possible, and that kind of growth makes love last.

Christian Faith Is a Developing Love Relationship

What does all this discussion of the stages of love mean in terms of a faith relationship with God? The point is simple yet profound: if Christian faith is a response to the love of God, it shares many of the characteristics of every other love relationship. We have seen that, although each relationship we experience is unique, our friendships and our other love relationships share common characteristics or patterns of development. We meet another person, we grow in knowledge of the other, we make a decision to respect and care for the other, and then the relationship grows deeper. So it is with Christian faith. Certainly each person experiences a unique relationship with God. Yet common characteristics seem to exist in the development of faith.

Christian Faith Begins Somewhere

Obviously faith must begin by somehow meeting God. Exactly when that happens may not be easily remembered. As in our relationships with parents, the origins of an individual's faith relationship may be hidden in a cloudy past. This would be particularly true when a family exposes a young child to many outward expressions of faith. Such expressions may include meal prayers, bedtime prayers, stories about Jesus, examples of Christian conviction by parents. These childhood experiences of faith can be so much a part of family life that a person never becomes fully conscious of their importance.

On the other hand, someone who recently became aware of the presence of God—perhaps through a very powerful religious experience of sacred Mystery—will often be able to identify precisely when his or her faith became real and recognizable. This stage in the development of a faith relationship with God might be what some Christians identify as the moment of conversion, the point at which they can say they met Jesus.

The insights offered by the community of believers must be confirmed in a person's own life.

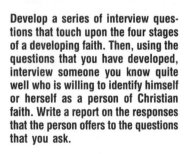

Develop a series of interview questions that touch upon the four stages of a developing faith. Then, using the questions that you have developed, interview someone you know quite well who is willing to identify himself or herself as a person of Christian faith. Write a report on the responses that the person offers to the questions that you ask.

Christian Faith Requires Knowledge

Once a faith relationship with God begins, a believer's knowledge of God must continue to grow. Catholic Christians often learn about God from their parents and then gradually become more involved in the larger religious community. Typically, Catholics celebrate Eucharist in the parish, listen to the reading of the Scriptures, experience the Sacrament of Reconciliation and perhaps Confirmation, attend weddings and baptisms, and so on. Catholics may also attend formal religion classes, either in a Catholic grade school or in a parish program. Slowly the knowledge of God and of Christian faith grows and matures.

Remember another point that has been stressed in this course: faith in God is not simply an intellectual issue; it is also a matter of the heart. Formal religious education and religious celebrations within a community of other believers offer marvelous insights into God. Yet these insights must eventually be confirmed in a person's private perspective on life—in his or her reflecting on life experiences, in encountering God in the wonders of creation, in sensing Jesus' Spirit within human relationships, and so on. Once a Christian acquires a personal worldview in which Jesus is Lord, he or she is ready for the next stage in the development of faith.

Christian Faith Demands a Commitment

This next stage is one you may not have experienced yet. This stage of decision is the moment when the Christian makes a commitment to assume responsibility for living according to the values of the Gospel. A very important point must be made in this regard: just as we cannot be forced to love another person, so we cannot be forced to love God enough to decide to be a Christian. Every Christian arrives at this moment on a unique schedule and by a unique route.

For example, you may be at a level of understanding about God where a firm decision about faith is just not possible. You may simply want to think more about faith or learn more specifics about Christian faith. Perhaps you are experiencing doubts and have a lot of questions about your faith that you want answered. The point is this: whatever position that you take in terms of your faith in God is perfectly acceptable, assuming that your search for truth is honest. No typical or average faith relationship exists.

Many people, young and old alike, suffer needless guilt when they have religious doubts. In fact, these doubts are very common during the development of religious faith. We must also remember that God's love is not dependent on the feelings of people. God loves unconditionally and without expectations.

On the other hand, you may feel good about your faith relationship with God and confident about your religious convictions. If so, these qualities make you neither better than others nor abnormal. To repeat: we are each totally unique, and that uniqueness is a treasure.

Every person arrives at the decision to be a Christian on a unique schedule and by a unique route.

Christian Faith Keeps on Growing

Once the decision is made to accept the love of God, the love relationship that we call faith becomes a lifelong process of continual growth and development. As is true with other love relationships, growth in faith will not always be easy. This growth includes both high points and low points, moments of great joy and severe doubt, times of intense closeness to God and times of great loneliness.

Yet this growth process is not boring and routine. Faith in God lived out with conviction and openness is exciting and fulfilling. "I have come so that they may have life," promised Jesus, "and have it to the full" (John 10:10). The believer knows that Jesus is true to that promise. In Christian faith, the believer is involved in a love relationship with sacred Mystery—that is, with a God whose infinite wonder and love expels boredom.

Learning to Live by the Spirit of Jesus

If you did the reflection activity suggested on page 252, illustrate how your friend or loved one has exhibited each of the qualities identified to the right as central to the art of loving. That is, give examples of how she or he has demonstrated openness, sensitivity, strength, and creativity.

Many people feel that loving is simply a natural human instinct, a spontaneous response to the love of another person. So the thought of learning how to love or of practicing love seems ridiculous to them. Yet loving is an art and so requires four of the same qualities demanded in learning other forms of art:

- openness—a willingness to learn and to change
- sensitivity—an ability to understand; in the case of loving, an ability to understand the needs of the one whom we love
- strength—the energy to undertake a lot of hard work
- creativity—specifically, a talent for finding new ways to express love and to respond to the loved one's needs

Any kind of art can be learned only with much guidance, and excellence can be achieved only with much practice. The same is true with the art of loving. Perhaps this is why we view those people who love well as special, even heroic. We know that they have achieved excellence in an art that demands tremendous skill and effort.

Developing a Christian Spirituality

As a love relationship with God, religious faith, if it is to achieve any real depth, demands the kind of hard work required by other forms of loving. Like the ability to love, faith is an art that requires a willingness to learn from personal experience, a sensitivity to the many ways God is revealed in life, a desire to make daily efforts at community building, and a creativity in responding to God's revelation.

The art of living out one's faith in God in unique, individual ways is called **personal spirituality**. Each person develops a personal spirituality according to his or her particular needs, abilities, and background. If it is a **Christian spirituality**, it centers around a common theme from Jesus' life and message as revealed in the Christian Testament. Namely, the Christian is called to live by the Spirit of Jesus.

Throughout the Gospels, we see that Jesus himself was led by the Spirit. He promised to send a Spirit who would lead people to truth, and then he shared that Spirit at Pentecost. The signs of the presence of that Spirit are identified in Saint Paul's letter to the Galatians: "The fruit of the Spirit is love, joy, peace, patience, kindness, goodness, trustfulness, gentleness and self-control" (5:22). How does a Christian learn to live by the Spirit?

That is, how can someone gain the openness, sensitivity, strength, and creativity to follow the impulses of that Spirit in daily life?

If Christians are to continually grow in their ability to respond to the love of God, they must take on the following four tasks:

1. Christians must constantly seek better knowledge of the meaning and message of Jesus.
2. They must then deepen their understanding through personal prayer.
3. They must also support and gain encouragement from other believers in the community of faith that is the Church.
4. Finally, Christians must reach out in loving service to the people around them.

Faith is an art that requires a desire to make daily efforts at community building.

These four tasks—centered on knowledge, prayer, community, and service—are at the heart of Christian spirituality. Let's explore each of these in greater depth.

Growing in Knowledge of Jesus' Life and Message

A growing love relationship with anyone requires a constantly growing understanding between the people involved. The initial knowledge that one gains of a person can lead to the commitment of love. That love in turn often drives a person to seek more understanding of the loved one.

The same is true about faith in God: A basic knowledge about Jesus and his message is required before the personal decision about faith can be made. Yet after that decision has been made, an almost unquenchable thirst for more knowledge develops. How do Christians grow in their knowledge of Jesus? To whom do they turn for more information?

The School as a Source of Knowledge

To some extent these questions are immediately answered by the situation in which you now find yourself—as a student attending a Catholic high school. The most obvious source of information about Christian faith for you as a student is the religious education provided by your school. Whether or not this will be an effective source is seemingly dependent upon two factors: (1) the quality of the courses you will take in religion and of the teachers who will direct them and (2) your openness and willingness to share personally in that process of education.

Admittedly, you have little or no control over the first factor. If you are blessed with good courses and teachers who can make faith come alive for you, be grateful for that gift. However, if a limited selection of courses or personality conflicts with individual teachers keep you from enjoying your religion classes, the process of learning can be difficult and you have little control over this.

The factor you *do* have control over, however, is your own response to the religious education that is offered you. Entering fully into the learning process—that is, listening to the opinions of others, sharing your own insights, thinking through the implications in your own life of what is taught, weighing alternative answers to the many questions a study of faith raises—can directly help to make your experience of formal religious education more enjoyable and beneficial.

Entering fully into the experience of learning can help to make formal religious education more enjoyable and beneficial.

The Bible as a Primary Source of Knowledge

Earlier in this course, we discussed at some length the central place of the Bible, particularly the Christian Testament, as a primary source of information about the message of Jesus. Reading the Bible with guidance, either by using sound study guides or by studying in the company of others who are recognized for their knowledge of and background in the Scriptures, will be best. However, although this caution remains valid, it should not keep you from your own private reading of the Scriptures.

Try this simple experiment: Keep a Bible next to your bed. Before falling asleep each night, read the Scriptures for just five minutes. Don't worry about analyzing what you read and don't feel that you must pray about it. Simply read for five minutes and then stop. You may find this exercise will develop into a very rewarding habit.

Where should you begin your reading of the Bible? One of the Gospels—preferably Mark's or Luke's—would seem most appropriate. If, after reading either one or both of these, you want to continue the practice of regularly reading the Bible, then you should ask your teacher or parish priest for a reading program to guide you.

The most influential source of information about the faith is simply other Christians.

If the thought of regular biblical reading does not appeal to you, take more advantage of the times when the Bible is read to you, particularly during the Mass. Listen as carefully as you can to what is read. Carry on a silent dialogue with the priest during his homily, asking yourself if you agree with or could add to his insights about the readings.

Finally, if you arrive at church prior to the start of Mass, look at and reflect on the scheduled readings for that day printed in the missalette. All these exercises can add greatly to your appreciation of the Bible as a marvelous source of knowledge about God.

In preparation for reacting to the next homily you will hear, imagine yourself as entering into a dialogue with the priest. Write a one-page response to the homily as if you were speaking directly to the priest.

The Community of Faith as a Source of Knowledge

Perhaps the most influential sources of information about the faith are simply other Christians who are willing to share their experiences. Christianity is not simply knowledge about someone or something. Rather, it is essentially a way of living, a lifestyle, a life stance that is based on a growing love relationship with God. Many other people are involved in this ongoing journey of faith—parents, teachers, and friends. Getting to know other Christians, listening to their stories of faith, and sharing one's own experiences with them can be an invaluable source of growth in the understanding of faith.

A comment might be added here as well about a characteristic of Christian spirituality that is particularly Catholic. The Catholic Church emphasizes more than other Christian Churches what is called the *communion of saints*. This term refers to the entire community of believers, both living and dead.

Christians at work in the world today offer loving service to others—service that deeply impresses even those who are not Christian. The inspiring work of Mother Teresa among the dying people of Calcutta, India, has rightly received much attention by the media. Yet each of us has likely met Christians whose goodness is so transparent that we would acknowledge them as saintly even if the world generally never honors them.

In their respect for holy people, however, Catholics more often revere saints who have died in service to the Lord. One dimension of the Catholic Church's liturgical year that we did not emphasize in our previous discussion is what is called the Church's *sanctoral cycle*. The Catholic Church celebrates most weekdays as the feastdays of particular saints. In its daily liturgies, the Catholic Church honors the memory of these individual saints who serve as striking models of faith for today's believers.

Because of their high regard for the saints of the past, Catholics have occasionally been accused of worshiping saints. Some people have suggested, for example, that instead of praying to God, Catholics pray to saints, especially to Mary the mother of Jesus. This interpretation of the Catholic understanding of the saints is inaccurate. Catholics do not venerate the saints *instead of* the Lord. Rather, Catholics look to and honor the saints *because of* what the Spirit of Jesus has accomplished through these special people. By looking at the works of the saints, Catholics discover both direction and encouragement as they work out a personal Christian spirituality.

Life as a Source of Knowledge

One's personal life experience is another vital source of knowledge about God and faith. God loves constantly and reveals sacred Mystery within life experiences. Reflecting on

Mother Teresa of Calcutta and Bishop Dom Helder Camara of Brazil serve as striking models for today's believers.

Determine who is your patron saint, that is, the saint after whom you were named. (If you were not named after a particular saint, choose one whom you would like to have as a patron.) Using resources from your school library, develop a brief biographical sketch of the saint. Be sure to note the day of the year on which the saint's feast is celebrated.

the glad and sad moments in daily life, being sensitive to world events, and then praying over these personal and social happenings in quiet reflection can provide a tremendous amount of insight about the journey of faith. Exercises like the keeping of a personal journal or diary can help a great deal in this regard. All in all, the opportunities for growing in the understanding of Jesus and his message are limited only by the imagination and the ambition of the individual. This growing knowledge is essential to the ongoing development of faith.

God loves constantly and reveals sacred Mystery within life experiences.

Deepening Knowledge Through Prayer

For a long time in the history of the Catholic Church, the most common definition of Christian faith was that it was an assent to truth, that is, an intellectual acceptance of the teachings of Jesus. The Church now teaches that such a view of faith in God is too narrow, too restricted to the intellectual level of life. Christian faith is much more than a mental exercise through which a person becomes comfortable with philosophical formulas and arguments. If faith in God were only that, a person's ability to grow in faith would be completely dependent upon his or her level of intelligence. Nothing could be further from the truth.

Believers need to learn as much as possible about faith, but if faith remains on the level of the intellectual beliefs, it is not faith in its fullest sense. Faith in God must go much deeper than the mind; it must touch the depths of the heart. The usual way that faith touches a person at this level is through the experience of prayer.

This chapter listed four ways in which Christians can grow in their knowledge of Jesus' life and message.
- List the four ways.
- Rank them according to how each meets your needs and desires.
- For each of the four ways, state two ways that you personally could increase your knowledge about Jesus.
- Write a brief summary of the results of this activity.

Prayer Is More Than Talking to God

Prayer is often thought about in the rather restricted sense of talking to God or saying prayers—as if prayer is simply a matter of repeating words in the hope that someone out there is listening to them. Thinking of prayer in a much fuller and more personal sense can help to improve our attitudes toward it.

One contemporary writer calls prayer "communication in a relationship of love." The word *communication* indicates that prayer is not a one-way process in which a person simply talks to God. Rather, communication implies that what is shared in prayer is a two-way exchange or dialogue. In a prayerful dialogue, the person shares his or her thoughts and feelings but also receives some feedback—that is, some kind of response from God. How does this happen?

Many times prayer does not require words.

The answer has much to do with the fact that the communication within prayer takes place within a relationship of love. People in love communicate in all sorts of ways, not just with words. Many times, in fact, words seem almost to get in the way of communication between friends. For example, many of us have had the experience of simply sitting for a long time in the presence of a friend without saying a thing. We might listen to music together, take a long walk in silence, or sit quietly by a lakeshore or on a hill, sharing a beautiful view. Does communication take place in such situations? Sure it does: we leave these encounters with friends feeling refreshed and also feeling closer than before.

Prayer works in a similar way. Some kinds of prayer, in other words, do not require words, and yet they are fulfilling dialogues rather than one-way monologues. We might ask, however: How does a person know that God listens? How does God talk back to the person praying? Let's explore some possible answers to these important questions.

Why Bother to Pray?

The conviction of believers is that God speaks all the time, communicating Mystery and inviting a response from people during each moment of their lives. The conviction that this is so is based purely on the belief that God truly loves us as individuals. Consider this: If you love someone, you need to be with that person, to share, to express yourself to him or her. If God loves, that love demands these same expressions.

If we do not believe that God loves us as individuals, of course, the whole idea of prayer becomes ridiculous. Why bother? God certainly does not need our nice words. If God does not care about us, all the talk in the world is not going to change the situation.

If we do believe that God loves us, on the other hand, not praying—not opening ourselves to the power and joy of a love that is without limits—would be silly.

Daily Life as the Content of Prayer

Because God loves each person individually, prayer must also be personal, unique, and centered on individual life experiences. So prayer can be a kind of dialogue with God simply about how life is going, about feelings, and about other relationships. We share these kinds of things in all love relationships.

How Does God Answer Prayers?

God's response to prayer will hardly be like a booming voice from out of a cloud! God responds to people in their inner selves and their inner needs because they reach out to God at that level. Consider the following examples:

- An attempt at prayer can open a person's mind and give him or her a better vision of life. God's response in prayer is therefore a clearer perception of what one's life is all about, where a person is going in life, and so on.
- God gives the power to live according to what one knows in the heart is true. Therefore God in prayer touches the will and strengthens a person's character.
- God calms the emotions in the experience of prayer, and prayer can bring peace to a confused mind and heart.

■ God in prayer can fire the imagination with new ideas, new possibilities, new ways of dealing with the world.

■ Finally, God can communicate through memories, allowing a person to learn from past mistakes and giving the encouragement needed to move into the future with hope.

Prayer can bring peace to a confused mind and heart.

Write a one-page description of an incident in which you or someone you know could claim that prayers had been answered by God. In light of the discussion of this topic, identify how God answered the prayers.

A believer can do much to improve prayer: exercises can be done, bodily positions can be assumed to help one pray, disciplined routines can clear one's mind for prayer, and so on. These methods are beyond the scope of this course; they may well form the content of an entire course during your religious education. The key principle to remember here, however, is that prayer is not only the recitation of memorized prayers at specific times and only in buildings constructed for that purpose. On the contrary, a person can pray all the time, simply by being in touch with daily life experiences and by trying to see God in them. God loves us constantly, and because of that love, God is with us all the time—loving, caring, and asking for a response in faith. Prayer is an essential part of that response, and an essential part of growth in spirituality.

Sharing Faith with the Community of Believers

The third dimension of spirituality is the practice of joining with others in the community of faith for mutual sharing, support, encouragement, and celebration. Jesus taught that faith in God is not to be a one-to-one relationship. In other words, Christian faith is not a matter of each believer living in isolation and pursuing a private relationship with God. Faith is ultimately a communal experience—that is, an experience that must be shared with others if it is to mature. That is precisely why the Church exists.

Christians have been called to live in community for two primary reasons:

1. The message of God's love promotes a sense of celebration. The believer has a desire to reach out to others in joy. When something great happens to us, we want to have a party, to get all the gang together to share our good fortune. This urge to celebrate one's blessings is one of the impulses for participating in the Church, the community of faith.

2. The actual living out of the message of Jesus can be very difficult. Trying to be all we can, trying to care for others, can be plain hard work, which cannot be done without the help of others who share our convictions. So the encouragement and support of other believers is vital.

These two reasons also serve to explain why the Catholic Church so strongly emphasizes the need for its members to gather for regular worship. The purpose of the weekly celebration of the Eucharist is not only to fulfill the duty to worship God. The Eucharist also is an opportunity for believers to celebrate their lives as Christians and to rededicate themselves to support one another in their mission to heal a suffering world.

The believer has a desire to reach out to others in joy.

The Church Is Believers, Not Buildings

The official gatherings of the Church are very important. Participation in the life of the Church takes place most visibly and directly through the sacramental life of the Church discussed in the preceding chapter. The sacraments allow Catholics to gather in community to reflect upon and celebrate the key events in their lives—the very events in which they discover God.

Yet the Church is not simply a place where people go to do certain things. Participation in the life of the Church takes place wherever believers live and act as persons of faith. Whenever Christians care for others, whenever they reach out with concern to those around them, the Church is present.

Parish Life as a Center of Communal Faith

Catholics engage in the sacraments primarily in parishes, which are often small communities that allow believers to get

A major concern of many parishes is that their high school students attending Catholic high schools lose their sense of belonging to the parish. Design a five-point plan for helping Catholic high school students remain in touch with the parish community.

The parish community will only be as alive as the faith of its members.

to know one another, to feel part of the same life experiences, and to develop friendships with one another. The parish also provides many opportunities beyond the sacraments and the other liturgical expressions of the Church. Examples include social events, service projects to help those is need, and a variety of programs to respond to specific needs in the parish. All these are opportunities for involvement in the community that we call Church.

A final note on this dimension of Christian spirituality: the parish community will only be as alive as the faith of its members. Unfortunately, many people view their parish communities as spiritual service stations: they go to Mass on the weekend to get filled up with enough spiritual fuel to get through the week.

This approach ignores the fact that people fuel the parish. The parish community is one in which individuals who are already growing in their spirituality come together to share the fruits of that experience and to celebrate it with others. People must participate in parish life, therefore, with an attitude of giving as well as getting. Strangely enough, the more that parishioners give, the more they gain in the gifts of the Spirit.

Reaching Out in Service to Others

Finally, mature Christian spirituality demands that believers seek personal growth for more than their own happiness and that of their local community. Indeed, the entire thrust of the message of Jesus is that Christians must always be using their talents to reach out to a wounded world—a world that desperately needs the healing touch of love.

Too many Christians feel that they are responsible for only themselves and for their own development. They figure that if they avoid doing bad things, they have done all that is asked of them. This is simply not the case. Christian spirituality is more than avoiding the bad. Rather, it is a matter of doing the good by stretching beyond one's own interests to help others. A major part of this attitude of service is a sincere concern that all people be treated with justice. Everyone must do as much as possible to alleviate the monumental problems of world hunger, for example, and work toward the time when the world can truly live in peace.

Can One Person Make a Difference?

Confronting the worldwide problems of justice and peace is an awesome task. These issues can seem so incredibly tough that a person can wonder about ever having an impact on them. The result can be feelings of frustration and despair. Such feelings can be particularly strong for adolescents who are also caught up in personal struggles concerning identity and relationships. How can someone who is already worried about getting a passing grade in a course or about resolving a conflict with a parent take on issues such as nuclear disarmament or world hunger? Some young people simply assume that these are adult issues for which adolescents are not responsible. Other adolescents, who want dearly to help eliminate social evils, experience great frustration or discouragement resulting from a sense of powerlessness.

Confronting the worldwide problems of justice and peace is an awesome task.

Actually young people can perform effective actions in the struggle against social injustice. To be effective, however, these actions require that young persons have a proper perspective, a willingness to work with others, and an understanding of their special abilities and talents.

Taking a proper perspective: Social evils such as poverty, world hunger, and racism can seem like monsters over which people have no control. Yet each of these social problems involves and affects individuals with names and faces, living in families in identifiable communities. The point is that we can deal with major social problems by confronting or helping an individual person in a particular way. We cannot hope to change an evil social system overnight, but we can begin to dismantle the system by dealing with one person right now.

Working with others: Caring, committed individuals working together can have widespread and long-range influence over the social conditions that oppress people. So participation in helping communities like the Church is important. Another reason for working with others is to gain a sense of support and affirmation. If we hope to have the strength to care for the needs of others, we must have our own needs met by people who care for us.

Understanding abilities and talents: We cannot share ourselves with others if we are not convinced that we have something of value to share. In evaluating our talents, we must not define the term *talent* too narrowly. For example, a sense of humor is a marvelous talent. Also, everyone treasures people who are good listeners. These are both tremendous gifts to offer to a group committed to the struggle against social injustice. The following list includes personality traits, all of which underlie important talents:

With a pencil, lightly circle all those qualities from the list of personality traits that you feel you possess to some degree. Then identify a service activity at your school in which the qualities that you have circled would be of value.

cooperative	loyal	encouraging
determined	enthusiastic	farsighted
joyful	attentive	outgoing
perceptive	responsible	generous
honest	persistent	thoughtful
persuasive	warmhearted	open-minded
imaginative	serious	practical
reliable	realistic	artistic
friendly	insightful	creative
logical	sympathetic	energetic

A major task of adolescents is to pursue educational plans that will strengthen their skills, uncover new talents, and thus expand their general ability to serve.

Can one person make a difference? Read the story of Trevor Ferrell on pages 272–273 for one inspiring example of a young person committed to the service of others. Of course, not everyone can hope to achieve the results that this incredible young man did. Few of us will have movies made of our lives or receive awards from a president or be invited to go to India to meet Mother Teresa. Yet each of us can have a positive effect on the lives of those around us. If millions of people made a commitment to do just that—remember that the Catholic Church alone has over 800 million members—the evil social structures that enslave so many people would begin to collapse.

Recall the story of the poor man at the beginning of this chapter. He felt that he had to leave home to solve his problems. Similarly, many Christians believe that the only way to engage in service to others is to travel to distant lands to work with poor and suffering people.

Working with others helps us gain a sense of support and affirmation.

In reality, that challenge is so demanding that most people cannot accept it. Again, the result is a feeling of helplessness. The opening story hinted at a different view, however. Heaven is to be found by discovering the richness of our own lives as they are. We do not need to look beyond our own homes and neighborhoods for opportunities to serve. The primary responsibility of Christians is to love those nearest to them. Christian service can be demonstrated just as truly by resolving conflicts peacefully at home as by marching against war. Likewise, Christian service can be demonstrated just as clearly in a kind word to a lonely classmate as in the gift of money to poor people. What can one person do? Mow the lawn or shop for groceries for a shut-in in the neighborhood. Read a book to a blind person. Offer to baby-sit for free for the single parent down the street. The more that we learn to love and care for

It all began one night in December 1983, when Trevor Ferrell was eleven. He and his parents were watching a news program about the growing population of homeless people in the United States. Trevor's immediate response was like many of ours when we hear about the more than two million Americans sleeping in subway and bus stations, in parks and abandoned buildings, and on the street curb.

"How can so many people be hungry and homeless in a country as rich as the United States?" we ask. "How can other people stand by and watch the pain and misery of these human beings?"

But Trevor realized something that many of us miss. "Other people" includes anyone who says,

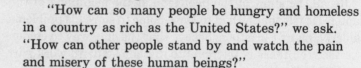

"Someone should do something" and then turns the channel, forgetting it until the next time. Instead, Trevor asked himself, "What can I do?" and then set about finding the answers.

The news show reported that Philadelphia alone had a homeless population of about ten thousand. At Trevor's insistence, the Ferrells drove eighteen miles to Philadelphia that night. "It was scary," says Trevor, "but I just went up to this street person and said, 'Here's a blanket for you and God bless you.' He looked at me and said 'Thanks very much . . . and God bless you.' "

Anyone else, eleven-year-old or thirty-year-old, might have been satisfied with this initial effort. But Trevor's desire to help was only increased by this late-night visit to Philadelphia. Trevor and his family continued to go out on the street, offering whatever they could get from relatives, neighbors, and friends to a grateful handful of homeless people. Their efforts were boosted eventually by their local parish, and soon other people, inside and outside of Pennsylvania, began to pitch in. Trevor's Campaign, as it came to be called, drew the attention of the nation, and then the world.

Through the help of many volunteers, the gesture made by the Ferrells on a winter's night continues years later as a van carrying food, blankets, and clothing makes "runs" into Philadelphia each night. Local chapters of Trevor's Campaign have grown nationwide.

And Trevor's Campaign doesn't only feed people. A large part of his program is geared toward helping the homeless get back on their feet. At Trevor's Place, a renovated building donated by a local church, up to

CAMPAIGN

one hundred homeless people are given shelter and, with the help of social workers, are assisted in finding new jobs and homes of their own.

As a leader, not only among those fighting the battle against hunger and poverty but among teens, Trevor has some definite ideas on what teens could be doing to make a difference. First, says Trevor, "Get involved. There are Salvation Armies and other groups who feed the homeless. Call these organizations in your area. Or, if you like to talk to people, find out where you can volunteer to read to blind people or to the elderly."

Whatever Trevor does in the future, one thing is certain: he has made a lasting impression on us all. His example teaches a lesson to teens and adults alike: within each individual is an incredible power to touch the lives of many. There is a Trevor Ferrell in all of us, and it's up to each of us to find him. (Adapted from Lee Radovich, "Trevor's Campaign," *Catholic Teen Magazine*)

274

Spirituality and Morality

The more that we learn to care for those nearest to us, the more likely we are to find ways to influence the lives of those far away from us.

A friend shares the following thought with you: "The world is so messed up that there is no point in trying to change it. Sometimes I just want to give up on life." Write a letter to your friend in response to his or her statement.

those nearest to us, the more likely we are to eventually find ways to influence the lives of those far away from us.

Most Catholic high schools provide opportunities for involvement in Christian service. Organized efforts for serving others on both a local and a global level are common in many schools. You might initiate or participate in some of the following activities:

- Join a walk to raise money for the Campaign for Human Development or for Oxfam, both of which support self-help projects worldwide.
- Organize a booth for career day to provide information on peacemaking professions.
- Volunteer in a soup kitchen or in a shelter for the homeless.

- Work on a school program to recognize the contributions of Martin Luther King, Jr.
- Start a letter-writing campaign or petition drive to make a state or national legislator aware of a particular justice issue.
- Begin a school group to study peace and justice issues.

Investigating such opportunities can help you discover how your particular talents and abilities can be of help in these efforts.

Christian Morality and Christian Spirituality

No comment has been made to this point about a central issue in Christian spirituality: Christian morality. Morality generally deals with decisions about right and wrong behavior. **Christian morality** deals with these issues in the context of Jesus' teaching about God's love and the human response to that love. We live in a world in which many Christian values have been seriously challenged. Young people today confront enormous difficulties with issues such as sexual promiscuity, the abuse of alcohol and drugs, cheating in the classroom, and so on. The burden on all those who are sincerely trying to live according to Christian values can be immense.

We do not have the space here to deal at length with these kinds of issues. A full understanding of and appreciation for Catholic Christian moral values and their impact in the lives of believers requires much investigation and discussion. This will very likely be the focus of an entire course in your high school religion curriculum.

Yet some very basic information on the meaning of Christian morality can be provided here. For example, people who sincerely strive to develop their personal spirituality along the lines presented in this chapter will be virtually guaranteed lives of moral conviction. In fact, true Christian morality cannot be understood apart from this commitment. The ways in which Christians choose to act in their daily lives directly reflect their belief that God unconditionally loves them and that they can best respond to that love by caring for others. Christian morality is, then, a result, or an end product, of a commitment to live out these values.

Your school might give you the opportunity to work on a program to recognize the contributions of Martin Luther King, Jr.

Young people today confront issues such as sexual promiscuity, the abuse of alcohol and drugs, and cheating in the classroom.

Making Moral Decisions as a Christian

In striving to make good decisions about tough moral issues, Christians look for guidance outside themselves as well as within their own hearts. This chart attempts to summarize both dimensions of the process of decision-making.

▶ Step 1: Define the Issue

Begin by defining the issue at hand as clearly as possible. In some cases, such as abortion or the morality of capital punishment, this may require considerable study and reflection. In other cases, such as stealing or destroying property, the issue may be more easily understood.

▶ Step 2: Seek Advice

After defining the issue, look for outside resources for information and guidance. Among those resources are the following:
- the values and teachings of Jesus as found in the Christian Testament
- the formal teachings of the Church
- the advice of respected people who possess deep faith and obvious goodwill

▶ Step 3: Reflect Honestly on the Consequences

Reflect on the morality of certain actions, decisions, and attitudes in light of the results they are likely to cause. The adjacent chart reflects solid Christian values.

▶ Step 4: Pray for God's Guidance

In prayer, the believer weighs the results of all the reflection suggested by the previous steps. The Christian asks God to guide him or her to do what is right and to reject what is wrong.

Once the Catholic Christian has seriously considered a decision in light of guidelines such as these, he or she can act with confidence. Does this seem like a lot of work? Certainly. Yet, those who care enough to work at their moral decisions are able to live in dignity and peace.

Actions, decisions, and attitudes are

RIGHT OR MORAL

when they produce all or some of the following results in the one acting or in those who are affected by the actions:
1. an increase in the ability to trust others
2. greater honesty in all relationships
3. a lessening of the sense of separation
4. an increase in an attitude of cooperation
5. a greater sense of self-respect
6. a stronger belief that people are generous and caring
7. a feeling of peace and joy in life

Actions, decisions, and attitudes are

WRONG OR IMMORAL

when they produce all or some of the following results in the one acting or in those who are affected by the actions:
1. an increase in suspicion
2. a feeling of phoniness in all relationships
3. a feeling of isolation or loneliness
4. an increase in useless competition
5. feelings of guilt and embarrassment
6. a stronger belief that people are greedy and selfish
7. a feeling that life is lousy

Making Moral Decisions as a Christian

How might a Christian act out faith in the daily circumstances of life? What kind of qualities characterize the believer who is trying to live the values of Jesus? How might the sincere Catholic go about deciding what is right or wrong in a particular situation? These, again, are complex questions requiring much study and discussion. However, some general guidelines regarding Christian moral decision-making can be helpful. The chart on page 277 attempts to summarize these in a simple and understandable way. Read the chart carefully and reflectively. Try to apply it to particular situations in which you have found yourself struggling to decide what is right or wrong. If time permits, your class may engage in applying the principles reflected in the chart to specific moral issues of concern to the class as a whole.

Choose one major moral issue confronting young people. Write a brief explanation of how young people could respond to the issue in light of the decision-making guide provided on page 277.

A Final Word: The Catholic School

You have come to the end of a lengthy process. While studying this book and sharing classroom activities, you have reviewed the essential dimensions of the Catholic Christian faith. You have learned that faith in God is not a flight of fancy but a sensible worldview. You know now that Christian faith, in particular, has stood the test of time and has touched the lives of countless millions of people. These individuals, motivated by the reality of God's love in their lives, have dramatically influenced the course of history. Where the Church goes in the future will be directly affected by the faith and works of all those who are Christians today.

As a student in a Catholic high school, you have a rare and wonderful chance to prepare yourself now for having an impact on the future. Try to see your high school career as a whole, as an integrated pattern of opportunities to grow in faith. You will be taking many religion courses, each of which can be an important step in your growth.

Yet that is only part of the story. Religion classes will allow you to reflect on Christian faith in a directed, organized way, but the study of religion alone cannot be viewed as a complete measure of one's personal Christian development. Many

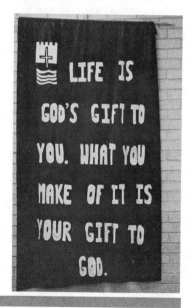

LIFE IS GOD'S GIFT TO YOU. WHAT YOU MAKE OF IT IS YOUR GIFT TO GOD.

Where the Church goes in the future will be directly affected by the faith and works of all those who are Christians today.

students have received perfect grades in religion classes throughout their school careers but have never acted on what they learned—they have never tried to live the implications of the message of Jesus in their personal lives. At the same time, many students who have had to struggle just to attain average grades in religion courses have lived the lives of true saints.

So your formal religion classes are only one facet of the opportunity for growth afforded by your school. You may also develop close friendships with many others—students and teachers alike. You will have many chances to gain experience of Christian community: You will be able to learn, to play, to pray, and to grow with others. You will be able to develop and share your talents with that school community. All of this is part of the Christian education afforded by the Catholic school. The high school years, it is commonly said, are among the most enjoyable and exciting of our lives. That can be a cliché, but such comments become commonplace only because they are true.

Write a letter to an imaginary eighth-grade student who will be taking this course next year. In light of your experience, advise the student on what to expect.

During your high school years, you will be able to learn, to play, to pray, and to grow with others.

Early in this course we discussed the fact that the adolescent years involve the greatest surge of growth and change that you will likely ever experience. Your body will change and develop rapidly. You will experience deeper friendships with others. You will grow in your ability to experience God and to share that experience with others. You have begun a marvelous journey. I wish you well as you pursue it.

Review Questions

1. Identify two possible meanings for the story of the poor man in search of the magical city of his dreams.

2. What two elements of Jesus' teaching relate to the story of the poor man? How does each element relate to the story?

3. What is the long-standing view of conversion within the Catholic Church?

4. Name the four traits that occur in the development of most love relationships.

5. Why is the full experience of a child's love for a parent often only possible when the child leaves home?

6. What are four common characteristics that seem to be present in every faith relationship?

7. Why is much of the guilt about religious doubts described as needless guilt?

8. What four qualities are required if a person is to grow in the art of loving?

9. Around what common theme from Jesus' life and message does Christian spirituality center?

10. Identify the four tasks in which Christians must engage if they are to grow in their ability to respond to the love of God.

11. What factor can students control in terms of their experience of formal religious education?

12. What is the meaning of the *communion of saints?* What role can this play in the development of one's personal spirituality?

13. How would you respond to a non-Catholic person who claims that Catholics worship the saints?

14. What definition of prayer is quoted in this chapter? Briefly compare this definition to the more common notion of prayer.

15. Explain why and how one can pray without using words.

16. Why might a person refuse to pray?
17. How does God answer prayers?
18. What are two reasons that Christians have been called to live in community with other believers?
19. What is wrong with the notion of the parish as a kind of spiritual service station?
20. State three qualities that people need to become positively involved in actions on behalf of social justice.
21. What does Christian morality mean?

Key Terms

conversion
Christian spirituality

Glossary

Pronunciation Key

ə	abut, was, above
a	mat, air
ā	fade, day
ä	farther, guard
e	bet
ē	key
i	tip
ī	fine
ō	boat
ù	pull, wolf
ü	flu
′	A stress mark precedes a syllable with primary stress.

Abba (′əb-bə). A uniquely intimate name for God used by Jesus. Best translated into English as "daddy," "papa," or "dada." Expresses the belief that God cares for people like a loving father.

Acts of the Apostles. A book of the Christian Testament, an extension of Luke's Gospel, depicting life in the early Christian community and the spread of the Christian faith through the travels and teaching of Saint Paul and others.

Adolescence (ad-əl-′es-ənts). The transitional stage in human development between childhood and adulthood.

Anorexia nervosa (an-ə-′rek-sē-ə-nər-′vō-sə). An eating disorder in which a person literally starves himself or herself out of fear of gaining weight. Ten to fifteen percent of sufferers of this disease die.

Apparitions. The appearances of Jesus to his followers after his death and Resurrection.

Ascension. The event in which Jesus, following his Resurrection and apparitions, disappeared from the physical world and passed totally into the presence of God.

Atheists ('ā-thē-əsts). People who deny the existence of God.

Bishops. The church leaders whose role and authority are based on that of the Apostles in the early Church. Literally means "overseer." In today's Church, bishops are leaders of dioceses.

Book of Revelation. The last book of the Bible—a visionary and highly symbolic work attributed to John, the author of the fourth Gospel. Also known as the Apocalypse.

Bulimia (byü-'lim-ē-ə). An eating disorder involving binge eating, in which sufferers gorge themselves and then use laxatives or force themselves to vomit.

Christian faith. The particular form of religious faith understood as the human response of believers to the unconditional love of God as revealed in Jesus. That response, an intellectual assent to the truth of Jesus' message, is also a response of the heart and ultimately of the total person.

Christian morality. The principles and processes by which Christians make decisions concerning right and wrong behavior. Best understood within the context of Jesus' teaching about God's love and the human response to that love.

Christian Scriptures. The entire Bible, comprising both the Jewish Scriptures and the Christian Testament.

Christian spirituality. The unique ways in which Christians live out their faith relationship with God. Implies a commitment on the part of the believer to live according to the message and values of Jesus.

Christian Testament. The collection of the sacred writings of Christians, including the Gospels; Acts of the Apostles; various Epistles, or letters; and The Book of Revelation. Commonly referred to as the New Testament.

Church. The gathering of those people who profess faith in the Risen Jesus and his message and who, through the power of the Spirit, live their lives in loving service to all people.

Consumerism. As a negative cultural value, the conviction that happiness can be achieved through the acquisition and consumption of material things.

Covenant. A special relationship experienced between God and people. In Jewish history, the Sinai Covenant was formally begun during an encounter between Yahweh and Moses on Mount Sinai. Christians believe that a New Covenant between God and people was established through the life, death, and Resurrection of Jesus. See also **Sinai Covenant.**

Conversion. The way in which a person comes to a commitment to God. In Catholic Christianity, the gradual, lifelong process in which the person of faith turns to God as the center of his or her life.

Culture. The total pattern of thought, speech, behavior, and social values that has been passed down from one generation to another within a given society. In a more restricted sense, the means by which such things are passed on—for example, the arts, music, literature, social customs, and traditions of a society.

Day of Atonement. A sacred Jewish feast in which faithful Jews repent of their sins. Also known as Yom Kippur (yōm-ki-'pùr).

Diocese. In the Catholic Church, a group of individual parishes within a geographical region over which a bishop has authority.

Doctrine. An official teaching of the Church or a statement of faith approved of by the bishops and the pope.

Dogma. An official doctrine of the Church that is considered so essential to Catholic faith that any rejection of it would imply rejection of the faith as a whole.

Ejaculation (i-jak-yə-'lā-shən). The release through the penis of the milky fluid and sperm cells known as semen (sē-mən). Occurs during a man's sexual arousal.

Embryo ('em-brē-ō). The name given a human at the early stage of development when the fertilized egg multiplies into a cluster of thousands of cells and settles into the lining of a woman's uterus. See also **fetus.**

Epistles. The letters, written by Saint Paul and other early Christians, that are included in the Christian Testament.

Eucharist. Another name for the Mass. Based on a word meaning "to give thanks."

Fetus ('fēt-əs). A developing human from about three months after conception until the time of delivery. Generally used from the time when the person begins to take on recognizably human characteristics. See also **embryo.**

Free will. The human capacity, given by God, to make choices about values, behavior, and so on. Also refers to the belief of Christians that God never interferes with the freedom of the individual to make such choices.

Gospels. The four books of the Christian Testament that recount the life, death, and Resurrection of Jesus. Credited to Matthew, Mark, Luke, and John.

Grace. The unconditional and undeserved love of God for people.

Hebrews. Those ancient tribes that made up the earliest ancestors of the Jewish people. Abraham, Isaac, Jacob, and their respective families and tribes were Hebrews.

Immediate gratification. The negative cultural value that leads people to avoid any suffering and to seek the instant satisfaction of their needs and desires.

Incarnation. The mystery of Jesus being both God and man. Literally means "in flesh." The term refers to the belief that God took on flesh in Jesus in order to become united with people.

Individualism. The cultural value that, in its negative form, promotes the rights of the individual while denying the needs of the community. Replaces service to others by an excessive desire to satisfy one's own needs.

Inspiration. God's influence upon human authors as they wrote the Christian Scriptures. Fundamentalist Christians believe that God literally dictated every word of the Bible to the human authors. Catholics, however, believe that the Bible is accurate and true *in all those things that are necessary for salvation* but that people need not believe that every word of the Bible is literally true.

Israel ('iz-rē-əl). A term with two primary meanings: (1) Israel was the name given by God to the patriarch Jacob. (2) The word also refers to the political makeup of the Jewish people during part of their history. As the Hebrews conquered Canaan, the territory was divided among "the twelve tribes of Israel," which were said to have descended from the twelve sons of the patriarch Jacob. These twelve regions gradually split up, with the ten northern tribes taking the name of Israel and the two southern tribes taking the name of Judah. See also **Judah.**

Israelites. The descendants of the patriarch Jacob, who was given the name Israel by God. Later they would be known as Jews.

Jew. A follower of Judaism. See also **Judah.**

Jewish Scriptures. The sacred writings of the Jews, which are also treasured by Christians. Preferred as the name for the collection of books in the Bible commonly referred to as the Old Testament.

Judah (ˈjüd-ə). One of the two kingdoms of the Jews, comprising two of the original twelve tribes of Israel. The kingdoms of both Israel and Judah were eventually destroyed, but a Remnant, or small group from the southern kingdom of Judah, survived.

Judaism. The name given to the religion based upon the Remnant who survived the destruction of the southern kingdom of Judah. See also **Israel.**

Judges. The great warriors who led the people of Israel against their enemies as the Israelites began to conquer the land of Canaan after the Sinai Covenant.

Kingdom of God. A term used by Jesus to describe the rule, or reign, of God over the hearts of people and also a new social order based on unconditional love of God and others.

Law. A statement of the responsibility of the Israelites in their covenant with Yahweh. Given to Moses by Yahweh on Mount Sinai. The cornerstone of the Law is the Ten Commandments.

Liturgical year. The annual cycle of religious feasts and seasons that forms the context for the Church's worship.

Menstrual (ˈmen-strəl) Period. The monthly event when the lining of a woman's uterus is shed. The shed lining flows out through the vagina in the form of blood and tissue. Also referred to as menstruation (men-strə-ˈwa-shən).

Messiah (mə-ˈsī-ə). The title given to the saving leader hoped for by the Jews. Based on a word meaning "the anointed one." Later applied to Jesus, whom some people believed fulfilled that hope.

Monotheism (ˈmän-ə-thē-iz-əm). The belief in the existence of only one God.

Mother of God. The special title given in the fifth century by the Catholic Church to Mary, the mother of Jesus. The primary intent of the Church in giving Mary this title was to reassert its belief in both Jesus' humanity and divinity.

Nicene (ˈnī-sēn) Creed. A communal prayer that expresses the major beliefs of the community of faith. *Creed* is based on a word meaning "to believe." The Nicene Creed, which is commonly recited in the Catholic Mass, was first developed in the year A.D. 325 during a church council held in the city of Nicaea.

Ovaries ('ōv-ə-rēs). The sex organs of a woman in which the eggs, or ova ('ō-və; singular, ovum), that are required for reproduction are stored and ripened.

Ovulation ('äv-yə-'lā-shən). The process in which a woman's ovaries release one mature egg, or ovum, on a monthly basis. If the egg is fertilized by a sperm, pregnancy begins.

Parables. Brief, easily remembered stories often employed by Jesus as a teaching method. They teach lessons by describing great truths in terms of common human events. Many times parables end with surprising twists intended to catch the listeners' attention.

Passover. The holiest and most celebrated Jewish feast, memorializing the miraculous liberation of the Israelites from Egypt during the Exodus. Lasted a week in the time of Jesus and included the ritual sacrifice of lambs in the Temple. This feast played a central role in the events surrounding the Last Supper and the Crucifixion of Jesus.

Patriarchs ('pā-trē-ärks). The key persons in history upon whom the religion that we now know as Judaism was founded. Literally means "father." The term is commonly used to identify the three very special Hebrew leaders—Abraham, Isaac, and Jacob.

Pentecost. A term with two meanings: (1) For the Jews, Pentecost is a great springtime feast celebrating the giving of the Law by Yahweh to Moses on Mount Sinai. (2) For Christians, Pentecost is a feast celebrating the gift of the Holy Spirit to the followers of Jesus after his death and Resurrection. Often referred to as the "birthday of the Church."

Personal spirituality. The unique way in which an individual lives out and expresses his or her faith relationship with God. Christian spirituality implies a commitment on the part of the believer to live according to the message and values of Jesus.

Pharisees ('far-ə-sēs). A group within Judaism that was conservative in politics but liberal in matters of religion in that they accepted new developments in Jewish thought. Their tendency toward legalism put them in conflict with Jesus.

Polytheism ('päl-i-thē-iz-əm). The belief in more than one god.

Prophets. The name most commonly associated with the special people in the history of the Jews who continually challenged the people to live in accordance with the covenant with Yahweh. Literally means "one who speaks out."

Puberty ('pyü-bərt-ē). The period in a person's physical development when the reproductive system matures. Accompanied by the appearance of secondary sex characteristics—such as body hair, change of voice, growth spurts, and so on.

Religion. The attempt by communities of people throughout history to express their shared faith through outward signs—including symbols, celebrations, statements of belief, and codes of behavior.

Religious faith. The belief and trust in a power beyond the self—that is, in a supreme being or a creator of the universe.

Resurrection. The event in which Jesus was raised from the dead by God.

Revelation. The self-communication or self-disclosure of God, in which sacred Mystery is made known by God to people. Literally means "to reveal" or "to unveil."

Sabbath ('sab-əth). The weekly day of rest and prayer for the Jews based on the creation story in the Book of Genesis. Lasted from what now would be Friday evening to Saturday evening. The Christian practice of Sunday worship has its origins in the Jewish Sabbath.

Sacraments. In the Catholic Church, the key ritual actions in communal worship—for example, Baptism, Eucharist, Confirmation. Literally means "sacred."

Sadducees ('saj-ə-sēs). A faction within Judaism that was liberal in politics but conservative in religious matters. Constituted the priestly aristocracy of the Jews.

Salvation history. The saga of God's loving action throughout the history of the Jews and the Christians. Refers to the belief that God is revealed in and through the events of history.

Scriptures. The sacred writings and texts of various religions. Refers, in Jewish and Christian religions, to the Bible. Literally means "writings."

Seven gifts of the Holy Spirit. The characteristics of Christian life that are made possible through the influence of the Holy Spirit—namely, wisdom, understanding, right judgment, knowledge, courage, love, and reverence.

Sexual permissiveness. The negative cultural value that regards sexual relations between people as a casual activity that can be routinely engaged in without concern for commitment or personal responsibility.

Sin. The breaking of the relationship of love between people and with God through selfishness. Often used to identify the effects of a breakdown of harmony, such as greed, cruelty, and injustice.

Sinai ('sī-nī) Covenant. The special relationship established by

Yahweh and the Jewish people during a dramatic encounter on Mount Sinai between Yahweh and Moses. In the Sinai Covenant, Yahweh promised to be the caring God of the Jews, and they in turn promised to follow the dictates of the Law.

Stereotype. An unfair characterization or judgment of people or things based on oversimplified and often untrue opinions or information.

Symbol. A special kind of sign that helps people give expression to experiences and realities that are too big for words. Refers to both objects (such as wedding rings or birthday cakes) and actions (such as hugs or handshakes). Symbols are commonly used by religions to express their beliefs and values.

Testicles ('tes-ti-kəls). The male sex organs that produce the sex cells, or sperm, required for reproduction. Contained in the loose pouch of skin under the penis called the scrotum ('skrōt-əm).

Theology. The academic field devoted to the investigation of God and of God's relationship with the universe. Literally means "the study of God." The term is often used in reference to particular religions, as in *Christian theology* or *Jewish theology*. The scholars trained in this discipline are known as theologians.

Tradition. Among Christians, the teachings believed to be handed down by Jesus and the Apostles. Among Roman Catholics, the essential teachings and practices that have emerged from the ongoing, lived faith of the Christian community. Includes the official decrees of church councils and popes that are considered true and authoritative.

Transcendence (trans-'en-dənts). The interior sense of a reality that goes beyond our physical, sensory experience; the sense of something or someone "out there," beyond us. Also refers to the experience of moving out from or beyond oneself.

Trinity. The central Christian dogma that there are three distinct persons—the Father, Son, and Spirit—in one God.

Uterus ('yüt-ə-rəs). The muscular structure within a woman's abdominal area in which a baby develops. Also called the womb. If a woman's ovum, or egg, is not fertilized by a male sperm, the lining of the uterus will be shed on a monthly basis. See also **menstrual period**.

Vagina (və-'jī-nə). The canal, or opening, in a woman that leads to the uterus. The vagina receives the penis during intercourse, and semen is deposited there. During birth, the baby is delivered from the uterus through the vagina.

Vocation. A strong inclination or desire to pursue a certain profession or way of life. Literally means "a call." In religion, the term refers to the sense a person has of being called by God to fulfill a certain role or to follow a particular lifestyle. Often used more specifically to refer to a personal sense of being called by God to the religious life as a priest or as a religious sister or brother.

Wisdom. In discussions of religion, a basic system of beliefs. What a religion holds to be true about the nature of God and about God's relationship with the world. The wisdom of Catholicism is embodied in the Christian Scriptures and in the body of teachings known as the Church's Tradition.

Worldview. A perspective on or understanding of life and its meaning. Serves as a context for and greatly influences one's attitudes, values, and relationships.

Works. In religion, the code of behavior that is central to the moral understanding and lifestyle of believers. For both Jews and Christians, this code focuses on the Ten Commandments and the values reflected in them.

Worship. All the celebrations and communal prayer forms of a religion. In Catholicism, refers to the seven sacraments of the Church as they are celebrated within the context of the annual cycle of feasts and sacred seasons known as the Church's liturgical year.

Yahweh ('yä-wā). The Hebrew name for God, variously translated as "I am he who is," "I am the One who is present," or "I bring into existence all that is." The Jews of Jesus' time held this name in such reverence that they refused to pronounce it, even passing over it when reading their scriptures.

Index

S

Sabbath, 121, 233, 240, 241. *See also* Sunday
sacraments, 206, 208, 222, 228–231; life of Church visible in, 267; presence of Jesus in, 174, 226–227, 231, 242; purposes of, 226; as religious expression, 189. *See also* celebrations, religious
sacred Mystery, 109; and faith, 89, 255, 257; finding words to express, 205–206, 209; God is, 82, 83; revelation of, 94, 95, 202, 262; sensing, in nature, 86, 224; and the Trinity, 214; universal belief in, 85. *See also* God, the one
Sadducees, 124
saints, 235, 262
salvation history, 119; complexity of, 136; in Jewish Scriptures, 134; and revelation, 95, 104–105
sanctoral cycle, 262
scribes, 194
Scriptures. *See* Bible
self-image, 87, 137, 144, 249; affected by cultural standards, 24, 27; developing, 50–51, 66–68, 72–73; and friendships, 32; and physical development, 25, 52–53; poem on, 34; and sexual identity, 31; and the world of *if onlys,* 48–49

service, Christian, 61, 182, 187–188, 194, 259, 262, 268–275
seven gifts of Holy Spirit, 180
sexuality, 24, 31–32, 34–35, 61
sexual permissiveness, 61, 64, 65
sin, 136–137, 154, 230
Sinai Covenant, 109–110, 112, 115, 117–118, 119, 123, 125, 195
social classes, 124–125
social development, 18, 31–35
social justice. *See* justice and peace
society. *See* cultures
Solomon, King, 112
Spirit. *See* Holy Spirit
spirituality, Christian, 242–243, 258–259; and Christian morality, 275; and communion of saints, 262; cultural attitudes toward, 55–56; and service to others, 268–275
spirituality, personal, 258
statements of belief, 89, 96, 188, 206
stereotypes, 51–57, 123
suffering, 61, 80, 120; can create feelings of transcendence, 87; challenges faith, 88, 136; and Christian service, 187, 194, 267; of Jesus, 152–153

Sunday, 240–242; dedicated to Jesus, 235; Easter, 238; worship on, has roots in Jewish Sabbath, 121, 233
symbol: definition of, 223–224; Jesus as, 227; limitations of, 209; need for, 222; purpose of, 231; as religious expression, 89, 96, 188; in sacraments, 226, 228, 230; in worship, 120

T

television, 63–64
Temple (Jerusalem), 112, 122, 124, 148; and early Church, 189, 195
Ten Commandments, 98, 110, 111, 117, 119, 123
testament: definition of, 115
testicles, 23–24
theologians, 84; role of, in developing Tradition, 210, 211
theology: definition of, 84
Thomas (Apostle), 171–172, 238
Thomas Aquinas, Saint, 84–85, 86
Tradition of Catholic Church, 205–216
transcendence, moments of, 87
Trinity, dogma of, 213–215
trust, 251; and faith, 76–77, 80–81, 88–89, 160; and friendship, 33, 80, 94; in God, 80–81, 81–82, 153. *See also* faith, Christian

Acknowledgments (*continued*)

The scriptural quotations are from the *Jerusalem Bible,* published and copyrighted © 1985 by Darton, Longman & Todd, Ltd., London, and by Doubleday & Company, Inc., New York.

The prayer on page 66 is from *Intimacy,* by Henri J. M. Nouwen, page 73. Copyright 1969 by Fides Publishing, Inc. Reprinted with permission.

The folktale on pages 71–72 is from *Story Telling: The Enchantment of Theology,* by Belden C. Lane. Saint Louis: Bethany Press, 1981. Sound cassette.

The story on page 86 is from *The Song of the Bird,* by Anthony de Mello, SJ, page 12. Garden City, NY: Doubleday & Company, Image Books, 1982.

The poem on page 89 is from *Markings,* by Dag Hammarskjöld, translated by Leif Sjoberg and W. H. Auden. Translation. Copyright © 1964 by Alfred A. Knopf, Inc., and Faber and Faber, Ltd. Reprinted by permission of Alfred A. Knopf, Inc. and Faber and Faber, Ltd.

The version of the Nicene Creed on page 216 is from *The Sacramentary* (New York: Catholic Book Publishing Co., 1985), page 368.

The extract on pages 272–273 is adapted from "Trevor's Campaign," by Lee Radovich, *Catholic Teen Magazine,* March 1987, pages 6–9. Copyright 1987 by The National Federation for Catholic Youth Ministry. Reprinted by permission.

Photo Credits

The Photo Source: Cover

Bettmann Newsphotos: pages 102 (right), 105, 113, 184, 192 (right), 211, 212, 250, 275

Paul Buddle: pages 16, 18, 24, 27 (bottom), 31 (top), 64, 79, 147, 174, 197, 199, 232 (bottom), 246 (bottom), 256, 260, 261

James Carroll: pages 6 (bottom), 22, 88, 128 (right), 133, 156 (bottom), 279 (left)

Jim Cronk: pages 11 (right), 59, 67, 92

Crosier Monastery, Rev. Gene Plaisted, OSC: pages 10, 14 (left), 19, 26, 36, 37, 38, 39 (right), 42, 56 (top), 70 (right), 77, 86 (bottom), 91, 107, 128 (left and bottom), 140, 156 (left and right), 160, 179, 183, 201, 204, 210, 220 (bottom), 230, 238, 239, 252, 253, 254, 257, 259 (left), 266, 267, 279 (right)

Vivienne della Grotta: pages 57, 58 (left), 75, 85, 203, 214, 224 (right), 233, 240, 269

EKM-Nepenthe: pages 6 (left), 8, 9 (top), 23, 29, 35, 39 (left), 40, 46 (left and bottom), 49, 52, 53, 58 (right), 60, 62, 65, 70 (left), 73, 83, 86 (top), 87, 97, 102 (bottom), 118, 135 (right), 163 (left and right), 169, 173, 192 (left), 222, 225, 234, 263, 271, 276

Michael Goldberg: pages 33 and 217

National Catholic Photo Service: pages 102 (left), 142, 207, 220 (left), 248, 262

Religious News Service: pages 94, 98, 117, 122, 213, 226

James Shaffer: pages 9 (bottom), 11 (left), 12, 14 (right and bottom), 20, 21, 25, 27 (top), 31 (bottom), 41, 46 (right), 50, 54, 55, 56 (bottom), 68, 70 (bottom), 80, 95, 96, 104, 114, 119, 135 (left), 136, 139, 143, 146, 150, 153, 158, 167, 177, 181, 182, 187, 188 (top and bottom), 189, 192 (bottom), 208, 220 (right), 224 (left), 227, 228, 232 (top), 241, 242, 246 (left and right), 249, 251, 259 (right), 264, 268, 274, 278

Steve and Mary Skjold: pages 6 (right), 223

The photographs on pages 272–273 are used with permission of Frank Ferrell for Trevor's Campaign for the Homeless. For further information contact: TREVOR, Box 21, Gladwyne, PA 19035.